# Dracula, Frankenstein and Friends

For Zoë, Alice and Martha.

And for Bela and Boris and the rest.

All rights reserved
Author: Michael Galley
Cover design: Michael Galley
Copyright © 2021 Michael Galley

# Dracula, Frankenstein and Friends

Michael Galley

'Ghosts of my childhood
Stay with me if you will…'

the Mountain Goats
*Outer Scorpion Squadron*

# CONTENTS

| | |
|---|---|
| INTRODUCTION | 9 |
| 1. I BID YOU WELCOME | 12 |
|     DRACULA (1931, UNIVERSAL, BROWNING) | |
| 2. HAVEN'T YOU EVER WANTED TO DO ANYTHING THAT WAS DANGEROUS? | 29 |
|     FRANKENSTEIN (1931, UNIVERSAL, WHALE) | |
| 3. ALONE BAD | 43 |
|     BRIDE OF FRANKENSTEIN (1935, UNIVERSAL, WHALE) | |
| 4. MEMENTORABILIA MORI | 51 |
| 5. ANGLO-FREUD! IN COLOUR! | 54 |
|     BRIDES OF DRACULA (1960, HAMMER, FISHER) | |
| 6. HE WENT FOR A LITTLE WALK! YOU SHOULD HAVE SEEN HIS FACE! | 70 |
|     THE MUMMY (1932, UNIVERSAL, FREUND) | |
| 7. THE WAY YOU WALKED WAS THORNY | 81 |
|     THE WOLF MAN (1940, UNIVERSAL, WAGGNER) | |
| 8. BUTLER-EATING BABIES AND HEAD-TO-HEAD BEDS | 93 |
|     SON OF FRANKENSTEIN (1939, UNIVERSAL, LEE) | |
| 9. BLOOD! MORE BLOOD! | 103 |
|     KISS OF THE VAMPIRE (1963, HAMMER, SHARP) | |
| 10. MAD? OR UNBELIEVABLE? | 120 |
|     DRACULA'S DAUGHTER (1936, UNIVERSAL, HILLYER) | |
| 11. ZOMBIE! | 129 |
|     PLAGUE OF THE ZOMBIES (1966, HAMMER, GILLING) | |
| 12. THE FANDOM MENACE | 137 |
| 13. MY BRAIN AND HIS BODY | 150 |
|     THE GHOST OF FRANKENSTEIN (1942, UNIVERSAL, KENTON) | |
| 14. DEATH IS THE MONSTER | 161 |
|     THE PREMATURE BURIAL (1962, AIP, CORMAN) | |
| 15. PERFECTION | 176 |
|     THE RAVEN (1935, UNIVERSAL, FRIEDLANDER), THE BLACK CAT (1934, UNIVERSAL, ULMER) | |
| 16. IF I EVER FIND PEACE I'LL FIND IT HERE | 184 |
|     FRANKENSTEIN MEETS THE WOLF MAN (1942, UNIVERSAL, NEILL) | |
| 17. QUOTH THE RAVEN | 194 |
|     THE RAVEN (1963, AIP, CORMAN) | |
| 18. THE MONSTER MASH | 203 |
|     HOUSE OF FRANKENSTEIN (1944, UNIVERSAL, KENTON) | |
| 19. A LOATHSOME THING | 213 |
|     THE REPTILE (1966, HAMMER, GILLING) | |
| 20. PUT IT OUT! PUT IT OUT I TELL YA! | 229 |
|     SON OF DRACULA (1943, UNIVERSAL, SIODMAK) | |
| 21. THEY ALWAYS DESTROY EVERYTHING | 237 |
|     THE EVIL OF FRANKENSTEIN (1964, HAMMER, FRANCIS) | |
| 22. 1977 – ANNUS HORRORBILIS | 247 |
| 23. IS THERE NO END TO YOUR HORRORS? | 259 |
|     HOUSE OF DRACULA (1945, UNIVERSAL, KENTON), FALL OF THE HOUSE OF USHER (1960, AIP, CORMAN) | |

# Introduction

Hello. My name is Michael Galley and I'm a horror film fan.

Visualise me stumbling reluctantly to my feet in order to shamefacedly utter that last sentence to my support group if you wish, but as the years have gone by I've found myself able to gather around me some few shards of self-respect which the gawkily self-conscious young man I once was would have found difficult to imagine, so I'd sooner see it as a declaration of pride.

I'm a horror fan for any number of reasons, but I *became* a horror fan for one specific one. Just over forty years ago I watched a late night season of BBC2 horror double bills on a series of Saturdays in the summer of 1977; a season that, typically, paired a Universal classic from the 1930s and 40s with a then still daringly modern Hammer or AIP film from the 60s, and was given the umbrella title of *Dracula, Frankenstein – and Friends!*

Though I've unceremoniously removed the hyphen and the exclamation mark, which smacked a little too much of an unwarranted jauntiness for my down-in-the-mouth liking, I've borrowed the name for the title of this book, partly because it seems to sum up what I'm writing about, and partly because it helps to emphasise just how significant and influential that season of films has been in shaping the person that I've become and some of the ways in which I see the world.

No child growing up in the 1970s could have been entirely oblivious to the ubiquity of the horror culture surrounding them, from the monster mags gracing the shelves of every newsagent's to the lurid box cover art of the Aurora monster kits glowering from every toy shop window.

Horror was everywhere, even sliding sinisterly into the gothic-tinged Public Information Films warning a generation of trembling schoolchildren to stay away from deep water and electricity pylons.

As a result, by the age of eleven or twelve I had developed a vague, unfocused interest in all things Monstrous. That interest was about to find its focus.

July 2nd 1977. Margaret Thatcher has yet to unleash her bile and malice upon an unsuspecting nation, and the miserable prospect of Monday morning's ritually humiliating swimming lesson is far enough away to be ignored for now. The long hot blissful summer holiday is so close I can almost taste it. Mum and Dad are still alive and well, and Tom Baker is still the Doctor. All is right with the world, for these moments at least.

Mum has, astonishingly, agreed to let me stay up late to watch a film that I've been pestering her about. BBC2 is about to show Bela

Lugosi in *Dracula*, and for one particular boy, cosy in the corner of a red sofa in a three-bedroom semi in an obscure suburban corner of Norwich, as well as for a whole generation of particular children of a pleasingly morbid cast of mind and a similar, self-dramatisingly adolescent sense of their 'outsider' status, life is never going to be the same again.

*"Die!!!!!! You will all Die!!!!!!!!!!!"*

# DOUBLE BILL ONE

## Saturday July 2$^{nd}$ 1977

DRACULA                                       22.10 - 23.45

FRANKENSTEIN                          23.45 – 01.10

# 1. I BID YOU WELCOME

## Dracula (1931, Universal, Tod Browning)

*'I am ... Dracula.'*
**Count Dracula (Bela Lugosi)**

This was the one. No question, no debate. Forget the incredible, masochistic skill of Lon Chaney's 1920s self-transforming portraits of deformity in films like *The Hunchback of Notre Dame* and *The Phantom of the Opera*. Take away Chaney's makeup and you're left with costume drama. Forget the lurid expressionistic stylings of Weimar Germany's *Caligari* and *Nosferatu*. Those are arthouse experiments, not genre films.

Most of all, forget the critical received wisdom that Tod Browning's 1931 *Dracula* is fatally compromised by its director's lack of technical ambition, by its lead actor's overripe, melodramatic style and that its last two thirds plod by in stagey theatricality. Forget the widespread idea that its failings are thrown into sharp relief by the simultaneously made Spanish language version shot by George Melford, and even more so by James Whale's 1931 *Frankenstein*, made only months later but light years ahead in terms of its maturity of vision and technical sophistication.

No, forget all that. *Dracula* was the one, the wellspring, the great original on which everything since has depended. The Spanish language version is an interesting piece of work in its own right, with a couple of very striking moments, and crucially it has novelty on its side – it remained unseen during the half century in which the Browning version became a legendary and very familiar icon of popular culture. But as the novelty wears off, it seems pretty clear to me that the Browning Lugosi film is the definitive version, and overall much the better of the two films. And Whale's *Frankenstein* is a glittering masterpiece, a towering achievement and a truly great film. But it is the *second* great horror film. *Dracula* is the first. Without the daring and ferocious originality with which *Dracula* made this strange new cinematic territory viable, *Frankenstein* would never have been made.[1]

There's a pleasing symmetry (which I confess gives me a worryingly disproportionate degree of satisfaction) to the fact that the horror film itself was born at exactly the same moment that I fell in love with it. It could have been otherwise, you see. I later discovered that there had been two previous horror double bill seasons on late night Saturday BBC2, a fact I found almost impossible to believe at the time. How could

---

[1] For a fuller exploration of why the film is so much better than its reputation, see *Dracula AD 1931* by Matthew Coniam and *Tod Browning's Dracula* by Gary D Rhodes.

you start anywhere other than here, with the unbeatable Universal cycle of the 30s and 40s? Why on earth would anyone choose to show anything else first?

Had I been a year older, there's every chance I might have started with the 1976 season, yawned a bit through *The Cat and the Canary* with Bob Hope or *The Mad Genius* without him, and drifted away forever. There were more double bill seasons to come, so worse still, I could have been a year or two *younger* in which case my first contact might have been with *Superbeast* or *Daughters of Satan;* a dread prospect far more frightening to me than anything within the films themselves.

Even now I sometimes envisage a scenario in which I am gasping my last upon my deathbed when a black-robed chess-playing Reaper straight out of Bergman's *The Seventh Seal* (I do occasionally watch films without werewolves in them) offers me the chance to play for an extra year or two of life. 'No' I croak feebly, 'not if it means rewriting history so the first horror movie I saw was *Zoltan Hound of Dracula* in 1981.'

But thankfully no; the synchronicity was delightfully exact and this was the moment, both for me and the genre itself. Chronologically the two events may have been forty-six years apart, but the on-screen instant was the same. About ten minutes in, Dwight Frye's Renfield nervously enters the vast, ruined hall of Castle Dracula. Huge, fairytale cobwebs dominate the mise-en-scène. Wolves howl. Rats, bats, insects and spiders scuttle and swoop.

So, bizarrely, do a couple of armadillos, whose own gothic career never quite took off like their animal co-stars. Spare a thought for all those black and white armadillos roaming the gutters of Hollywood's skid row muttering 'It should have been me.'

Lugosi stands in full evening dress, a knowing smirk playing across his striking features, half way down a crumbling stone staircase. And what a staircase.

Anyone ever inclined to dismiss the horror movie as a low budget form, marred by its shoddy production values, should be strapped to a chair with their eyes sellotaped open in front of a screen showing the entire 30s output of Universal horror films on loop, marvelling at those lofty, magnificent sets until they promise never to utter such lazy second hand shite ever again. I'd be hard pushed to think of a better sustained series of production designs in the whole history of cinema.

And then it happens. The true birth of the horror film. Slowly, richly, enigmatically, each heavily accented syllable weighed and relished, Lugosi intones 'I am – Dracula. I bid you welcome.'

Many have argued that the tragic downward spiral of Lugosi's later career was due in large part to his failure to ever master the English language, some even claiming, wrongly, that in *Dracula* he is delivering his lines phonetically, without any comprehension of their meaning. A quick look at a filmed interview of the time, or any of his other early thirties performances (which don't involve the heavy pauses he gives the vampire Count) would be enough to see the argument doesn't hold water. Lugosi's English elsewhere is strongly accented, but perfectly competent, even fluent. Admittedly, his delivery is ripe for parody – yes, I'm looking at you *Sesame Street*'s Count von Count – but the mannered, stately delivery, including the occasional oddly placed emphasis, was an entirely deliberate choice on the part of Lugosi and Browning, and for my money an incredibly effective one. The sonorous musicality of cadence he brings even to a line as apparently banal as 'We will be leaving … tomorrow … evening' lends it a strange, moody portentousness which has to be heard to be believed.

In a career move which has often been cited as the other main factor behind his later struggles to find decent parts, or even to work at all, Lugosi reportedly turned down the role of Frankenstein's Monster before it was offered to the then unknown Boris Karloff, on the grounds that the Monster had no dialogue. I strongly suspect this version of events is apocryphal, but as far as I'm concerned if this was indeed the truth of the story then Lugosi was absolutely right. His Dracula is a remarkably potent piece of physical acting – the slow, deliberate pacing, those extraordinary hands, the potency of his gaze and statuesque command – but the incredible power of his vocal performance is, if anything, even more exceptional. So to fail to give him dialogue would be to waste a crucial element of Lugosi's very real star quality.

And what dialogue he is given here. 'Listen to them. Children of the night. What music they make.' 'The spider spinning his web for the unwary fly. The blood is the life, Mr Renfield.' 'I never drink – wine.' Every one a winner, and all of those within the first twenty minutes.

Certainly the lush richness of the dialogue was one of the reasons I fell so immediately in love with the film. Even at that age I loved words, the sound and the shape of them, and Lugosi's dialogue was instantly memorable and instantly quotable, like many of my favourite things – Python sketches, or *Withnail and I* for instance. It's this, in the end, which makes all those critical commonplaces about how cheap and stagy and talky the film becomes in its later sections irrelevant to me. Yes, it would be nice to see that wolf running across the grounds of the asylum rather than being told about it, and yes it would be nice for Lugosi to be given a more dramatic curtain call than a limp off-screen groan, but to automatically assume that 'talky' is such a terrible insult to bestow on a film is to miss a central point about the *nature* of that 'talkiness'.

Of course cinema is different to theatre, of course film can be much more than pictures of people talking, but great actors delivering great lines don't necessarily need prowling, moody camerawork of the sort *Dracula* delivers in the magnificent opening castle scenes in order to hold an audience riveted. It's also a legitimate use of the medium to allow the camerawork and technique to become invisible for a time while the actors and the dialogue hold centre stage. In fact, it seems to me perfectly fair to say that one of the many and varied palaces of delights — some visual and technical, some not — which this greatest of all art forms is capable of, is bringing us closer to those great actors delivering great lines than the theatre ever can.

Anyone still inclined to regard the last hour of *Dracula* as dreary, dull and disappointing should take another look at the two, equally powerful confrontation scenes between Lugosi's Count and Edward Van Sloan's steely Van Helsing. Despite the single, 'stagy' drawing room setting and without any showy filmic techniques to distract us, the battle of wills which culminates in Lugosi's beautiful rendering of 'For one who has not lived even a single lifetime — you are a wise man, Van Helsing' is enthralling, intense and genuinely epic.

In fact, it was at least in part this epic nature to the conflicts at the heart of the film to which I found myself responding. Even today, I love stories which, like *Dracula,* deal in Good and Evil on a grand, apocalyptic scale — the season finales rather than the ordinary episodes, the vast end-of-the-world-is-nigh sweep of those kind of narratives — and even more so back then. I never much liked *The Fantastic Four*, preferring the stark realism of *Spider Man Comics Weekly* (strange how a 10-year-old sees things), but a couple of years earlier I had been completely floored by the issue with Galactus on the front, the sky filled with fire and meteors, the sun blotted out, The Silver Surfer as the horseman of the apocalypse, all that.

Albeit in a different genre, *Dracula*'s sheer Gothic romanticism; the crypts and the bats; the fogs and the storms; the castles and the crumbling abbeys, seemed of a piece with that kind of storytelling. The decay and the death. Death as a concept, in all its power and endless, incomprehensible strangeness, is a universal preoccupation of course, but perhaps most preoccupying of all in adolescence, when the reality and the truth of it begins to present itself for the first time, but remains somehow fresh and unbelievable, undimmed by painful experience.

There are many things that make the film compelling viewing, but central to all of them is Lugosi's extraordinary power and charisma. Most aficionados tend to argue that Karloff was the finer actor – Bela versus Boris is the horror movie fan's equivalent of 'are you a dog person or a cat person?' – but whatever the role, and especially when, as here, the role was worthy of him, Lugosi possessed an intensity on screen that is completely unrivalled. It's impossible to take your eyes off him – the audience is every bit as hypnotised as Frances Dade's morbidly romantic Lucy or Helen Chandler's doll-like Mina. If Karloff's Monster is the great acting performance of horror cinema – the actor subsumed entirely by the character – then Lugosi's Dracula is horror cinema's greatest *star* performance, role and actor becoming effectively a single entity.

It's hard now to describe just how much I loved that 1977 BBC2 screening, and just how much of the rest of my life was set in motion by that otherwise unremarkable hour and a half in front of the telly. I didn't so much watch the film as wallow in it, rolling it around my eyeballs and savouring each frame the way a wine taster swills a fine Burgundy. Except I was definitely going to swallow, not spit.

I remember the feeling of that summer night with an absolute vividness which no number of passing years or alcohol-zapped brain cells seems to diminish. Of course I've seen *Dracula* many times since, and I understand a bit about how memory works. Of course I'm idealising; I'm distorting; conflating the original event with later ideas and memories; incorporating other experiences. Still, who cares? I remember it, so there.

But *why* did the film impact on this 12-year-old so profoundly? It is a great film, certainly, despite what its detractors and doubters might suggest to the contrary, but even I would have to admit that I find it marginally less impressive now than I did way back when. And even then, in a world where classic black and white movies from the 30s and 40s were still a familiar and regular part of the schedule on the three available TV stations rather than, as now, having to be specifically sought out in the wilder regions of the subscription movie channels, I was still aware that I was watching something oddly remote and archaic.

Shown to today's younger generation, as, against my better judgement, I have occasionally done to classroomfulls of disbelieving students, Lugosi's performance tends to inspire one reaction: gales of laughter. Never teach a text you love, I was once sensibly advised. Teenagers will trample it viciously underfoot, laughing in your face as they do so, leaving your poor heart bruised and bloodied on the floor.

Knowing this, I'll even defensively try to forestall their reaction in the way I introduce the film, droning on about context and the passage of time. Worse, I'll sometimes even join in, siding with the adolescent philistines against my beloved Bela just to show how hip and aware I am – and dying a little inside as I do so. So why should it have been so different for me, at a similar age, back in 1977?

There's been a marked shift in the cultural landscape, I think. Today we live in the age of detachment and distance. To really *believe*, to be totally passionate about anything, to genuinely and unabashedly fall for something, as I did for horror movies in a no holds barred, hook line and sinker heart on the sleeve all cliché's welcome kind of way is growing harder and harder in these 21$^{st}$ century too cool for school days of ours. We're almost always a step back, at one remove from the world around us. We live our lives inside inverted commas. We can say anything because everyone knows we don't really mean it. We don't mean anything, and so in turn nothing means anything to us. And so nothing matters, except being in on the joke. It's the postmodern curse; the inability to view anything without the layers of irony and cynicism which inevitably intervene between us and our experiences.

The idealistic 'we can change the world' daydreaming of the 1960s, even the earnest political ideologies of the 1970s and 80s are laughable to us now, their passionate conviction and hopeful sloganeering rendered risible by disillusion and the changing landscape, but they've been replaced with nothing more worthwhile than a sneer.

It's encoded inescapably into our language, into our speech patterns. Words like 'Epic', 'Awesome' or 'Legend' which once commanded a distant view of the sublime are now commandeered into service as epithets to describe – usually at one further remove from existence on Twitter or Facebook – the most mundane and routine of experiences and people.

The twenty first century isn't unique in this. A quick scan of Pope or Fielding would quickly demonstrate an eighteenth century facility with utilising the once epic and legendary to offer ironic comment on the triviality of contemporary experience.

But much as I love the cheerful cynicism of the eighteenth century novel or the wit of an Augustan mock heroic couplet, it was the urgent sense that something vital was missing from this detached world view that led the Romantic revolutionaries to rediscover Passion with a capital P. With their sometimes overwhelming, almost dangerous, earnestness, Blake, Coleridge, Wordsworth, Shelley and Keats were all driven by their rejection of the perils of an age which, like ours, seemed led by irony and the curl of the lip. And Gothic horror, let's not forget, is Romanticism's disreputable cousin.

Today's triumph of irony is little wonder, of course.

So much of the world we now inhabit is plastic and artificial and fake, drawing a kind of knowing, self-mocking attention to its own artifice, from the hollow strains of The X Factor musical landscape that envelops us through to the ironically labelled 'reality' shows which don't represent any kind of reality anyone is ever likely to encounter unless they travel across the vast infinity of interstellar space to consider the nature of real life on the planet Bollocks: from our phone tapping, kiss and telling 'free' press to our laughable, and laughably inept, post-spin doctoring post-Blairite post-new-new Labour post-plastic coalition post-Cameron post-Brexit, pandemically-engulfed BoJo Tory 'government' (and that one really belongs in the inverted commas), that it's no wonder we choose to view everything, whether it deserves it or not, in the same way.

Over-earnest belief, closed systems of thought, the fraudulent, the fundamentalist and the empty; they *need* a cold and cynical eye to be cast upon them, but when we can't differentiate, when everything becomes the same, then nothing has any value. We preclude real involvement, real belief, real love, and we're *killing* ourselves. A vision of the future we're making? Simon Cowell's face, forever.

Well not here. In this tiny corner of the 21st century I can mean what I say, just as I did back in 1977. There can be a way of viewing films like *Dracula* as the very definition of kitsch, as though the only conceivable pleasures to be found in old horror are of the sniggering, knowing, 'so bad its good' variety, and … I…HATE…IT. *Dracula* is not 'so bad it's good'. It is not 'bad' at all; in fact, it's not even 'good', it's *magnificent*, and it doesn't need me to apologise for it, as I have done too often, on the grounds of age or context or the conventions of melodrama or anything else. And irony, that most precious and delicate of comedic techniques in the hands of an Austen, and that ugliest and laziest way of cheapening and demeaning the genuinely beautiful and transcendent in the hands of the rest of us, had nothing whatever to do with the way in which my twelve-year-old self fell so suddenly, desperately and unexpectedly in love with the performance of a long dead Hungarian actor in a film made four decades and an apparent millennia of technological advances previously. 1977 makes me the *Star Wars* generation remember, this screening of *Dracula* coming only months before I saw George Lucas change the very idea of what was possible in the cinema.

No irony involved; this was the real thing, and I fell for *Dracula* on its own terms, not mine. Something which was to be true only rarely when, later (much too much later as it happens), I was to fall for actual flesh and blood people rather than flickering black and white celluloid ghosts.

So if not irony, then what? To begin with the most obvious and comment-worthy element of the film to have resonated in my adolescent psyche, it would not need the most ardent of Freudians to discern a degree of sexual significance in *Dracula*, and indeed in the whole mythology of the undead bloodsucker. The dark, domineering lover. The kiss of the vampire. The bite as symbolic penetration. *Dracula* as seduction motif. *Dracula* as sadomasochistic fantasy. Dracula as the sexual liberator of repressed female desire. As the id to society's ego. As homoeroticism. I've read them all. Admittedly I hadn't read them all when I was twelve, but looking back I don't feel there's much doubt that a part of the reason for the film's marked impact was that I was responding powerfully to a touch of the old subtext.

If you look at the evolution of the vampire film since 1931 it won't take you too long to come to the conclusion that, in the genre as in the rest of society, subtext grows ever more overt. In the 50s and 60s Hammer added heaving cleavages delightfully to the mix, and by its nadir in the 70s was dealing almost exclusively in bare-breasted Scandinavian lesbians. Then there's Brad Pitt and Tom Cruise in one another's arms in *Interview with the Vampire* (whatever did Scientology have to say about that, little Tom? Did no-one *notice?*) After a certain point it's no longer subtext so much as ... well, text.

By comparison, of course, the Lugosi version is relatively chaste and sedate. But make no mistake, the subtext is there, and it's powerful, particularly when you bear in mind that I hadn't seen those other films yet, and by and large nor had anyone else I knew. Sublimation was the order of the day, and just like a whole generation of obsessive stamp-collecting or butterfly-pinning Victorian schoolboys before me (because those cold showers could never be quite cold enough, could they?), I found something into which I was able to channel some of my dawning sexual awareness and energies.

And to a painfully shy and spotty 12-year-old like me whose plan for getting a girlfriend consisted mainly of lying on my bed and waiting hopefully ('*Talk?* To *girls?* Are you *insane*?'), sex was a dark and troubling mystery, just like *Dracula* itself. Alluring, enticing, preoccupying, but secretive, furtive, somehow unknowable and unknowably intense. My sexual experience at this point was restricted to a strange and growing relationship with Leela, the leather bikini-clad companion to Tom Baker's Doctor, brilliantly played by Louise Jameson – albeit a rather distant and one-way definition of a 'relationship' given that it was conducted entirely via once weekly 25 minute doses of Saturday teatime television and some occasional single-handed and inexpert under the bedclothes fumbling. Actually, 25 minutes in front of a screen and a bit of a wank? Perhaps it was all rather more 21$^{st}$ century than I'd realised.

Of course I knew the basic 'who's meant to put what where' facts, but sex existed for me only in the imagination, in an overheated fantasy world, and it was this humid and sticky world which those coded old horror movies plugged straight into. And the fantasy possibilities they offered, like the idea I might be able to work a little of Bela's hoodoo over Shirley Chambers, who sat opposite me in double Art once a week, ('You vill be mine, Shirley Chambers … mine') thus circumventing the obvious impossibility of actually speaking to her, was desperately appealing.

I'm a long way from understanding how the adolescent mind works today – if I understood that a bit better my day job might be a tad easier than it is – but it's been very interesting for me to see the impact of the recent, now almost exhausted, vampire craze. *Buffy the Vampire Slayer,*

*Twilight,* and *The Vampire Diaries* may wear their adolescent sexual yearning rather more obviously on their sleeves than the old Universal and Hammer movies I grew up on, but it's clear to see that the symbolic representations of that overheated fantasy life still strike a chord – it's just that in today's world that breathless audience is almost exclusively female.

The male horror audience has largely decamped to the zombie as its monster of choice (slow, unthinking, unfeeling and *hungry* – it doesn't get much more male than that). As a result, vampires have transformed into 'a little something for the ladies', as an otherwise educated man recently described the orange juice beside the bottles of Stella in his fridge to me without a hint of face-saving irony.

The reason for this seems fairly clear. Even in this apparently more equal society, with gender roles and expectations no longer so absolute or so clearly defined, it remains much more difficult for girls to approach, or more importantly to be seen to approach, sex and desire in as direct and straightforward a way as boys. The double standards remain. The identical behaviour makes him a 'player' but her a 'slag', so the coded fantasies of the vampire story – the ultimate bad boy if ever there was one – strike home powerfully. The majority of teenage boys are well versed in the twilit and degraded world of the most explicit internet porn while grown women still hide behind the tasteful grey covers of *Fifty Shades of Shit*e.

For all that, however, I think I have to concede that the sudden rush of adoration I felt while watching *Dracula* came also from another and altogether more specific and personal need. The sexual imagery, after all, is there for everyone to see, but not everyone who saw the film finds themselves more than forty years later writing thousands of words on the subject, Aurora glow in the dark monster kits watching over their shoulder while they swig coffee from a mug with a fangs out Christopher Lee on it in a horror-memorabilia filled shed at the bottom of their garden. I entered into my lifelong relationship with the film and the rest of its demon kind because of something more direct and more particular.

Despite the rather cosy – and not untrue – portrait I recall of the moments leading up to that first encounter with movie horror, in many ways I was in fact a very unhappy twelve-year-old. I was secure at home with solid, loving parents, but in the outside world I was lost and miserable.

School was another, entirely separate world, and it was one I found completely impossible to cope with. The shithole to end all shitholes; school was a series of savage hierarchies, with me at the bottom of all of them. It would be wrong, of course, to try to give the impression that my high school was a cross between a Siberian Gulag, Room 101 and the lowest circle of hell; only that if you were trying to make a film about such a place, using it as a location would have enabled the production designer and the set decorators to put their feet up for a while.

Not that it was appreciably worse than any other state school in the 1970s I don't suppose, and perhaps even better than many. God, they were awful places. All those freezing mobiles; all that institutional snot green paintwork; the spam fritters and the semolina puddings (what the hell *is* semolina anyway?); the narrow gloomy corridors and the toilets of death - and all of it stale with the smell of decay, despondency and defeat. If, as it has become a cliché to say, the 70s really were the brown decade, at least some of that brownness – brown Cortinas, brown leather jackets, white dog poo for contrast, even tank tops – has attained a kind of *Life on Mars* retro chic. But not the schools. In the brown decade, they were the brown of mud and shit.

Me, I attended our local Grammar School, but only for a single year before (in accordance with the nobly egalitarian ideals that characterised the educational thinking of the day) it merged with the neighbouring Secondary Modern to become fully Comprehensive.

This conflict surrounding educational policy was one of the key philosophical battlegrounds fought between progressives and traditionalists that defined the 1970s. The debate, which rumbles on in education even today, runs something like this. On the one hand, it's clearly criminal that academic selection exiled the majority of the population to second class status from the age of eleven and the dream of replacing such an immoral system with a single, fair and equal access to education for everyone ought to be impossible to argue with.

On the other hand, it would be equally hard to argue with the assertion that grammar schools offered bright working class kids a shot at a life and opportunities inaccessible to their parents' generation, and, as it turned out, all but inaccessible to the generations which came after them. It's a fundamental condemnation of our society that there is less, not more, capacity for social mobility now than there was forty years ago. Part of the reason for this is that the closure of grammar schools like mine, however awful those schools were, saw a generation of aghast middle class parents who would previously have been perfectly happy with a grammar school education for their children now doing whatever it took to pull together the fees necessary to send them into the private sector.

In this way, the idealistic comprehensive reforms of the state system had the unforeseen side effect of handing a massive financial boost to struggling independent schools which might otherwise have disappeared altogether by the 1980s. Ironically, the drive towards fairness helped perpetuate, rather than eradicate, the inequalities within the system by propping up a truly elitist education eligible only to the few who could afford it. Most ironically of all, the Education Secretary who closed more

Grammar schools than any other was not Labour's Shirley Williams, but Margaret Thatcher, who held the post in the Heath government of the early 70s.

Whatever the merits of the philosophical arguments however, what is undeniable from my own personal experience of the change is that at the time and on the ground it was the worst of all possible worlds. We grammar school 'elite' retained a separate uniform until we outgrew it, were educated in separate classes in that ghastly parody of a ghastly public school, marked out as swotty gits by our grammar school tie but surrounded in the corridors by the full warp and weft of the comprehensive world in all its rich tapestry. We might as well have been given targets instead of badges on our blazers.

Not that I can pretend I found solidarity and comradeship within my narrow band of grammar school classmates. Au contraire. They hated me, and made that fact very clear. At the time I found it baffling and incomprehensible; everything I did, everything I was, was apparently laughable, ridiculous and wrong, but I didn't understand what I was supposed to do or to be instead. Looking back, of course I can understand, and far from feeling any resentment I'm inclined to side with my tormentors and against my weedy and wet, snotty and self-pitying twelve-year-old self.

For one thing, I wasn't blessed physically. Tall, gangly and very, very skinny (oh, how my middle aged self wishes for that problem now), with buck teeth, big ears, a crooked nose and unfashionable hair. And spots.

I discovered rather to my surprise in later life (somewhere in the nanosecond that came between acne and grey hair) that I wasn't bad looking. Not Johnny Depp, admittedly, but not Michael Gove (a man with a face that looks as though it was designed to loom through a porthole in a 1950s atomic age horror movie) either. Looking now at old photos I can see that back then there was really nothing wrong with me that wasn't wrong with everyone else too.

In any case, it's how we feel that is more important than any kind of objective reality. As time has gone on I've known many people who look like the back end of a particularly ill-favoured Routemaster to be extremely successful sexually, and by contrast many others who manage to combine statuesque good looks with all the attractiveness and allure of a pot plant. It's probably enough to say that at the time I felt ugly, and so I was.

For another I was, and still am, a natural obeyer of the rules with an instinctive and inbuilt fear of authority figures that amounts to a kind of dread of being caught out – a fact that has probably prompted my political sympathies into their lifelong leftist, anarchistic anti-authoritarian shape as a reaction against my forelock-tugging, cap-doffing personal instincts. Those instincts kept me well away from the smokers and the snoggers and the drinkers in the legendary realm behind the bike sheds, away from the popular naughty boys and the even more popular naughty girls and resolutely out of the in crowd.

We were also poor. Not in a *Boys from the Blackstuff* where is the next meal coming from kind of way, but sufficiently poor to mean I was aware of looking a little shabbier, a little different from most of the people around me. We lived in a biggish 30s semi in a decent area, which we mortgaged rather than rented, we had a car, we even once went on a week's holiday, but the holiday was to Southsea, not the Costa Del Sol, the 30s semi was a bit run down, and the car was a rusty 60s Singer Gazelle rather than an anonymous Ford. On the rare occasions my mum picked me up (my dad didn't drive) I used to slide down in the seat until I was almost horizontal to try to avoid being spotted.

I wore a faded blazer and too-skinny tie, a crucial year before the days when skinny ties became punk-fashionable, both of which had been handed down to me from my elder sister. For a time in between my school shoes falling apart and us being able to buy a new pair I was despatched in a pair of the steel toe-capped brown suede safety boots my mum wore to her factory job. It seems odd and a little irritating to me now that in the full knowledge of the kind of stick I was going to get for that I didn't simply refuse, but somehow you just didn't do that in our house. Instead, off I toddled to my inevitable doom looking like a slightly less butch Rosa Klebb. I don't mean to imply that there weren't other kids who were just as badly off, and many worse, but they all seemed to have personalities which could defuse it as a target for bile rather better than me.

Not only was I ugly and poor, I was clever enough to stand out a bit and stupid enough not to hide it. My mum was a Geordie and my dad fairly broad Norfolk, and the result of the combination for me was a standard English accent which, combined with a strangely pompous and antiquated way of expressing myself (not sure where that came from really; I think it was just liking words, and not seeing why certain phrases or bits of vocabulary should be out of bounds) marked me out as 'posh'. Crivens! Those deuced fellows gave me the very devil of a time for it!

Early on I remember overhearing another boy – Darby was his surname I think, though he was always known as 'JD' (the closest I got to a popular nickname was 'Bender') asking where he could find our cookery-teaching form tutor. Eager to be helpful, I pointed to a first storey window I'd clocked earlier and said 'She might be in that room. I can see cookery utensils in the window.' Handy hint, younger readers. 'Utensils' is not a word to bandy around lightly if you want to be a popular 11-year-old. Poor and posh is a tricky combination to carry off at the best of times, and I couldn't carry it off at all.

I couldn't even manage the one option which my taste in music and books (and even horror movies as time went on) might have made possible, which was to find some kind of safe haven in a sub culture of what would now be called 'alternative' like-minded kids. Today I would have had a ready-made outlet – I'd have been a goth or an emo – and in fact I was soon to find a bit more of a secure identity as I discovered and embraced punk and new wave for similar reasons. I saw some of myself in Costello's geeky speccy intelligence and sneer, in Rotten's howl of anger and the curl of Strummer's lip. Back in the summer of 77 though, my mum-bought clothes and my conventional once-every-six-weeks-regular-as-clockwork-down-the-road-to-Adrian's-unisex-stylists-haircut told against me.

In truth my mum and dad's salt of the earth solid working class respectability precluded that kind of escape route, which I wouldn't really begin to find until Sixth Form. They were both clever people, and books were embraced in our house rather than feared as strange alien invaders from another world – not so long ago I saw a perfectly pleasant fourteen-year-old I was tasked with inculcating with a love of Shakespeare and the Literary Heritage physically recoil from a pile of paperbacks at a school book sale as though they were somehow mysteriously slimy and contaminating. We weren't like that. The local library (remember them?) was a fortnightly fixture in our lives; we watched 'Play for Today' (though mum's verdict was almost always a variant on 'what a funny ending' or 'what was that all about then?'), but truth be told neither mum nor dad had an 'alternative' bone in their body. There simply wasn't the frame of reference for that process of osmosis that comes from having the right books and music lying around, the right films to have seen, the right holiday destinations to have experienced.

Of course at the time the cultural horizons of most people I knew were fairly limited and I'm not suggesting that I was sneered at or beaten up because of my lack of knowledge of Italian neo-realist cinema, only that the one sub-culture I might have had some kind of instinctual connection with was closed off to me.

No, I was very much on my own, and a 'natural victim' as the teachers who can't be bothered to do anything about it (and today I proclaim myself a proud member of their number) will tend to label the bullied to avoid the much more difficult task of confronting the pack.

There was one point above all the others though, which shamed and humiliated me more than everything else put together. I cried. At eleven and twelve years old, at high school, I still cried. I didn't mean to. I wasn't trying to earn sympathy. I wasn't attention seeking. In fact, I was desperate to *avoid* attention, and I'd have done anything to stop it but I couldn't. It just happened. Part of it was simply a natural reaction to being singled out and bullied and victimised, but often it came out over the most trivial stuff. 'I lost my PE kit!' 'Carl Pennington nicked my Doctor Who book!' My wailing reaction to that sort of thing would, obviously and not unreasonably, only heap further abuse upon my snivelling head. Of course I now recognise the self-perpetuating cycle. I cried over trivial stuff because I was profoundly unhappy about pretty big stuff (or at least pretty big to a twelve-year-old whose life was mainly school), and because I cried, more nasty stuff would happen to make me unhappier.

While I may still be prone to a few more tears than the average fifty something – though I've never compared notes on this with anyone: who knows, maybe there are whole legions of middle aged men who can't make it through the last half hour of *ET* without sobbing like a baby – I don't really think I'm especially thin-skinned or sensitive in my true nature. 'I was benevolent and good. Misery made me a cry-baby' as Mary Shelley has her articulate monster outsider almost say.

My days at school were grey with boredom and a barely suppressed hysteria always bubbling just under the stagnant water of the cesspit. For some time before I sat down to watch *Dracula* I'd been bullied and miserable; picked on at school by girls – often by older girls I didn't even know – for being ugly and unattractive, and all the time by boys of my own age for being gay and swotty and posh, and it didn't help at all to know that I wasn't. And it was into this world that Lugosi strode on the 2$^{nd}$ of July 1977, his screen presence one of complete, assured, commanding power.

Outlandish, heightened and stylised as my alternative bohemian self that never was could ever have aspired to be. Intelligent, yes, but also strong and powerful, as charismatic and enigmatic as my ideal self might ever have wished. Above all, controlled and in control. He was tall and erect, each odd gesture of the hands and fingers held with rigid precision. I slouched and stooped and stumbled. For all his evil, Lugosi's Dracula was a man absolute in self-possession and purpose, utterly secure in his own skin. Small wonder that an adolescent so insecure, so uncertain, so *opposite*, should identify so completely. To a bullied child, filled with self-doubt and uncertainty, the one I had been waiting for, my dark Messiah, had come. Lugosi was my dream self.

How could I resist? When he spoke those famous first lines it was me, far more than Dwight Frye's Renfield, who Lugosi was welcoming into a new world; a fantasy land where I would find many of my fears and obsessions, my desires and fascinations, played out in coded form; a dreamscape I was never really to leave.

Here in front of me was a rich and stylised world, endlessly fascinating and endlessly enjoyable, a world sumptuous and alien enough to enable me to lose myself entirely and forget the unhappiness of the everyday completely, and yet paradoxically a fantasy world in which I could also *find* myself, because these films for me were not simple escapism. I didn't develop a sudden love of glamorous MGM 30s musicals, for instance, and fixate upon Fred Astaire and Ginger Rogers – creatures of equally extraordinary and alien physical grace and beauty as Lugosi in their own way. A love of show tunes and Busby Berkeley might have taken my later life in an entirely different direction.

When I discovered the horror film, I found that through it I could view and confront difficult truths about myself and the world around me, but in distorted funfair mirror form. I recognized the selves and the worlds I saw, but they were drawn in such heightened, expressionistic shapes that they became not only manageable - it was possible to adore them, to luxuriate in them, all because of the exotic version of life that Lugosi introduced to me that summer's night in 1977. It's no exaggeration to say that those summer double bills saved me at a time I desperately needed saving, offering me some sense of validation and worth which I was otherwise entirely lacking.

Of course I was never consciously aware of all this back then. I didn't reflect on it – vampires not being good with reflections (see what I did there?). I only knew that I loved the films, deeply and totally. I never really *thought* about them at all. Or rather, I thought about them all the time, but in an entirely uncritical way that could hardly be called thinking in any meaningful sense. They filled my head (excerpt from M.Galley's stream of consciousness circa 1977: "*…belalugosi's brilliant isn't he yeah really brilliant yeah really really brilliant I wonder what frankenstein would have been like if he'd been in it really brilliant I should think yeah but karloffs great too him and lugosi in the raven was really brilliant…*") but I never really considered *why* they meant so much to me or why they colonised the inside of my head in quite such an alarmingly inane way.

In some ways I'm only becoming fully conscious of it now, as I write, and so perhaps only now am I beginning to truly realise just how much I owe to these films, how much they gave me at a time when I needed it most, and how deeply, deeply grateful I am for the comfort, and the joy, and the genuine inspiration they offered me. So, with apologies to one of my later heroes, George Orwell:

To the past and to the future; to whatever genius was controller of BBC2 Summer scheduling back then; to the disappearing concept of Public Service Broadcasting; to Universal Pictures; to Karloff and the Chaneys; to Hammer Films; to Cushing and Lee and Corman and Price, and to all the rest; and above all to Bela Lugosi, who himself lived at times a lonely and haunted life, old friend from my loneliest and most haunted days: from the age of irony; from the age of *Love Island;* from the age of Cowell and Cameron and Trump and BoJo; from my long gone and long ago twelve-year-old self and his middle aged child – Greetings. And thanks.

## 2.  HAVEN'T YOU EVER WANTED TO DO ANYTHING THAT WAS DANGEROUS?

### Frankenstein (1931, Universal, James Whale)

*'In the name of God? Now I know what it feels like to <u>be</u> God.'*
**Henry Frankenstein (Colin Clive)**

I didn't watch it.

Just pause for a moment, dear reader, to reflect on exactly what that means. To today's Skyplusing, netflixing, i-playering, rapidsharing, AmazonPriming, youtubing, blu-ray-buying generation it means absolutely nothing. In our world it has become almost impossible to 'miss' something you want to see. Everything (or almost everything) is always available somewhere, somehow. But this was 1977. I wouldn't own a video recorder for another decade. And in 1977, nobody owned them, and there were no digital channels to endlessly repeat everything on a loop cycle forever.

No, I didn't watch it, and that meant that, as my fannish obsession rapidly overtook me, I had no idea when, if ever, I might have another chance to see James Whale's masterful 1931 *Frankenstein*. In fact, BBC2 re-ran many of the Universal classics in a much less well-remembered season in 1983, two years after these double bills seemed to have come to a natural end. However, I didn't see *Frankenstein* then either, because I spent that long post-A level pre-university Summer of 1983 unsuccessfully Kerouacing my way across France, spectacularly failing to get off with all those free and easy Brigitte Bardot lookalikes my over fertile imagination had conjured up. Firstly, I discovered those fantasy girls didn't seem to exist, and secondly that even if they had existed, my fond hope that being barely able to speak their language (literal as well as metaphorical) would make me oddly intriguing and irresistible had been just a tad over optimistic.

I have a feeling the infant Channel 4 also ran a series of classic horror movies on a Friday night in the mid-80s sometime which would almost certainly have been my first encounter with the film. But that's six, maybe seven years later. *Seven years* before I got my second chance, by which time I was a longhaired student living in a scummy shared flat in Northern Ireland getting bladdered on Guinness and worshipping at the shrines of Joyce and Orwell rather than Karloff and Lugosi. The obsessive and self-absorbed 12-year-old boy from the summer of 77 to whom seeing the film would have really *meant* something had long since ceased to exist. The world by then was an utterly different place. All of which makes for a salutary lesson that opportunities in life are there to be taken, and may often be one time and one time only deals.

Of course I read about the film in the few Horror Movie books which I began to accumulate as birthdays and Christmases and saved pocket money allowed, cursing the madness that had come upon me and taken me to my bed rather than leaving me rapt in front of the TV screen. I studied stills, pored over the opinions of Alan Frank and Denis Gifford and Carlos Clarens, watched all of the sequels and lapped up the flashbacks to the original in both *Bride of Frankenstein* and *Ghost of Frankenstein* as this finest of all the BBC2 horror double bill seasons unrolled through the summer. So I pieced together a version of the film in my head long before I finally saw it. But nothing could substitute for that long gone and once only opportunity which I had allowed to slip through my fingers.

I would like to be able to console myself with the idea that it had not been my fault; that it had been out of my control. I would infinitely prefer to be able to shift the blame elsewhere, to be able to say that mum had drawn the line at the end of the first half of the double bill. That would have made some sense, at least.

Bedtime in our house was normally accomplished with militaristic zeal and rigour. It had been 9 o'clock without fail for years, although I think by this point a slow war of attrition had pushed the frontier back as far as half past, allowing me to watch some of the shows – often quality American import sitcoms like *MASH* or *Rhoda* – which occupied that crucial 30-minute slot in the schedules. It was perhaps as late as 10 or half past on a Saturday because it wasn't a school night – hence I shared the nation's brief, unlikely fixation with cop buddy series *Starsky and Hutch*. But the sudden and unprecedentedly indulgent laissez-faire flexibility I encountered on this particular night caught me totally off guard. Never mind a paltry half hour here or there, my newly liberal mum seemed to dismiss the very existence of 'bedtime' with a nonchalant wave of the hand.

I suspect in hindsight that she may have caught the glimpse of new fanaticism in my shining eyes as *Dracula* unspooled before me and, warm-hearted as she always was, saw some of that 'child aglow at Christmas' wonderment in my reaction which meant that she could not bring herself to curtail this sudden new love.

Both my parents were always exceptionally tolerant and encouraging of my odd fixations – for many years mum could, if pressed, list every Bond villain up to Stromberg in *The Spy Who Loved Me*; dad picked up my Spiderman comic from the newsagent every week without fail, and the battered and cherished copy I still own of *The Doctor Who Monster Book* was a present he brought back for me from the only training course I ever recall him being sent on. A couple of days in Portsmouth. Anyone else remember the days before training courses made us all worry about all the things we didn't know and hadn't been worrying about not knowing before because we didn't know about not knowing them?

I think now that their willingness to accept and embrace my embryonic fanboy was because they saw in these sudden rushes of excitement and wide-eyed enthusiasm something of the little boy they remembered, as opposed to the increasingly withdrawn and taciturn adolescent I was becoming.

In any case, whatever the reason, with no advance warning mum simply asked me if I was going to watch the next film. She didn't want to see it – she remembered *Frankenstein* as 'all flashing lights and noises', a critical response to Whale's landmark of cinema not shared, I was to discover, by Gifford or Frank et al – but I was welcome to stay up on my own if I wanted to.

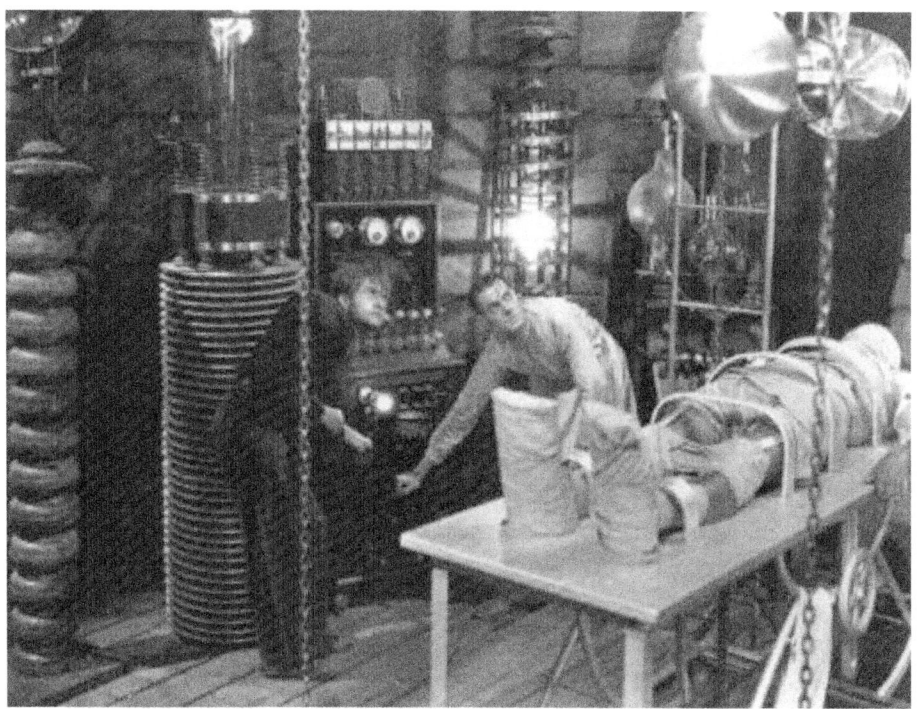

*James Whale's 'Flashing Lights and Noises.'*

So *Dracula* – literally the most fantastic thing I had ever seen – had finished, and where I had taken it for granted that at this point I was to be despatched to my little box room at the back of the house a sudden and spectacular possibility opened up to me of prolonging this magical night even further. Unable to believe my luck, there was only one thing anyone in this wondrous position could say. 'No mum, that's OK. I'll go to bed.'

Wait, what? 'No mum, that's OK. I'll go to bed?' Cretin! What was the matter with you child?

What could have possessed me? I'd just seen the best film ever – the progenitor of a genre that was immediately to become a desperate obsession – but opted not to bother with *Frankenstein*, not the first in the cycle, but certainly the most influential. It was Karloff's monster, rather than Lugosi's Dracula, who lurched his poignant way through a series of sequels, almost inventing the now industry standard idea of the 'franchise', in that as in so many ways years ahead of its time.

Was I tired? Nobody is that tired. Believe me, by the time the next Saturday double bill rolled around it wouldn't have mattered if I'd just escaped from a month or two as the victim of a CIA sleep deprivation experiment, I'd still have propped my eyes open for the hour and a half it took to enjoy the second film.

Perhaps it has to do with a certain inborn and instinctive caution that is a strong part of my psychological makeup; a caution that has kept me, for instance, working in the same room in the same building at the same job for the past thirty years. I enjoy teaching, but I'm in little doubt that fear of change has more to do with this almost unheard of immobility than contentment with things as they are. It's a personality trait that has made most of my life less a question of 'seize the day' than 'wait and see the day after tomorrow'. 'Carpe Diem' be damned, 'hang on a mo' is my motto. *Dracula* had been such an intense experience that, fearing either disappointment or total overload, I took the safe option and went to bed rather than risk either. 'Haven't you ever wanted to do anything that was dangerous?' Colin Clive's Henry Frankenstein asks in exasperation early in the film. I'm afraid my reply would be an unequivocal 'No.'

In later life we had a very hard time surrounding the birth of our first child – I use 'we' in that self-aggrandizing, right-on, new man sense which actually means my wife suffered rather a lot very bravely while I stood around uselessly on the sidelines trying not to snivel – involving miscarriages, an ectopic pregnancy and eventually an emergency caesarean and a haemorrhage which resulted in a seemingly endless blood transfusion on the operating table while I held my newborn daughter and wondered if my wife was going to die in front of me. A couple of years later, blessed with a beautiful daughter and my wonderfully still alive and still wonderful wife, in a way that was rather symptomatic of the same spirit that had cost me *Frankenstein* so long before (although admittedly relating to a marginally more significant subject), I had a very vivid sense of having 'got away with it' and after such a narrow escape was bitterly and adamantly opposed to the idea that we should push our luck any further.

Like most good moles, however, I find the wild-eyed adventurousness of your average water rat irresistibly attractive and, fortunate to say, with her customary abandon my significant other overruled my needless fears and objections and as a result we have a second and equally extraordinary daughter.

This is the complete set though, finally, definitively and absolutely – and I love complete sets; obsessive collecting being somehow DNA spliced with the horror movie gene – this last sentence being included in the unlikely event that my wife, still on occasion worryingly broody, should ever overcome her aversion to horror films enough to be reading this.

Not everything can be put down to inborn instinct however, and inevitably I now see that a part of this reticence, this reluctance to simply grab things I want with both hands, stems from my family and the kind of home I grew up in.

By contrast to what I've said about my time at school, my home was a place of absolute warmth and security. It's possible in fact that this stark contrast between two mutually exclusive spheres of existence helps explain my immediate acceptance and embrace of the horror films that I was discovering, which of course have the idea of duality at their very heart. Dr Frankenstein mirrored by his monstrous creation; poor tormented Larry Talbot and his Wolf Man alter ego; by day one way and by night another (no, sorry, that last one's from *Shrek*, but you get the idea). My own life contained two entirely separate states of being and I was a different person in each; it couldn't have been much of a leap to see Jekyll and Hyde as no more than an accurate symbolic reflection of what to me was simply an everyday reality.

My parents were a fixed point of complete certainty; they loved both me and my sister, and one another, with an absolute, unquestioned and unquestioning devotion. I didn't worry about them; I didn't really have to think about them at all, they were just *there*, and I knew they always would be. I'm sure I'm not alone in this. The past is another country, and one that didn't seem to include divorce or separation in its customs. I don't know how unusual this was, but I literally did not know anyone with divorced parents back then – glancing around my classroom today it seems quite hard to find a kid without them.

Even in the context of the time, however, I think there was something exceptional about the degree of comfort and – for want of a better word – *cosiness* that enveloped me as a child. Life was birthdays and bonfires and long long hours of back garden football and the deep warm butterflies of Christmas and of course I know, I know, part of this is just that aching A.E. Houseman land of lost content blue remembered hills rose-tinted recollection of a middle aged man looking back on what has passed away, but part of it is simply *true*. That's how it was.

Life was unvarying, untroubled routine. Up at the same time each day and to bed at the same time each night. The same meals on the same nights each week. Coffee made with milk boiled in the same pan at ten past eight every night (never eight, always ten past) and always signalled by some tuneless humming of whatever piece of music it was that accompanied the Nescafe ads of the time. Mum and dad never quarrelled. Never swore. I barely remember a raised voice – except for the annual blazing one-or-two-too-many-fuelled Christmas rows about the most bizarrely innocuous of subjects. I recall one, which reduced most of the house to tears of rage and frustration, about John McEnroe, and another about my failure to 'play in the street', mum having somehow failed to notice a slight build up in traffic between the Newcastle of the 1930s which spelled childhood to her and the reality of living on a 1970s main road.

No, things at home were safe and secure; mum and dad valued peace and quiet and gardening (they were both tall, but in most other respects it was a bit like being raised by hobbits), and although my adolescent self was unable to share the warm nostalgic glow which now suffuses all my memories of home, the worst he would have been able to say about it was that he sometimes found the environment just a little *too* safe, to the point of being a tad stifling. The Sex Pistols' *Never Mind the Bollocks* for instance, was banned in our house, always a much stricter and more effective censor than even the stuffily paternalistic BBC of the day, and had to be surreptitiously smuggled from Andy's Records into my bedroom to hide between the ELOs and Manfred Manns.

Above all, I was loved, in a comfortably quiet and undemonstrative way.

I suppose that what I'm driving at here, with all the limited insight and perspective that the passing years have given me, is that our home was like a bubble of cosiness separated invisibly from a colder, harsher outside world, but like all bubbles it could only exist with the agreement of all inside not to pop it. I think in the end it was this that was at the root of my failure to grab the chance to watch the film, and in the longer term to allow other, more significant opportunities in life to slip by.

I didn't ask to stay up for *Frankenstein,* even though it was clear nobody would have minded if I had, in exactly the same spirit in which I never shared a single word about what was happening to me at school. I think I can see now that I was keenly aware of the need to avoid ever being too excessive or too demanding in anything, in case it troubled the secure surface of our little world. Problems simply weren't permitted access to the bubble of our lives, and to introduce them – whether in the shape of something as trivial as the slightly unusual idea that I would stay up after everyone else had gone to bed, or more seriously that I was quite miserable for a lot of the time – would have been a breach of the unspoken contract we'd all signed up to that we would live in a place quite separate from the anxieties and the fears and the worries that existed *out there,* outside the bubble.

All this was never voiced, or made explicit. I just somehow knew, or felt, that however much I might want to, staying up for the film was *the wrong thing to do.* At least until the next week, by which time the selfishness that inevitably goes with all true obsessions made me happily set aside such qualms.

As a child I accepted the never stated rules that underpinned the serenity of our house unquestioningly. Children are good observers, and have an instinctive understanding of the clues they witness; on the rare occasions problems of a fairly average and everyday sort intruded on their lives, mum and dad struggled to cope. We had a cowboy builder do an extension once, who did the usual trick (and not an unreasonable one, given the irregular nature of so much of their income) of booking up a few jobs simultaneously and flitting between them, so that the deadline for completion slipped further and further away during days and weeks of nobody arriving to finish the work. When he did appear one day, mum physically keeled over during the ensuing confrontation.

Of course it's not the worst parental crime in the world – in fact it's no crime at all – to make your home a safe and softly spoken bubble world, and I speak now as someone all too aware of the terrible parenting decisions I'm sure I'm in the process of making. We do our best with the hand we're dealt, and I'm afraid Philip Larkin with his deepening coastal shelves, his man handing on misery to man and his fucking-up parents may have been right, though he can still piss off for being such a dreary misogynistic right-wing professional pessimist. What I finally begin to see now, however, with that recognition of a shared humanity with your parents that only comes later in life – and sometimes after they've already gone – are some of the reasons my mum and dad *needed* to build a home so utterly calm and untroubled.

I remember being fascinated when I was very young by the cover of a book – I don't remember the title at all – which showed a boy reading the same book, which in turn showed the same boy reading the same book, and becoming preoccupied with the idea that, starting with me if I sat and held the book in the same way as the boy on the cover, the sequence must literally go on getting smaller and smaller *forever.*

Dealing with the past is a bit like that. Begin to get to grips with yourself and you have to look further back to see why your parents were that way, which takes you to their parents and on and on in an inescapable nexus of cause and effect ad infinitum. However, I promise to delve no further into the past than the early lives of my mum and dad, since this is a book about horror movies rather than about infinite regression. I've got to leave some territory to Aristotle; after all, he was kind enough not to mention *Frankenstein Meets the Wolf Man* in *Posterior Analytics*.

What I am now capable of realising is that, in different ways, both my parents had experienced traumatic childhoods a million miles removed from the security and stability of mine.

The success of *Angela's Ashes* and *A Child Called It* a few years ago spawned a competition to discover the most heinous and appalling backgrounds it was possible for anyone to come from and publish exhaustive and prurient accounts of the horrors their authors had endured, to be drooled over with sadistic, almost pornographic glee by their wet-mouthed readers. The vogue for the misery memoir was a ghastly, *genuinely* ghoulish phenomenon which fortunately seems to have abated with the diminishing returns on the publisher's balance sheets, and by the standards set by some of those dreadful books, and, sadly, by comparison with the truly appalling circumstances that many people have endured, mum and dad didn't have much to complain about, but that's not the point. It ain't what you do, it's what it does to you.

Mum was the youngest of three children, born in 1931 into a picturesque, everyone knows everyone, you could leave your front door open, children playing in the streets and fields kind of Northumbrian village in which her dad cut a dashing and well respected figure as a local fireman. Well respected until people found out he was having it off with the local lady of the manor that is – all very Catherine Cookson, isn't it? My gran Kitty had altogether too much pride and self-respect to turn a blind eye, with the upshot being that she ended up having to feed and clothe three young children – Cath, George, and Ann, my mum – as a single mother in pre-Welfare State, depression era Newcastle. Times were Jarrow March tough for everyone back there and then, but perhaps especially for a woman on her own with three kids. She coped on her wage as a cleaner in the hospital, supplementing it by – as quite a few people did at the time – running a 'pub' from her front room.

Mum worshipped her own mother, but never talked much about her dad, with whom she had no contact at all when growing up: although she did tell me much later that she'd visited him in hospital when he was dying and felt absolutely nothing for a man who was a total stranger to her. I am fairly clear that she carried a sense of betrayal with her from that very, very young age, and lived with a sense of men as essentially predatory and untrustworthy. I think that accounts – as far as the mysteries of love are ever to be accounted for, which isn't far, truth be told – for her falling so completely and irrevocably for a man as gentle and placid and essentially *reliable* as my dad and creating a world of security never to be called into doubt, as our home.

Like mum, my dad had known childhood poverty and hardship – that's *real* poverty, by the way, not the clapped out car, shabby school uniform version that was a part of my 70s childhood – born in 1929 in a tiny cottage on the then still very rural outskirts of Norwich.

I live in Norwich myself, and love my home city, with its two rivers and its castle and cathedral and university, and as such of course I bitterly resent the patronising view of the city trotted out by lazy metropolitan journalists which suggests that twenty first century Norwich is still somehow essentially *quaint* and rural – I drive a Toyota, not a tractor, and we even have running water and electricity these days – but back then there was certainly a measure of truth in the image. Small holdings all around, livestock in most back gardens – my dad earned a bit of extra pocket money from the old lady at the end of the street by collecting eggs from her vicious and terrifying goose, a mission he was only able to accomplish by pinning the spitting monster's scrawny neck against the wall with the Y end of a handy clothesline prop.

All very Lark Rise, with my granddad's wages as a slaughterman the only income and four young children – Doreen, (or Auntie Dodo as she was known forever afterwards to us), Gerald, my dad Roy, and Derek, the youngest. It was a crowded poverty that sent my dad into the Royal Navy as soon as he could join up, although it was no real sacrifice to him as it turned out; he gained a trade as an electrician and as much male bonding as he could have wanted.

Never an obviously testosterone-fuelled, hairy-knuckled, sloping-forehead version of a man's man, nonetheless dad always enjoyed all-male groups and cliques and seemed to actively seek them out in a working life that included the railways and the prison service. Life as a sailor also gave him the opportunity, as a green, know-nothing provincial boy to travel as far and as widely as any young nineteenth century gentleman on 'the tour'. Strange how the navy offered the working classes opportunities and experiences usually reserved for the very few; in later life dad took great pleasure in watching travel programmes and repetitively announcing 'been there … been there…' as each new and exotic destination was Judith Chalmersed into our living room.

There's no doubt in my mind, however, that it wasn't a very real, but widely shared and essentially unexceptional poverty that formed the key formative experience of my dad's early life, but the teenage death of his younger brother Derek.

I said earlier that mum hadn't talked much about her father when we were growing up, but compared to my dad she was loquacity itself. Always a quiet man, he was tight-lipped to the point of neurosis on the subject of Derek; sufficiently so to make that famously terrible interview between Parkinson and Robert Mitchum (Mitchum: "yep…nope…yep…"

for twenty minutes) seem like the sort of gushing weepy confessional that Piers Morgan would be proud of. Until I was legally an adult I didn't even know dad had had a younger brother because he had literally never mentioned his name.

Even after all this time I'm still not sure how much of this was about protecting us from the harshest realities of life for as long as he could and how much was about his own inability to confront the pain he continued to feel all his life at the monstrous unfairness of the loss, although I strongly suspect both played a part in roughly equal measure. I sometimes wonder how my relationship with the glorious morbidity of all these death-fixated movies might have been different had I been born into an earlier generation, one in which it would have been odds on that I would have come to know real loss, real bereavement, at a much earlier age than I did.

I'm still uncertain of the details – which I'd have gathered eventually from dad's exhaustingly garrulous elder sister (my Aunt Dodo) although I don't have any recollection of the specific occasion – perhaps because at the time I first heard the story I would have felt a certain shamefaced guilt that somehow *I shouldn't know this* and therefore allowed the specifics to slip away over time into the vaguest possible form. It was a part of dad's life he'd chosen never to share, and for his sake it seemed somehow intrusive and ugly to dwell on it. In broad terms, however, I know there was some sort of accident – although 'accident' makes it sound more appropriately dramatic than it was; in fact, it was an incident terrifyingly banal and commonplace, like being hit by a football or something – which, because of complications caused by Derek's pre-existing diabetes – ended up being terminal.

I remember once (I'm not sure how old I would have been, but young, certainly pre-Lugosi by some years) playing with a pair of grown-up steel and black binoculars which, along with the hard brown leather case they lived in had interested me from as early as I can recall, and dropping them on the kitchen floor. They didn't break, but dad went very quiet (more quiet, that is) and mum flew into an inexplicable rage, which in the almost preternatural placidity of our home seemed all the more bizarre and out of proportion.

It was only many, many years later that I came to understand. The binoculars came up in Dodo's account of Derek's last days – my granddad (who I never met but was a hard man by all accounts, a survivor of the trenches and German gas) returning teary-eyed from seeing his dying son and describing how his youngest wouldn't complain, wouldn't whine, but only wished he could see out of the window a bit better to fill the time. 'Poor little bugger', my granddad said, and spent money they didn't have on a pair of binoculars which had been passed on to my dad after Derek's death.

I suppose I could expend a bit of energy and research to find out more of the story but that really isn't the kind of approach I'm taking here. I'm not trying to write about objective facts, but about subjective memory. It's the vague, inconclusive version of these stories that are a part of me, that have helped shape me, not dates or clinical diagnoses. In much the same spirit, the sharper eyed amongst you, dear readers, will have noticed that there hasn't been much analysis of *Frankenstein* in a chapter supposedly about the film, but that's as it should be. I didn't see it at the time, so the impact of the film on me wasn't direct – it was as a mistake, a loss, a missed opportunity, that I experienced it, and that's what I've tried to reflect.

One single comment I will make at this point however. For many years (and probably including this 70s screening I think) it was impossible to see the film in full – censorship had expurgated Karloff's accidental, and entirely innocent, drowning of a young child, and also Colin Clive's wild cries as his creation stirs for the first time ('In the name of God … now I know what it feels like to *be* God') which were seen as, respectively, too hideously painful and too blasphemous to be allowed to assault the delicate sensibilities of the audience of the day.

Of course it doesn't need saying that the censors who took their cack-handed scissors to *Frankenstein* were idiots, but I think it's also worth acknowledging that they were responding, albeit absurdly, to a genuine coldness and brutality within the film.

It is unremittingly bleak, with none of the leavening wit and high-camp which characterises the rest of James Whale's Universal output (*The Invisible Man, The Old Dark House, Bride of Frankenstein*). No concessions are made. The film has a raw edge, presenting us with the cold dark truth of a harsh and empty world, an essentially godless universe in which people are fundamentally *stuff*, not spirit. It's a film without the religious, Manichaean idea of Evil or Good – only blind mischance and misguided, misaligned humanity.

All of which might be an appropriate point to make, even though it was years later when I finally saw the film, since it's a world view which – though I don't share it entirely – has come to represent a significant element in the way I see and respond to the world around me.

Rather to my surprise, I discovered in my later teenage years that dad was a militant atheist. He was very tolerant of others' beliefs (mum was a non-practising Catholic by this point, but always retained a vague, optimistic sense of a loving God above, an afterlife to be shared and a great respect for the church) but in his own private convictions his atheism was strident and severe.

At about 15, for instance, I found myself taking an interest in the slightly more offbeat end of commercial cinema, which was as close to arthouse as a provincial teenager of my background was likely to get, but lacking any similarly inclined friends and being a bit too timid to go to cinemas on my own, I prevailed on my dad's good nature to go along with me to stuff like David Lynch's *The Elephant Man*, Werner Herzog's remake of *Nosferatu*, Woody Allen's *Manhattan* and the like. It was walking back together from this last one (still perhaps my favourite of all Allen's films) at Norwich's Odeon, that he stopped at the queue outside the other cinema the city had to offer (the ABC, if anyone else remembers those) and took me into *Life of Brian* which for weeks previously I'd been pleading unsuccessfully with mum that I should be allowed to see. A chance like this to cock a snook at a non-existent god was just too hard for him to resist, and he laughed longer and louder than anyone else in the cinema.

Part of this, of course, is about simple truth. Non-belief is a given; it's for believers to have to explain and justify themselves. We atheists are right, until somebody – or Somebody – can prove us wrong. Though of course we'll look bloody silly on Judgement Day when He pops up to do just that. Dad was, in the best sense, a sceptic and a rationalist - traits I've inherited in part, although coupled uncomfortably in me with an alarming degree of new age credulity: Mulder and Scully constantly arguing in my head.

The other part, however, I have no doubt was owed in kind to his lifelong anger at the cold indifference of a purposeless universe which could have allowed his young brother to die so cruelly, brutally early.

*Frankenstein*, in other words, is the kind of film my dad might have made (had he had any interest in horror movies, and had he been a 1930s Hollywood film director rather than a 1970s hospital electrician, which is all a bit of a leap admittedly, but bear with me, I know what I mean). Because the film's bleak secularity is, in the end, more inimical both to the platitudes and to the genuine comfort offered by religious faith than any more immediately controversial but ultimately church-friendly horror fare, like *The Exorcist, The Omen* or, I'm forced to admit, *Dracula*.

So, with no disrespect to the genius of James Whale, I'm paying my own personal tribute here to a slightly different, alternate timeline, parallel world version of the film. Boris Karloff (or '?' as he was billed at the time) as the monster in *Frankenstein; Or, Up Yours the Almighty*, a film by Roy Norman Galley, the kindest-faced, gentlest-hearted director never to make a stir in cutthroat Tinseltown. And that's a movie I *would* have stayed up late to watch.

# DOUBLE BILL TWO

## Saturday July 9th 1977

BRIDE OF FRANKENSTEIN        22.50 – 00.00

BRIDES OF DRACULA            00.00 – 01.25

## 3. ALONE BAD

### Bride of Frankenstein (1935, Universal, James Whale)

*'Alone Bad. Friend Good.'*
**The Creature (Boris Karloff)**

Now I was hooked. *Dracula* had been a glorious surprise, *Frankenstein* a missed opportunity; it was with a week's wait and *Bride* that I truly succumbed to obsession. I suppose it was inevitable, though I do sometimes wonder what might have happened if the following week's offering had been instantly forgettable – one of the largely undistinguished and indistinguishable *Mummy* sequels for instance. Would *Dracula* have forever remained an extraordinary one-off in my mind?

I doubt it. I think I'd have persevered; the grounds for symbiosis between the awkward, uncomfortable adolescent and the awkward, uncomfortable genre were almost certainly too fertile to have dried up so easily, but you never know. As it was, however, the possibility never arose, since the next Saturday served up what is widely regarded as the very best horror film ever made.

*Bride of Frankenstein* is exceptional in many ways, not the least of which is in being a sequel which surpasses the power of the original – not a claim anyone is likely to make for *Halloween 3: Season of the Witch* or *Blair Witch 2: Book of Shadows*, say. It's also unusual in the degree to which it has gained an audience beyond fans of the genre – there's even an extended reference in the film of Nick Hornby's *About a Boy*.

Mainstream critics have always been more than a touch sniffy about horror movies, but *Bride of Frankenstein* is the exception, receiving almost universal acclaim as the foremost example of its kind and one of the most important films of the 1930s in any genre. Perhaps this is because the distinctive characteristics and idiosyncratic vision of James Whale, the film's director, are so clear for all to see here that *Bride* can be regarded more as an auteurist masterwork than a production line genre piece. Rarer still though, in the light of this wider acceptability, is that the film never condescends to its genre; never appears to be craving the more rarefied air of critical respectability at the expense of its deliciously perverse horrors – no-one could accuse Whale's masterpiece of being a horror movie for people who don't like horror movies.

What makes *Bride* so special is difficult to define, but perhaps it lies in the fact that no other film within the genre represents quite so perfect a commingling of so many disparate elements. There's a literate and subversive screenplay; beautiful cinematography and lavish set design;

Whale's incredibly deft blend of sly, dark humour and absolute, unbearably touching sincerity; Franz Waxman's majestic score which is by turns lush, romantic, witty and profound (the earliest horror movies had been slow to pick up on the possibilities of the soundtrack; both *Dracula* and *Frankenstein* feature only diegetic sound and beyond this unfold in eerie silence); Jack Pierce's makeup designs scoring a fantastic double whammy with both the reprise of the Monster and Elsa Lanchester's extraordinary Bride; and of course Ernest Thesiger's arch, bravura, scene-stealing performance as Dr Pretorius.

Even so, the film isn't *quite* perfect. I for one could happily do without the excruciating Villa Diodati 'how I wrote the monster' prologue with Gavin Gordon's agonisingly ill-judged Byron desperrrrrrrately r rolling and 'enunciating' in a toe-curling attempt to connote … *something*, though I've never been quite sure what, and Una O'Connor's shrill comic turn as housekeeper Minnie grates more than it amuses.

*'May I present my latest composition, entitled "Rrrrround the rrrugged rrrrocks..."'*

Nonetheless, the film's pleasures are endless and immaculate, and chief among them is the pathos and beauty of Karloff's performance. For me, no-one can top Lugosi and Vincent Price for presence and charisma, but if, rather than these qualities, one values range and subtlety and nuance then, along with Peter Cushing, Karloff was the finest *actor* to be associated with the genre, and he's never better than here.

It's a commonplace to suggest that the Universal films create pathos: a sense of their monsters as victims, but in fact in the later films in the Frankenstein cycle it's very hard to see the truth of the claim. No disrespect towards Lon Chaney Jr., or Lugosi, or Glenn Strange who between them filled the role of the Creature (the term Karloff always preferred to the M word) from *Ghost of Frankenstein* onwards, but in those post-Karloff films the character is largely seen as no more than a snarling signifier of 'danger', to be brought to life, smash something, or someone, before a handy fire disposes of him all over again. Or perhaps a handy swamp, to avoid appearing overly formulaic. In Karloff's delicate hands, however, the creature is truly an innocent; child-like in his helpless, hopeless capacity for destruction and always, irrevocably and tragically, more sinned against than sinning.

The power of *Bride* doesn't only lie in the exceptional quality of the text itself, of course; the social context of the film's production lends it a greater resonance. Horror movies have always been closely attuned to their own particular zeitgeist, holding a distorting mirror up to the events and anxieties of their times, from Lon Chaney's post WW1 studies in disfigurement and amputation to the cold war fears of the 50s atomic age monster movies, and it's easy to see Karloff's 1930s monster as a veiled comment on a tormented and vengeful proletariat in the midst of the Great Depression. The costume design, with those ill-fitting clothes and asphalt-spreaders boots, underlines the metaphor persuasively, and it's tempting to see the monster lumbering disconsolately across the landscape as the carnival reflection of Lennie from Steinbeck's *Of Mice and Men* (a part which, in a pleasing co-incidence, first made the name of Universal's soon-to-be monster of choice for the 1940s, Lon Chaney Jr.); a portrait of rootless, hopeless, itinerant labour, shambling and lost, unaware of its own strength and innocently, mindlessly destructive; an archetypal role filled for many of us in the ugly 80s by Alan Bleasdale's Yosser Hughes.

And it was in the 1980s that class as a concept and a social reality became a very vivid and immediate issue for me. For one thing, Margaret Thatcher *made* it an issue, placing her own psychotic, pathological hatred of we proles at the heart of the political agenda of the day and politicising an otherwise apathetic generation as a result. But it wasn't a battle that was only fought on the picket line at Orgreave or in the burning inner cities. For me it was more personal than that. A fully formed product of the Welfare State and the first member of my family to go to university, I found myself surrounded, for the only time in my life, almost exclusively by the middle classes.

I'm pleased to be able to say that I never tried to hide or deny my class and my background; less pleased to have to admit that I rather exaggerated my working class credentials, wearing them like another badge alongside the shiny tin circles declaring my support for CND, the Anti-Nazi League and The Clash which adorned my baggy student overcoat. Lacking the self-confidence to compete on a level playing field with all those Guys and Jeremys, I used my class as a readymade shortcut to 'cool and interesting', cultivated a vocal pomme-frite on my shoulder, and created a not completely fictitious but still essentially fraudulent identity for myself as working class hero and angry young man.

Cringing inwardly each time my friends exposed a little more of my working class lack of sophistication – each time I didn't know the difference between Caerphilly and Camembert, Muscadet and Chablis, or Bensons and Gitanes – I'd defend myself by adopting an increasingly Stalinist party line on what kinds of knowledge were bourgeois and trivial, and revealed not my basic ignorance but my housemates' pampered incomprehension of what real life was like out there in the real world (which meant the urban jungle that was Norwich as far as I was concerned).

'Mushrooms are middle class,' I once declared decisively, arbitrarily condemning them with ruthless politburo efficiency to the same gulag to which I'd previously exiled wax jackets and champagne and caviar and Virginia Woolf. The basis for my anti-mushroom edict was that we never had them at home (the ultimate arbiter of all class matters), although I later discovered this was due to a bout of food poisoning suffered by mum and dad before I was born, rather than anything intrinsically anti-proletarian in the hapless fungi themselves. I think it's fair to say I was not a fun guy (see what I did there?) to be with at the time.

All this formed the spine of my academic concerns and focus. Angered by what I saw as his patronising and sentimental approach to his working class characters, I wrote a snarling and superficial attack on Dickens, a writer I later came to love with all my heart; an undergraduate dissertation on Orwell, surely the most class conscious of all novelists; and for my MA turned my attention to Robert Tressell's wonderful and still too little-read radical novel *The Ragged Trousered Philanthropists*. Oh, how the Establishment trembled! I made sure that my well-thumbed copies of Marx's *Early Writings, Das Kapital* and *Communist Manifesto* sat snugly between my big red-spined biography of Che Guevara and my copy of Mao's little red book in the most prominent and easily noticeable section of my bookshelves – nudging Denis Gifford's *Pictorial History of Horror Movies* and Alan Frank's Movie Treasury *Horror Movies* onto the next shelf down. And of course, as a Literature student in the 1980s Terry Eagleton and his book *Marxism and Literary Criticism* became second nature to me. Or almost, anyway.

Something in me held back, just a little. The strictures and tenets of an exclusively ideological analysis of Literature always felt somehow inhuman, dehumanising, and blinkered to me. Something in me always wanted to shout 'there's more to *Women in Love* than base and superstructure and ideological state apparatus!' For all its innate conservatism, mainstream Leavisite criticism always felt much closer to the true heart of why I loved books and stories than the Marxist or Structuralist terminology I found myself trying to ventriloquize.

Perhaps it came down to the fact that I could imagine actual flesh and blood proletarians like my dad, who, without the benefit of a university education had a wide but patchy reading history that took in Shakespeare and Wilde and Dickens and Sterne alongside sea stories and cowboy books and Howard Spring and Leon Uris, reading, understanding, and even enjoying a 'Great Tradition' literary critic like F.R. Leavis, but I couldn't see the same being true of the likes of Lukács, Barthes or Derrida.

The rigid, impenetrable language itself formed a block, which suggested to me the formation of a new elitism, and which was simply not shaped to catch a sense of what it was to love, to feel, to be fully human in the way in which you can through and within literature.

This is perhaps partly why, persuasive though it is on some levels, the 'Monster as proletariat' reading of *Bride of Frankenstein* doesn't quite work for me. For one thing, the Universal movies are filled with representations of the working class, and by and large they're the ones brandishing the pitchforks and the burning torches and baying for Karloff's blood.

At best I think you could argue that the monster represents the abyss of dispossession and underclass despair which, in their worst nightmares, the respectable working class fear tumbling into. And of course it's at times like these, and like the 1930s, and like the 1980s, times of recession and depression, that the nightmare comes closest to the surface. Karloff's shambling giant is the homeless, friendless, penniless monster we might become if the bank forecloses and the factory shuts down, if the multinational downsizes and we're undercut by third world sweatshops, if we're made literally and figuratively redundant by austerity budgets and Brexit and public spending cuts and even pandemics. Of course the truth is we're always skating on thin ice, but in days like these we can feel the chilly water nipping at our toes.

It was this kind of combined working class fear and pride which sent my poor old parents almost apoplectic with worry every time I exceeded yet another student overdraft limit, wringing their hands with anxiety as each new threatening letter from my bank manager slapped onto the doormat when I escaped my debts by running home for the holidays.

For all that however, I still don't feel that the resonance of the film and of Karloff's performance in particular, is ultimately to be defined in terms of class anxieties or class consciousness. It's a broader, more universal sense of longing which pulls so relentlessly at me. In the end *Bride of Frankenstein* carries the power it does because somehow, mysteriously, it puts me in touch with the *yearning* that seems to me to be a central component of the human condition.

I'm not ashamed to say that, sentimental and religiose though it may be, the blind hermit scene (parodied so beautifully by Mel Brooks in his affectionate pastiche *Young Frankenstein*) moves me profoundly to this day, and that Karloff can bring me close to tears with the simple movement of his hands as he sees his newly animated 'bride' for the first time – so full of tenderness and loneliness and hope. The point, in the end, is that Karloff's monster is *us,* all we ordinary types, we who Nietzsche considered the bungled and the botched, the great mass of unfiltered humanity, filled with failure and defeat and self-loathing and cursed with hopes and dreams and empty wishes.

I'm as moved as I am by Karloff's pitiable little circling of his hands in supplication and shy welcome towards Elsa Lanchester's Bride because I've *felt* the intensity of that simultaneous hope and trepidation and fear in the face of longing and desire. I *am* the monster in those moments. Not that I was stitched together with spare parts from stolen corpses and animated with a brain handily labelled 'abnormal', although as I move through my fifties this seems increasingly possible each time I look in the mirror, particularly on a Monday morning.

Nonetheless, awkward and clumsy and naive, helplessly hopeful, I am the monster. And so are you. And this is the true secret of this most enduring of all horror movie icons. A creature from the wildest realms of fantasy, a half man with a flat head and electrodes through his neck who becomes, in Karloff's tender care, Everyman.

At university, as a pale student of the Arts (unhallowed or otherwise), I knew a breathtakingly beautiful girl named Evelyn Wilson with hair the colour of falling leaves and eyes bluer than summer, the girl that all the songs and poems are about. She wasn't my dream girl, as it turned out, as I'm one of the tiny percentage of the population in the fortunate and – if we're truthful, exceptionally rare – position of ending up married to my dream girl. In quite another sense, however, Evelyn was my *dream* girl – a figure from a fantasy world who seemed to have stepped, fully-formed, out of my dreams – though never into my arms, sadly, despite the song.

There's an achingly poignant moment in *Citizen Kane* where Orson Welles' old editor Mr Bernstein describes a girl in a white dress with a parasol he once glimpsed, for a few seconds only, on a passing ferry. 'I don't believe there's been a month gone by since then that I haven't thought about her,' Bernstein concludes wistfully, the rapture of the memory serving to underline his idealisation of not only the unknown girl, but of his own lost youth.

I did get to know Evelyn a bit better than Mr Bernstein and his mystery girl – by now I was nearly twenty so this wasn't quite Shirley Chambers in double art once a week any longer – and we even shared a house for a little while. Not as intimate as that makes it sound I'm afraid, since there were four or five other people in residence at the time, but there's something pleasing about being able to say, however misleadingly, that we lived together.

Still, for all that, Evelyn never became completely real to me. She always carried a hint of the impossible and the insubstantial with her. I wasn't in love – I now realise I didn't know what the word meant at the time, although I spent quite a lot of time spouting rather drunkenly and melodramatically about it – but it wasn't a question of lust either. It was more like an odd and distant and strangely spiritual sort of worship – closer to the courtly than the romantic concept of love.

Whenever I picture myself back then, and recall the rare occasions I was in any way close to her, I also see Karloff's little circling palms-up hand gestures and soft, pleading half-moan. However inarticulate and however naïve, they seem to express a universal wonder at the possibility that the dreamed of and the longed for might actually be, or become, in this moment *real* – and touch, and connect, and fill the gaping empty hole at the heart of everything, and also the dawning, ever-present foreknowledge that such a thing can never be, or at least never for the likes of us. Never for the bungled. Never for the botched.

Believe me, I can be as cynical as the next man if he's a particularly cynical sort, and like you I have my own Joe Strummer patented garage-based bullshit detector for the cloyingly sentimental and self-satisfied, and I find it making me hesitate before adding this last thought. But one of the lessons I've been taught by some of my favourite things – like Dickens and his pitiable infants so easily and cheaply mocked by Wilde, or David Lynch's *Blue Velvet* with its achingly sincere teenagers dreaming of the robins of hope, so often and so wrongly assumed by overly knowing audiences to demand an ironic reading, or *Bride of Frankenstein* itself come to that – is that we need to understand the place and value of sentiment when it's an expression of *truth*, and to deny ourselves that truth and that joy for fear of appearing somehow simple or smug or schmaltzy is to deny ourselves a huge part of what makes life worth living.

It's now more than thirty years since I was that callow student, and more than forty since I first saw *Bride of Frankenstein,* and I hope I've attained a modicum of greater maturity than I was capable of at either point, but I never cease to wonder at my own good fortune – that in this most real of real worlds I have found absolute contentment and love in the central relationship of my life, that such a thing actually *can* be for one as bungled and botched as me (take *that*, Nietzsche), and I never fail to marvel at the world of truth and hurt and yearning and despair that a man whose real name was William Henry Pratt understood so perfectly and was able wordlessly to convey in the gesture of a second or two.

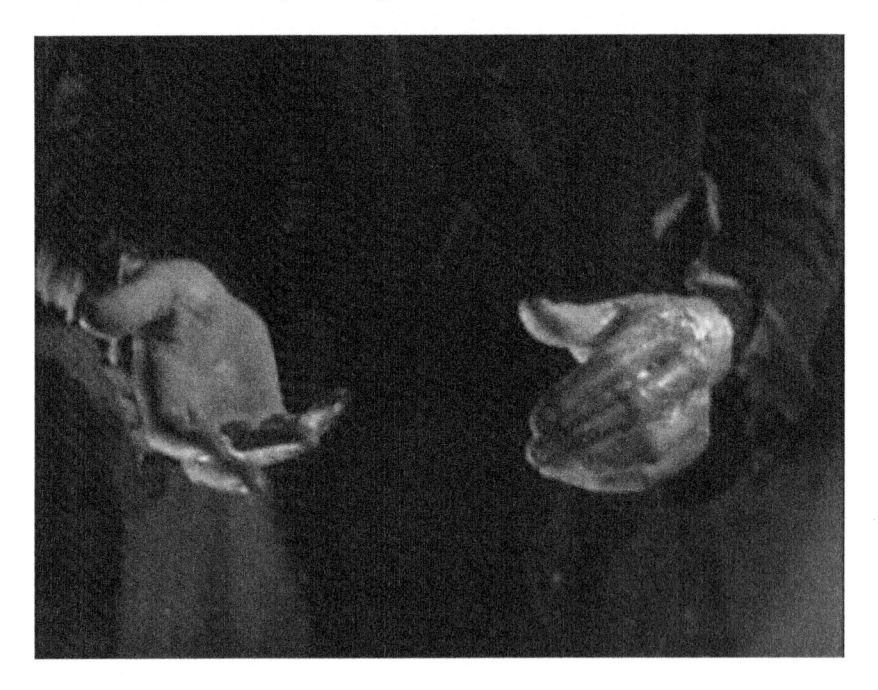

# 4. MEMENTORABILIA MORI

I have a novelisation of *The Bride of Frankenstein*.

It was published in 1978, and I came across it in a Norwich newsagent at some point that year. I'm not sure it's even possible to convey the bliss of that entirely unexpected surge of wonder – the sense that even amongst surroundings as concrete and mundane as the bookshelves in John Menzies it was possible to be touched by the divine. And being touched by the divine was an altogether more palatable experience than being touched by a smelly old pervert in a dirty mac, as I was a year later among those same bookshelves.

Back then, you see, it was still possible to be surprised by joy. The existence of something wonderful did not necessarily involve foreknowledge. Prior to glimpsing the book in a heart-stopping moment of disbelieving wonder, I had no idea at all that such a thing was available. Nowadays, with all our browsing histories recorded by Blade Runner AI central, all those 'available for pre order…58% of other customers who looked at this also bought…if you liked that you may also like this…we thought you might like to know about..' personal recommendations thrust the world of your desires ever more assertively under your nose.

You can't stumble accidentally across a book you never knew was even possible any more. Such a sudden, transcendent moment of delight, immediately followed by an onrushing defensive certainty that this was too good to be true and this had to be a dream because surely in truth there could be no brave new world that had such novelisations in it – all that has been search-engined out of existence.

That's not entirely a complaint. My shelves are groaning under the weight of much loved books and DVDs which I wouldn't ever have been able to access without those search engines and a lot of internet persistence. American imports of obscure – and not so obscure – 30s and 40s and 50s horror films never released over here, reprints and remaindered copies and rare books bibliofindered into my fetishistic fingers.

I had a bit of a collection as a 70s horror fan back in my teens – mainly the Aurora plastic monster kits, but also the Gifford and Frank books, David Pirie's *The Vampire Cinema,* Allen Eyles' *The House of Horror* (a particular favourite that last one, since not only did it offer a wealth of production information about Hammer films, it also included a sixteen page photo appendix of Hammer's leading ladies in various stages of undress to which my teenage self turned very frequently for research purposes). I still own all of them, but a combination of house moves and breakups and relocations and parental indifference to the future fortune a mint condition Aurora Jekyll as Hyde might bring, means I wouldn't now own any of them without having tracked down replacements from eBay and amazon and sellers around the world.

My *Bride* novelisation, though, is an original – the self-same copy I grasped and gasped at, heart pounding, mustering (either from my pocket money or by shameless begging and pleading) the 75p necessary to make the wondrous object my own nearly forty years ago.

It's just a slender little paperback – the cover a simple illustration of the bride herself with lurid green skin and a border of faux Gothic wallpaper. Re-reading it as I've just done, I would have to say it's very well written, by the wonderfully and almost certainly pseudonymously named Carl Dreadstone about whom I know absolutely nothing else, although the entertaining little three-page introduction by the brilliant Ramsey Campbell makes me suspect he may have been the book's true author. But viewed in one way – and perhaps the only rational way – it's nothing special.

So why does it – and by extension, all those other fannish collectibles, mean so much to me, and to the other souls like me? A while ago, on a particularly nice spring morning my wife and kids came and sat for a while in the memorabilia-lined shed in which I write. After a while she turned to me, her face assuming a pained expression suggestive of the most profound disappointment imaginable, and said, her voice a curious mixture of fondness, bafflement and exasperation, 'Why do we have two Hammer Horror shoulder bags hidden in the corner?'

Beyond the desperate nit-picker's defence that we only had one *shoulder* bag, because in fact the *Curse of Frankenstein* one was actually a *messenger* bag, not a shoulder bag at all, I found myself rather at a loss for an answer. These were secret purchases you see – picked up quietly in a *TV and Movie Store* sale maybe a year or more ago – and slipped incognito into a space between two free standing bookshelves, themselves creaking and groaning with a wealth of not dissimilar objects.

Don't trouble to lie, by the way. You're a secret purchaser too – we all are, whether it's shoes or handbags or teapots or magazines or novels or downloads or whatever it is that our partners can't see the need for or the value in. Because of course, rationally there is not and cannot be any value whatsoever. We just *want them*. I have two entirely functionless secret Hammer bags because I wanted them, no better defence.

But *why* did I want them? What is the appeal to a fifty-year-old family man of a plastic glow in the dark Aurora Creature from the Black Lagoon, or a NECA Wolf Man headknocker? Why did I want yet another near identical Bela Lugosi biography, or to replace books I'd already read a hundred times by the time I was fifteen solely in order for them to accumulate dust on a shelf? Come to that, why did my thirteen-year-old self even want the novelisation of *Bride of Frankenstein*, in the first place? After all, he'd already seen the film.

The answer, I think, lies somewhere in the gap between evanescence and permanence. Back in the pre-video days of 1978, a novelisation was your only means of holding on to or reliving the experience of the film. Remember those Target Doctor Who books from the 70s and 80s? It was only through them that I was able to encounter old Hartnell and Troughton stories – and they remain the best available form of many of those episodes, given the BBCs unfortunate habit of wiping the original videotapes – or to re-experience, or re-imagine the Pertwee or Baker stories I had seen. *The Web of Fear* by Terrance Dicks was my favourite – with its purple spine, and a grim-faced soldier, laser beams shooting from the eyes of a Yeti in the Underground, and Pat Troughton's marvellously craggy face all on the cover. In almost every other respect, all those episodes of my favourite show were gone forever immediately after their transmission.

In the same way, these Saturday night Horror Double Bills were the very definition of ephemeral. They spanned maybe ten weeks across a summer – rushing by as summer holidays do as a kid – to be watched and relished once and once only before disappearing almost as quickly as the career of a winner of *The Voice*.

I was desperate for anything which might help me grab hold of the experience, to retain a stronger sense of how that film *felt*. As time went on I got into the habit of desperately scribbling down credits and a few lines of dialogue onto scraps of paper as I watched, managing handwriting much speedier and more efficient than I was ever to be able to achieve in exams. If we ever had a copy of *Radio Times* – it had to be *Radio Times*, because back then it published only the BBC listings while *TV Times* did ITV and you had to buy both if you wanted to know everything that was on – I'd wait eagerly for the end of the week and then rip out the listings for the previous two films. I obsessively borrowed, renewed, borrowed, and renewed the two horror movie books my local library could offer – Carlos Clarens and Denis Gifford – and would have given anything to find any small way of holding onto the experience for a little longer than the running time of the films themselves.

Some time ago I came across a wonderful article by one of my favourite contemporary novelists, Jonathan Coe, in which he describes a lifelong obsession with Billy Wilder's wistfully elegiac *The Private Life of Sherlock Holmes* and its legendary lost footage, and he finishes by concluding that it hadn't been the complete version of the film he'd been searching for all those years but *'something even more unreachable: trying to recapture, somehow, the sense of wonder, of comfort, of security, of perfect happiness I felt when I first saw the film on that Sunday evening, when it made me forget, for two blissful hours, my fear of returning to school the next day. It is that young self I have been trying to bring back to life.'*

    For me that is precisely the desire at the heart of my obsessive consumption: of my fetishistic compulsion to hold, to possess, and to *own*. In a better world, or in a better adjusted individual, there would be no need you see. We should experience a film – like a piece of music, a painting, a novel, or a play – with our eyes and ears, in our heads, in our own responses, and that should be enough in itself. The craving to own, to possess, should be entirely foreign to the world of art. But it isn't. We fans dwell in a twilight nether world somewhere between the arthouse and the marketplace, forever caught in the mid-ground between the temple and the moneychangers.

    The desire to have the film, the experience, the sensation, available and ready whenever and wherever, is the desire to freeze time's cruel, onrushing indifference. Collecting, prizing, owning – these are our buttresses against time's predatory nature; these are the fantasist's anti-death medicine.

    We horror fans are not alone in feeling the instinct, by the way. It's not intrinsic artistic merit that makes parents hang on to their kids' pre-school paintings, or that makes holidaymakers experience huge chunks of their surroundings through a camera lens rather than head-on.

    All of that *stuff*, that plastic mass-produced rubbish and those production line paperbacks; they matter to me because, like the extraordinary magic of quantum entanglement (in which the tiniest particles of existence are mysteriously connected and will, simultaneously, behave in identical ways regardless of the distance between them, almost in effect being in two places at the same time), they put me, however briefly and emptily, in vivid and immediate contact with specific frozen, golden moments: moments in which it's always a Saturday night in the 1970s and mum and dad are sleeping contentedly upstairs and I'm 12, with a lifetime of limitless possibilities ahead of me.

    The idea that those moments are simply *gone*, and will not, cannot, come again is a surrender to death, to extinction: an acceptance of our flickering mortality. I shall not yield so cravenly. I choose to fight, in my own way, to retain and redeem and recapture those lost moments, to fix them in place, to make them mine forever in a world outside the transient and the temporal. I don't know if an Aurora Dracula or Carl Dreadstone's eternal *Bride of Frankenstein* novelisation were what Dylan Thomas had in mind when he urged us to rage, rage against the dying of the light, but until the immortality pill comes along they'll have to do for me.

# 5. ANGLO-FREUD! IN COLOUR!

## Brides of Dracula (1960, Hammer, Terence Fisher)

*'Land of dark forests, dread mountains and black, unfathomed lakes. Still the home of magic and devilry…'*
**Unnamed Narrator**

Colour! This one was in colour!

    A fact which I was only able to appreciate because my dad's best mate – a family friend who we called 'Uncle' Michael (does that still happen?) – had a big win on the football pools and bought us a colour telly out of his winnings at some point in the mid-70s. It's easy to forget looking back now that although colour broadcasting had begun in the 1960s it took most of the next decade for colour sets to become the norm. Even as late as 1977, the year I lapped up *Brides of Dracula* and also the year in which sales of colour TVs outstripped black and white for the first time, perhaps as much as half the population were still watching everything in monochrome.

    Mostly, I wouldn't have minded. I've always loved black and white – for its subtle chiaroscuro, its pools of expressionistic shadow and light, the way in which it creates a readymade short cut into a world of dreams and fantasy through its poetic, self-evident distance from the prose-coloured world that's always just *there* in front of us, and perhaps most of all for its pleasing ability to generate a smug, artier-than-thou sense of my own sophisticated cleverness as I went to see such out of time 80s big screen black and white movies as *The Elephant Man* and *Stardust Memories*.

    Nonetheless, there was always a certain thrill in the glorious Eastman colour of the second film on the bill when, as here, it turned out to be a later Hammer movie rather than a 30s or 40s Universal classic. I didn't understand such distinctions quite yet of course, since at the time my fixation with the genre was only a week old. In the broadest sense I'd heard of Hammer horror, but only in that pop culture way in which the words are just somehow out there in the ether, a part of the fabric surrounding us, a few vague impressions, maybe the title of a weird Kate Bush single. I didn't really know what Hammer horror was.

    For this briefest of spells, before I'd read any more, or seen any other films, this Peter Cushing vehicle might have been a direct sequel to Lugosi's *Dracula* which had so thrilled me a week before, rather than, as I later discovered, the second (and Dracula-less) entry in an entirely separate cycle of movies centring around Christopher Lee's lean, fanged and red contact-lensed version of the Count and Cushing's sharp and agile interpretation of Van Helsing.

Beginnings are always like that. There's no shape yet, just a cloud of delightful mystery and sensation, discovery and possibility. When you begin writing fiction, for instance, at first there's just the beautiful vague cloud of maybe and what if, which you gradually begin to tame and fashion into this specific thing here which you're actually writing – you create focus, and if you have the luck and the talent, maybe a kind of truth, but it also gets so much smaller than the ocean of the maybe that you had to swim in in the first place.

It's like falling in love. For all its passionate intensity, in the beginning that other person is still a mystery, only a vague idea of themselves. You may not be able to think about anything or anyone else, and can find solace only in dropping your beloved's name into every conversation, however unrelated – "Hundreds killed by a hurricane in America? Zoë's cousin went to America once…"- but the truth remains that you don't know that much about them.

It's only as time goes on that they refine themselves from that *possibility* of a person into the *actual* human being who stands ever more specifically in front of you in this exact and actual shape. A shape made up of the things we discover, like a sculptor chipping away at the stone to reveal the form that had always been waiting in the block. If the love is to last, then that shape will still be wonderful in your eyes, but inevitably it's now *defined*, hemmed in by fact, and so very much smaller than the infinite possibilities it had encompassed before.

The birth of any obsession is like this. Our own ignorance allows us to swim, however briefly and blissfully, in a *potential* world, a world where Lugosi may have frolicked in lurid colour opposite Cushing, Karloff might have won the Best Actor Oscar for *Bride of Frankenstein*, and *Lust for a Vampire* was even a tenth as good as its title. Until our own irresistible need to *know* narrows that world down to the shape of the single and the concrete at the expense of the abstract and the infinite.

For my ignorant twelve-year-old self though, viewing the film for the first time without preconceptions of any sort, what struck me most – after the lush, sumptuous beauty of the colours, courtesy of Jack Asher's luxuriant cinematography and Bernard Robinson's wonderful designs – was the sheer Englishness of the whole enterprise.

The great literary originals – *Frankenstein*, *Jekyll and Hyde*, *Dracula*, *The Hound of the Baskervilles*, the ghost stories of M.R. James – all have a decisively English soul, a surface composure quivering with barely repressed passion and hysteria, a national and cultural identity that is both indefinable and immediately recognisable. I know at this point someone will inevitably wish to point out, quite rightly, that *Dorian Gray* and *Dracula* were both written by Irishmen, *Jekyll and Hyde* and *Baskervilles* by Scotsmen, and Poe was American, but for my money the point still stands. Whether the writers were born from it or simply made it their spiritual and creative home, there's something in the English soil – a sense of history perhaps, of ancient mysteries forever lurking round the corner or behind the monument, or perhaps something in its landscapes, its misty moors and its barren flatlands, the bleak beauty of its desolate coastline, its haunted palaces and its foggy alleyways – which is particularly fruitful for the dark imagination and which means that Gothic horror has always had a peculiarly English identity.

However, for all their reliance on the literary source material and despite their emphasis on the fairy-tale qualities of their middle European settings; for all that the key figures in the evolution of the studio and amongst its creative personnel were European émigrés, the Universal movies are resolutely and unarguably American, not least in their relentlessly modernising approach.

The passage of time had leant the 1930s themselves a surface patina of nostalgia even by the summer of 1977 which rather disguised the boldly contemporary settings the Universal films had largely adopted, readily deploying many of the stock character types of America in the jazz age. Lugosi's Dracula, for instance, is essentially the lounge lizard and the Valentinoesque Latin lover of so many contemporary Hollywood movies, while Helen Chandler and Frances Dade as his victims are bobbed 20s flappers rather than Victorian maidens. In this, as in their eager adoption of a figure as all-American as Lon Chaney Jr. during the 40s, the Universal cycle looks and feels American to the core.

This is not intended as a criticism. Perhaps I'm a cultural philistine, but although I'm as capable as the next man of bluffing my way through a conversation about Ozu, Renoir, Bergman, Fellini, and the rest, it seems to me self-evident that cinema is an essentially American art form and the greatest cinema is American cinema, if not always geographically then at least in sensibility.

Hitchcock, the greatest director of them all, only produced his very finest work once he became absorbed by America. And though Hollywood turned its back on its own home-grown cinematic genius, Orson Welles, his best works – excepting the sublime *Chimes at Midnight* – were *Kane*, *Ambersons* and, later, *Touch of Evil*. In other words, the handful of films he was able to make in America. Add to the list Howard Hawks, Frank Capra, John Huston, James Whale, Scorsese, Coppola, Kubrick, Lynch, Woody Allen and, blazing the trail for a later generation of indie filmmakers (and an entire gender), Ida Lupino, and I think it's undeniable that nothing that has come from outside the States can rival what has come from within it in terms of scope and grandeur and intensity.

Where else could have produced *Casablanca, The Maltese Falcon* and *The Big Sleep? The Searchers, Rio Bravo* and *True Grit? Some Like it Hot* and *Sunset Boulevard? Jaws, The Godfather, Star Wars* and *Close Encounters of the Third Kind? Taxi Driver, Mildred Pierce* and *Now Voyager? Top Hat* and *High Society* and *Singin' in the Rain? North by Northwest* and *Silence of the Lambs? Citizen Kane, It's a Wonderful Life* and *Psycho?*

So there's genuinely no sub textual lip-curl of disdain when I suggest that the Universal horror films are wonderfully, meltingpotaliciously American in tone and feeling, but it's also true to say that for me there's something very pleasing about the fact that it took a small family owned production company called Hammer, operating shoestring productions out of a tiny studio in an English country house to finally bring horror back home to England.

As I've pointed out, I wasn't aware of any of this production background when I first watched *Brides of Dracula*, but I felt every inch of the sheer Englishness on screen, from the production designs and performances which render the geographically condensed middle Europe of the film's ostensible locations in terms of the Home Counties, to Hammer's crucial decision to give their movies a Victorian setting, perhaps the period when England appeared at its most 'English'.

Of course, Hammer's version of England has nothing to do with flags and parades, nor with putting the Great back into anything, and it's not in any sense aggressive or imperialistic. Much closer to the mark was Orwell (or quoting him, lord help us, John Major) with his vision of an England of warm beer and cycling spinsters and long evening shadows on village greens, but of course that England was always a fading nostalgic fantasy, and one made more so with each passing year – except in the cosy-crimed all-white world of Midsomer. Nevertheless, some of that quiet, precise, benevolently ordered and essentially rural country, struggling to restrain and contain the seething forces of disorder and chaos simmering below, has strong echoes in the world created by the Hammer movies.

It was a fictional English world I already knew intimately, from Conan Doyle and H.G. Wells and Kenneth Grahame and C.S. Lewis and Agatha Christie and Enid Blyton and *Stig of the Dump* and more particularly from *Doctor Who* in its Terrance Dicks, Barry Letts and Jon Pertwee era, a world of irascible squires, affable poachers and nervous vicars; a world of retired majors, amateur experts and gentleman heroes who found it hard to suffer fools gladly but always saved the day by doing the decent thing; a world of good chaps and rough, sometimes sullen and threatening, though often good-hearted, lower class types; a world that would like to have dreamed it was timeless and rather feared it was not; and perhaps most of all a world in which monsters lurked in the dark corners of its tranquil landscapes. A world, at least in its Hammer incarnation, in which everyone was Michael Ripper.

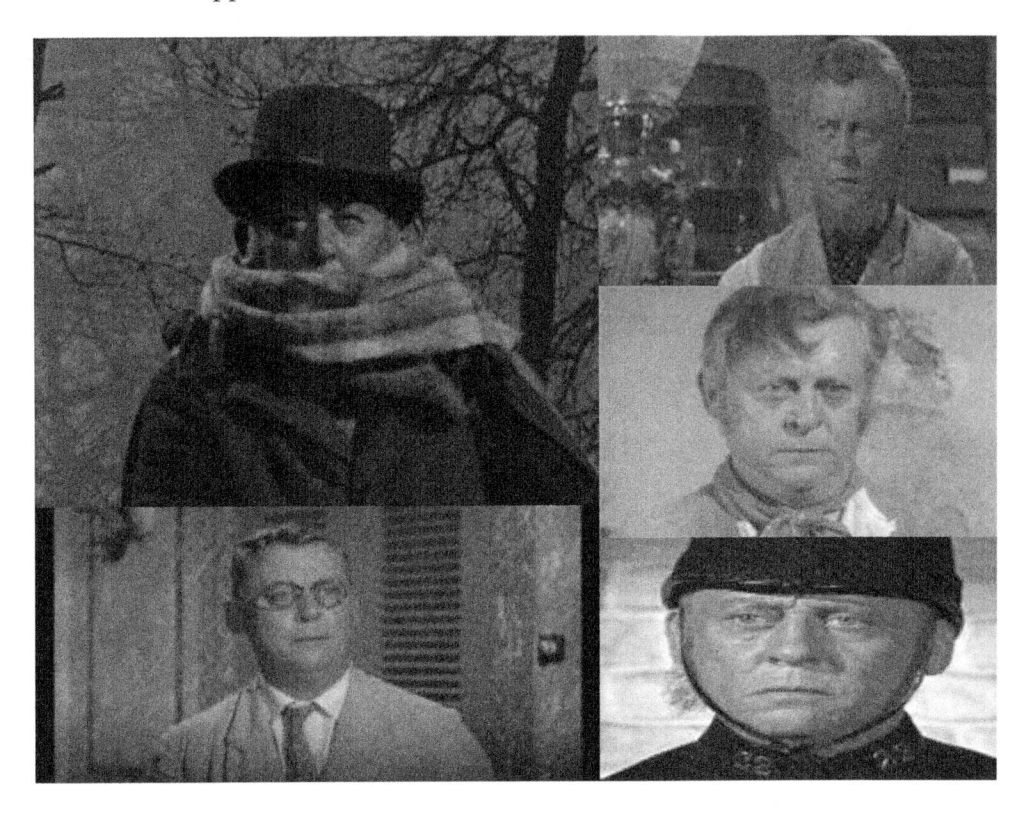

There is a tendency among critics to see this nostalgic picture of England, most especially in its Gothic form – and in the Hammer films in particular – as essentially parochial, xenophobic, even racist, and it's certainly fair to say that, in common with pretty much every area of the British media at the time, the films do not directly represent the increasingly multicultural society in which they were made, with 'the foreign' (whether the 'mysterious East' in *The Reptile* or Haiti in *Plague of the Zombies*) often embodying a source of threat.

For me, however, to leave the point there is a fundamental mistake, and one which spinelessly concedes the sense of what constitutes an English identity to the bigots of UKIP and the EDL and the BNP and the Brexiteers.

Crucially and demonstrably, England, even in its nostalgic, backward-looking Hammer guise *is* absolutely and irrefutably multicultural in its essential soul. Look no further than Christopher Lee's patrician features, which allowed him to spend most of the 60s and 70s flitting with equal facility between English aristocrats and swarthy continentals – and perhaps the less said about his Fu Manchu in this context the better.

60

We are a mongrel race, and that is something of which we should be justly proud. Anglo-Saxon. The clue is in the hyphen. We are also Celts. We are Roman, and Norman. On the East coast, particularly, we are also Scandinavian, thanks to some wild oat sowing by those marauding Vikings with their Danelaw and their horny helmets. All mixed up with the remnants of the Ancient Britons who preceded them all. And round my way there's also a strong Flemish, Walloon and Dutch influence dating back to a wave of persecution-escaping immigration in the 1600s. Oh, and back in the twelfth century a sizeable and prosperous chunk of the population of my home city were Jewish. Then the racists and the bigots got at them, just as, in today's world, they'd dearly love to do to the asylum seekers, the refugees, the Asians and the eastern Europeans.

For more than fifty years, since the first major influx of citizens of the former colonies, England's most recent brand of hairy-knuckled hate-mongers with their staring eyes and their sloping foreheads have been spewing out their venomous bile, but what they want you to forget is that, despite its sea borders, the English spirit, the English identity, has always, and wonderfully, been most truly defined by an inclusiveness, a blending of cultures, far more so than much of continental Europe. And I do mean *English*, very specifically, incidentally.

I find the word 'British' harder and harder to use with any conviction as time goes by. It speaks of an outdated and rather ugly sense of Empire and expansion, of fluttering Union flags and the last night of the Proms which says nothing to me about my sense of my own identity or my place in the wider world. It seems to me that those definitions are only meaningful when they are either very small and local or very large. It means something that I'm a member of the human race, sharing a common identity with the rest of the world's population (except for the lizardy illuminati of course). But the small ones mean something too. One, I'm a member of my family; two, I'm from Norwich; three, I'm East Anglian; four, I'm English, and only after that do I see myself as British or any other such loose conglomeration of associations.

In my idealistic and internationalist twenties I vociferously denied that any of this meant anything at all – there was no such thing as national identity, I declared; this was just a lie designed to allow our rulers to send us to war against our neighbours, blinding us to the truth that a plumber from Bristol has far more in common with a plasterer from Mainz than either of them do with the posh officers giving them their orders. I still stand by that to a degree – the madness of narrow nationalism, of 'are you one of us or are you *other?*' can be seen all too easily in the world around us, and leads ultimately and with a terrifyingly remorseless and insane logic to the ovens of Auschwitz, to the flying of planes into tall buildings, and to the public execution of the shipwrecked monkey washed up in Hartlepool during the Napoleonic wars because the locals took the poor hairy little jabberer for a Frenchman.

Nonetheless as I grow older I do find there is *something*: a vague, but palpably real sense of Englishness which lurks both within and around me – some loosely defined sense of intimacy, of belonging, which makes me warm to the sight of a red post-box or bus, which allows me to be every bit as interested in the latest score from the Test Match as an English binman or an English aristocrat.

Of course the exact nature of that *something* is much easier to acknowledge than it is to define – but its outline is a love of the quiet life; a gentleness which is perhaps born more of an almost metaphysical dread of making a scene than a genuine tolerance (just ask someone from the Windrush generation how real the much-vaunted English tolerance is); a restraint which masks the depth of an unseen iceberg of hidden feeling; a resigned, nagging sense of disappointment in things as they are, and, perhaps as a corollary to that disappointment, a consciousness of the past, almost an aching for it, which at both a personal and national level is so intense as to approach the unhealthy.

A sense, in other words, of the English spirit perhaps never embodied more completely in one individual than in the shape of Peter Cushing.

My sister and her husband live in Westgate on the Kent coast, and I try never to allow a visit to them to go by without a private pilgrimage round a few miles of coastline to the Tudor Tea Rooms in Whitstable, where Peter Cushing took tea almost every day, at a quiet table tucked unobtrusively behind a pillar. There's a melancholy to seaside towns, particularly of the more genteel variety, a kind of faded, out-of-season beauty which somehow seems to fit Cushing's quiet, inward quality like a blood-stained surgical glove, and which becomes all the more poignant when you know how he pined for the loss of his wife Helen through the last decades of his life.

I picture him, quiet and immaculate, sedate and restrained, the very model of an English gentleman, sipping tea alone at that little table, and all the time a wild pain and loss gnawing invisibly and monstrously at his broken heart, and not only do I feel a terrible sympathy, but also somehow a much greater and more immediate understanding of the furious intensity he lent his best-known characterisations; an unparalleled – and I'll say it again, an utterly English – ability to suggest both an eerily aloof composure and a wild, frantic desperation. Implacable, icy, and unperturbed on the surface, and turbulently, chaotically human beneath it.

There's an insignificant little sequence in one of his lesser-known films, *The Blood Beast Terror,* in which Cushing, playing a somewhat fastidious police inspector, rebukes his sergeant for allowing some tea to slop out of the cup and into the saucer. Perhaps a minute or two later, at the end of the scene, Cushing scrapes the bottom of his china cup against the edge of the saucer, a barely perceptible flicker of distaste fluttering across his usually impassive features. In one sense it's absolutely superfluous – a split second of 'character business' which would have gone entirely unmissed had Cushing not chosen to throw in such a subtle little flourish in a largely unimpressive low budget quickie, but that tiny moment for me is quintessential Cushing; exquisitely judged, perfectly suggestive of an entirely English quiet outrage, and typical of the extraordinary attention to detail he brought to every role, making him easily the most versatile of the great horror stars, slipping with ease from dotty enthusiasm to steely determination to coiled–spring tension to narrow-eyed evil to wild-eyed whimpering panic.

He truly was the most extraordinary of actors, gifted with a rare talent and a meticulously controlled and studied technique which, uniquely, enabled him to inhabit Van Helsing, Baron Frankenstein, Sherlock Holmes, Winston Smith, Grand Moff Tarkin and the big screen Doctor Who with equal conviction and grace.

Those two 1960s Doctor Who Dalek movies, incidentally, directed with real panache by Gordon Flemyng and made by Aaru – a kind of sister brand to Amicus, the production company which staked its own claim on the horror genre of the 1960s and early 70s with its highly enjoyable series of present-day portmanteau films – were a regular Saturday daytime and school holiday TV treat. They had made Cushing as reassuring a presence in my earlier childhood as his respective co-stars, *Record Breakers'* Roy Castle in the first film and Bernard Cribbins from *Jackanory* and *The Wombles* in the second. Had there only been a third film with *Blue Peter's* John Noakes as Cushing's companion in *Tardis* some kind of BBC Childrens' Programmes cuddliness quotient overload would probably have made my head explode.

Cushing's Dr Who is an absentminded, charmingly dotty English professor, rather than William Hartnell's much more acerbic, alien and mysterious figure from the TV series at the time (and yes, 'Who' was actually the character's surname in the Dalek films, unlike the TV version who is called The Doctor, not Dr. Who. Except once or twice in the early years when he actually does seem to be called Dr. Who after all). Nonetheless, Cushing inhabits the role whole-heartedly, reprising it in all but name a decade later in another highly enjoyable Amicus fantasy adventure called *At the Earth's Core*. His skill was such that I never found it difficult to accept that the cosy Saturday afternoon Dalek-defeater of my childhood was now the much icier Van Helsing, or, as I was to see before long, the downright monomaniacal Baron Frankenstein.

As predictable in my tastes as most fans of old horror movies and *Doctor Who*, I'm also a Sherlock Holmes aficionado – my childhood was filled and endlessly enriched by my discovery of the stories, then the wonderful Basil Rathbone/Nigel Bruce films of the 30s and 40s which were a similarly regular feature of the BBC's 1970s schedules. Later I came to love the daring and manically committed Granada TV performance of Jeremy Brett, and now, with no little reluctance – even the same sense of betrayal of one's childhood heroes that many of my generation faced when forced to accept that David Tennant was every bit as good as Tom Baker or Jon Pertwee – I would have to admit that the extraordinary performances of Benedict Cumberbatch and Martin Freeman in the BBC's *Sherlock*, are as near as dammit the definitive version. It's high praise indeed, therefore, for me to say that the meticulous precision of Peter Cushing's Holmes, first essayed in Hammer's endlessly enjoyable 1959 version of *The Hound of the Baskervilles* and, as I discovered only relatively recently through the wonder of DVD, further refined in the 1960s BBC series, is fit to swap deerstalkers with the best of them.

As Baron Frankenstein and Van Helsing, he embodied two of the three pillars on which Hammer's extraordinary achievements were built (Lee's Dracula being the third of course), and I don't think he was ever better than he is here, in *Brides of Dracula*. The blinkered, condescending and – let's be honest – snobbish attitude of the critical establishment to the talent at work in genre pieces never fails to irritate me. A few years back I saw the previously mentioned Bernard Cribbins appearing as Wilfred Mott in David Tennant's final episodes as the Doctor, and he gave a performance of such immense subtlety and sensitivity, so filled with feeling and nuance and tenderness, that had the identical characterisation been given by some established theatrical gent in a quiet little social realist drama about dignity and old age I have no doubt the performance would have been showered with the BAFTAs and the plaudits it so richly deserved. Coming from him that sang *Right Said Fred* in a slice of Christmas sci-fi fun for kids though, it passed relatively unnoticed.

In similar vein (no pun intended), the role of Dracula's arch enemy has been attempted on film – and walked through – by no lesser theatrical luminaries than Laurence Olivier and Anthony Hopkins (thespian Sirs both), and anyone with eyes to see would have to acknowledge how completely the much less lauded Cushing trounces them both. For one thing, Cushing, Lee, and director Terence Fisher had the good sense to jettison Stoker's clumsily accented dialogue, and in losing the foreign baggage rendered the conflict between Dracula and Van Helsing in terms of an enthralling battle between the iron wills of, respectively, Lee's animalistic, icy, aristocratic entitlement and Cushing's stiff, puritanical, bourgeois morality.

Of course, although this was my first encounter with Cushing in the role, *Brides of Dracula* was Hammer's and Cushing's second stab at the character, and for me the film undeniably suffers because it lacks the central presence of Lee's Dracula from the first film. David Peel's Baron Meinster is a very different animal, and the awesome shadow cast by Christopher Lee is even more deadly to the somewhat fey vampire villain than the shadow of the windmill sails which Van Helsing manoeuvres to finish him off in the film's highly effective climax. Nonetheless, *Brides* is a remarkable achievement, and I can well understand why for many it represents the high watermark of Hammer Horror.

What does strike me now, however, in a way that entirely escaped my twelve-year-old self, is just how startlingly Freudian the whole enterprise is. I first read Freud when I was in my late teens, starting with the *Introductory Lectures on Psychoanalysis* and *The Interpretation of Dreams*. He took me entirely by surprise, partly because I hadn't expected such complex and original thinking to be rendered in prose so witty and accessible, and partly because I'd never previously realised I wanted to shag my mum and murder my dad. *Brides of Dracula* should probably have led me to suspect as much however.

Freud has been much derided over the years: for an intrinsic sexism; for drawing wild generalisations from researches on a very narrow, homogenous sample group; for thoughtlessly assuming that memories of child abuse were always fantasies rather than actual recollections; for too emphatic an emphasis on sex as a sole determinant of human behaviour and personality; and for giving a bizarre degree of credence to his friend Wilhelm Fliess's frankly weird theory that the centre of neurosis was in the nose, and could be rooted out with a bit of unsurprisingly disastrous nasal surgery.

For all that, however, Freud's approach was revolutionary for me. What I recall best from my early reading of his work was the sense of a new world being opened up. It was what Freud referred to as parapraxis which most immediately impressed me – the sense that these tiny and everyday moments of apparent accident, slips of the tongue, forgetting your keys, taking a wrong turn, revealed an undiscovered continent of hidden processes and motivations. Whatever the validity of Freud's clinical techniques and theories, what he taught me as a teenager, with all the force of genuine revelation, was that the world was not entirely as it seemed to be on the surface, and that much of what went on inside me remained a mystery to what, as Freud helped me realise, I could only loosely consider to be my self. He was not its inventor, but before Freud the idea of an unconscious mind had never really been fully formulated, and it is a concept which continues to echo and reverberate to this day.

*Brides of Dracula* unfolds like the archetypal Freudian dream, in a much deeper and more resonant sense than more conscious efforts to incorporate Freudian theory into the cinema – like the Dali designed dream sequence in Hitchcock's *Spellbound* for instance.

Initially Meinster is held in chains by his domineering mother. Freed from the metaphorical apron strings by a beautiful young girl, Meinster immediately puts the bite on his mother before infiltrating a nearby girls' school. Symbolic father Van Helsing must then sternly penetrate the matriarch's body with his stake and holy water. There is a startling sequence in which Meinster's servant acts as a perverse sort of midwife encouraging one of his victims to push her way out of the grave.

*Don't Call the Midwife!*

The boarding school scenes have something of the moist, Sapphic yearning of LeFanu's *Carmilla*. And ultimately of course, Meinster, more than a little camp throughout, successfully sucks on Van Helsing, with the appalled vampire hunter only able to burn out the 'evil' (of vampirism, or homosexuality?) from his soul with a literal branding iron applied to the bite and a good splattering of holy water. I'm not sure what Freud's thoughts on fangs were, but I can make an educated guess. Sometimes a cigar may be just a cigar, but not in this case I think.

It's not only *Brides of Dracula* of course. There's something about horror films which makes them uniquely placed to illuminate and embody the hidden and repressed. Freud himself could have made a decent horror writer – his ideas on the uncanny are profoundly unsettling – while Jung's shadow selves might almost have been designed to describe the denizens of the horror film. I have no doubt that, given the chance, both Freud and Jung would have been avid Saturday night horror double bill viewers – though not in the same room of course, or Freud would have kept fainting.

Freud described dreams as 'the royal road to the unconscious' and if cinema is the art form closest to the sensation of the dream then as Mark Gatiss pointed out in his *A History of Horror* 'horror films are the most dream-like of all.' Often it's overt; a part of the film maker's intent and focus, as in Carl Dreyer's *Vampyr,* or pretty much all of Roger Corman's Poe Pictures. But even with less intent and ambition, even amidst the worst and most obvious of slashers or cheapo mad scientists, isn't there something of the elusiveness and the unfathomable strangeness of the dream? The darkness, and the shadow at the bottom of the stair? The strange door at the end of the corridor?

It's this, to me, that's the true, beating tell-tale heart at the core of the horror film's appeal. The explanation usually offered for the apparently irrational and illogical pleasure audiences are able to take from being scared and horrified in the cinema uses the analogy of a rollercoaster. The films, it suggests, offer their audiences the adrenaline rush of a fearful, even life-threatening situation but from a position of complete safety. I've never bought it.

I've seen more horror films in my time than anyone probably should, and can honestly say that real fear has only ever once been a part of the experience. I watched Nicholas Roeg's intricate, majestic 1973 masterpiece *Don't Look Now* when I was 13, and was terrified beyond measure by the film's shattering climax (SPOILER ALERT – jump directly to the next sentence if you've never seen the film, and yes, I am aware that the nature of my prose style may mean that reaching the next sentence requires a leap of BobBeamanesque proportions), in which the mystery figure in the red coat is revealed to be not the benevolent spirit of Donald Sutherland's dead daughter but the dwarf-like serial killer who is to murder him.

Every time I turned out the light I saw that face – malevolent, malformed and mocking of all human hopes. Every time I closed my eyes, haunting my dreams for weeks, there was that slight, sneering shake of the head – was it aware of what Sutherland was hoping for? How could it have known? I can state categorically that pleasure was no part of my response to *Don't Look Now,* the only horror movie which has ever genuinely frightened me, and to this day I find it almost impossible to return to the film.

I've steeled myself to it twice over the years, and the effect was hardly diminished at all by age and experience. In fact, in many ways now that I have daughters of my own the film inspires an even deeper dread.

Fear, in other words, is not what I go to horror cinema for, and I didn't like it on the one occasion when that was what it delivered.

Neither, I think, is there any vicarious sado-masochistic pleasure for me to be found in the genre. I don't enjoy the current vogue for 'torture porn' – in films like *Saw, Hostel,* and *The Human Centipede* – although I certainly don't presume to pass any kind of judgement on the audience for those films, since I've read enough archive material to know that the same howls of outrage hurled at them today were once directed almost word for word at the now-tame and nostalgia-friendly works of Universal and Hammer.

Images of pain, suffering or humiliation are actually comparatively rare in the horror films I hold most dear, and even where they do occur – Lugosi's cackling delight in his Poe-inspired torture chamber in *The Raven,* for instance – those moments are so poetically heightened as to transform them into something of an altogether different order, bearing roughly the same relation to genuine violence as the 'It was the lark' love scene from *Romeo and Juliet* does to a 'Teen Babe loves Cock' video on Pornhub.

No, it seems to me that what audiences and fans truly gain from horror is an uncertain kind of recognition. Freud identifies the key to the experience of the uncanny as being a potent combination of the familiar and the strange, and explains it as the return of the repressed. In a truly dream-like way, and without the need for years of hideously expensive and dubiously effective psychoanalysis, horror allows us to explore our own unconscious selves, and this idea of self-exploration is the central pleasure films like *Brides of Dracula* continue to offer me.

Whether it's a shadowy something in my own psyche or a universally resonant collision of archetypes from the collective unconscious, in some mysterious way these movies are, like the lover in Shane MacGowan's *Rainy Night in Soho,* the measure of my dreams. I don't believe it is likely that I would ever be able to establish exactly how or why *Brides of Dracula* speaks to me so profoundly, but I think I'm sufficiently self-aware to recognise that what I'm responding to in its potent blend of sex and death, the sumptuous and the barren, the rational and the instinctual, the real and the dream-like, is a vague, half-formed sense of myself, of my many different selves, playing out an elaborate, enigmatic, flickering dance on the screen in front of me.

It's a heady cocktail – of the film's on offer in this season perhaps only Edgar Ulmer's 1934 *The Black Cat* can rival it for sheer, delicious revelling in perversity – and also a very, very beautiful film to look at. The combination is seductive and irresistible, and if you've never seen the film I urge you to surrender to its bizarre temptations forthwith: always much the best response to temptation, I find.

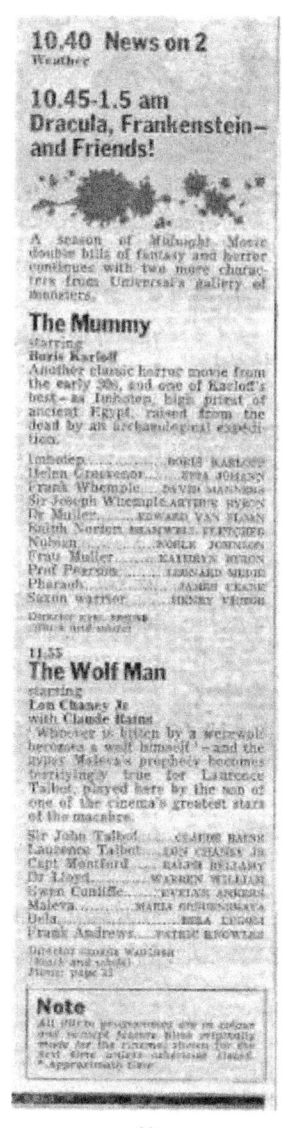

# DOUBLE BILL THREE

## Saturday July 16th 1977

THE MUMMY                  22.50 – 00.00

THE WOLF MAN            00.00 – 01.25

# 6. HE WENT FOR A LITTLE WALK! YOU SHOULD HAVE SEEN HIS FACE!

## The Mummy (Universal, 1932, Karl Freund)

*'Do you have to open graves to find a girl to fall in love with?'*
**Helen Grosvenor (Zita Johann)**

Mummies have never really done it for me. This isn't a psychological revelation – no Norman Batesing intended. I've just done my Freudian bit in the chapter on *Brides of Dracula* anyway. No, it's the lumbering bandage-shrouded variety that have always left me a little cold, dating right back to the faint disappointment this screening gave me for the couple of minutes between it ending and *The Wolf Man,* which I immediately loved, beginning.

I'm not sure quite why this should be so. I'd shared some of the strange fascination with all things ancient Egyptian that had overtaken the nation in the early 70s following the brouhaha which accompanied the Tutankhamen exhibition in London, and became fixated with a Schools History type folder which my sister owned, all fold-outs and little envelopes full of reproductions of letters and documents about Carter, Caernarvon and King Tut. I'm still a sucker for those 'book as artefact' kind of publications and have more of them than I can afford littering my shelves.

And the Tom Baker Doctor Who story *The Pyramids of Mars* which had been shown a year or so before had thrilled me with its barrel-chested robotic mummies and its Egyptian gods as von-Daniken style ancient aliens. A little later my Aurora plastic glow-in-the-dark mummy kit was loved just as much as the others, and when I came to read Bram Stoker's mummy-themed 'slightly less well-known than that other novel of his' *The Jewel of Seven Stars* I adored its musty, oppressive, claustrophobic atmosphere.

But the films themselves? Universal made a total of five mummy films, and Hammer managed four of their own, not to mention Stephen Somers' more recent franchise combining the Universal character with some light-hearted Indiana Jones high-jinx, and the best I could truthfully say about any of them is that I find them OK. Perhaps it's because, after all the fuss about the resurrection itself, everything tends to be a bit downhill - the films' stomp and strangle narrative strategies making them the original progenitors of the stalk and slash glut of Jasons and Freddies that ultimately so denuded the horror film in the 1980s.

And so my memories of this screening of the great grand Mummy of all that came after are rather less vivid than for many of the other films in this original run of summer double bills. I know I was bowled over by the opening five minutes, and if called upon – which I never was, oddly – could perfectly reproduce Bramwell Fletcher's mad, giggling delivery of his 'He went for a little walk' response to Imhotep's revival, but beyond that I can remember only a vague dissatisfaction. The fully made-up version of Karloff's mummy was glimpsed for a matter of seconds and only in this one scene, and the dusty and de-bandaged Ardath Bey guise in which he spends the rest of the film seemed to me a much less impressive presence. The film moved at a drearily funereal pace, plodding stodgily through its narrative as slowly as a limping mummy, a charge more often and less fairly levelled at Browning's *Dracula*, of which *The Mummy* is in fact virtually a disguised remake. All of which means that I have rather less to say about this one, given that it's impression on me at the time was relatively low-key, and so I'm going to try a different approach at this point.

I'm screening the film now, as I write, and I'm going to record my impressions as I watch, re-assessing the disappointment of a twelve-year-old from my middle aged perspective. The completist in me insists I have the Universal Mummy boxset in my collection, but it's not a film I've returned to often so I'm coming to it relatively fresh. Picture these words being scribbled into my notebook as the film unfolds before me, and this section operating in real time with all the tension of an episode of *24* – but without the explosions, the chases, the imprisonments, the tortures, and the miracle recoveries. And there's considerably less shouting.

So, here we go. Before I even get the DVD out of its case there's a strange, fluttering sparkle of excitement, even love. And make no mistake about it, I love these films. Not in the trivialising way we overuse that most sacred of words to describe our feelings for the banal and the mundane ('I love chips' or 'I love TOWIE'). Equally not in the more fully integrated way I love my wife and kids of course. No, this is more like an adolescent crush, in all its joy and fervour and occasional shamefaced guilt.

I get all warm and fuzzy as I slide the disc into the eager and welcoming openness of the DVD player, tingling with anticipation for the moment I will hear those bright and breezy brasses as the brave little plane circles the spinning black and white globe of the Universal logo, so full of hope and promise. And it's on a Saturday night of course, just as it always was so many years ago when BBC2 screened its blissful summer seasons, expanding my mind and enhancing my life in the process.

Of course, to accept the essentially adolescent nature of the obsession like this is to invite an accusation of stunted development, of an infantile and particularly pathetic kind of childishness. It's a charge that's hurled around a lot in newspaper think pieces by – usually right wing – commentators to account for everything from the apparently unforgivable crime of adults being prepared to be seen publicly reading the Harry Potter novels, to the waste of license payers money on an overgrown children's show like *Doctor Who*, to the great dumb guns and big bang rattle and hum of the summer blockbusters that are said to have been destroying 'proper cinema' ever since *Star Wars* reared its obscenely populist and profitable head.

So be it. Anyone who's ever been an adolescent will know how intense and overwhelming first loves are. They're not grown up, but they're not trivial either. They *matter*. They shape us. And we never forget them. Of course, most people reading this paragraph will be thinking of a first girlfriend or boyfriend, while I'm thinking of Bela Lugosi and Boris Karloff. Still, I'm not so sure there's a difference, in the end. And believe me, I'm all too aware of what that says about me.

The picture appears. There's the globe and that little plane. I know I've mentioned it before, but I'm so in love with that little plane. I say 'little', though if the globe is to scale then the plane is roughly the size of South America. I adore those production company logos. RKO Radio with its giant mast bleeping out a call that *King Kong* is about to begin, 20th Century Fox with its searchlights and buttonholingly assertive brass jingle which, for me, is always announcing *Star Wars*. But of all of them, it's the Universal one that thrills me most to this day, and most of all in this, it's original and most primitive form (by the late 30s the style was slicker and more assured, but though the globe remained, the plane and the poetry had gone). Something about that old plane, circling the whole slow spin of the whole wide world, is so suggestive of adventure and daring and danger that it is the perfect precursor to any horror film.

There was always a divide amongst lovers of these double bill seasons, which, in their archetypal form paired a 30s Universal with a 60s Hammer or AIP, as to whether you preferred the black and white ones or the colour gory ones. I heard Mark Gatiss – a man I could listen to for hours on almost any subject, but most of all on his love for horror – describe in an interview somewhere how he always felt he was just sitting through the old film waiting for the real thing to come later, but in my heart I was a Universal man.

I loved the Hammers, but I always felt they were essentially straightforward and prosaic, 'rattling good yarns' certainly, but not much more, while the 'old ones' had some of the timeless magic of myth or fairytale. I think a lot of that preference might be to do with the fact that I came to Denis Gifford's wonderfully warm, witty and nostalgic *Pictorial History of Horror Movies*, with its sniffy and shockingly unfair dismissal of Hammer as a modern day Monogram (the poverty row studio that churned out cheapo creepers in the 40s with Rondo Hatton or a down on his luck, visibly ageing Lugosi), before turning to Alan Frank's equally lovely Movie Treasury *Horror Movies* with its clear preference for the shock of the new. Impressionable and young, the theorist that gets at us first will often have a lasting influence. Thus my Pavlovian drool over the Universal logo with its brave little plane.

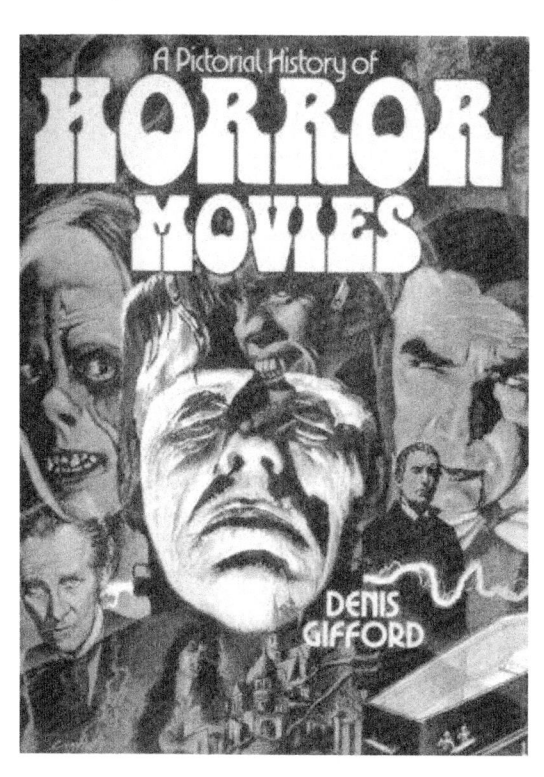

And then the film itself. A few snatches of *Swan Lake*, again – the same haunting theme that introduced both *Dracula* and *Frankenstein*. I know it's a confession only of my own ignorance and limitations, but classical music has never really engaged me. Opera and indeed all forms of classical 'singing' always sound weird and forced and histrionic to me, and although I can enjoy the odd 'Popular Orchestral Classics' kind of thing – anything where it's got a recognisable tune – I'm never going to happen upon a piece of classical music that can stir my soul like *Positively 4$^{th}$ Street, Waterloo Sunset, Baloo My Boy, This Ole Heart of Mine, Train in Vain, William it was Really Nothing, Up the Wolves* or *(The Angels Wanna Wear My) Red Shoes*. Rather than the music of evening suits and opera glasses, I respond to the directness of music from the fields and the streets, the work of intelligent peasants rather than the work of the educated and the trained. Those intelligent peasants might be anonymous fifteenth century balladeers or Lennon and McCartney, but what they all have in common is being common, like me. Of course I know that this says much more about me than it does about the relative merits of classical and popular music, but these few moments of *Swan Lake* were among only a handful of encounters with 'proper' music which did anything other than alienate me.

On the back of its use in the early Universal films (for which it is absolutely perfect) I got hold of a recording of the ballet, and listened at first obsessively, then a bit more dutifully, and then finally found myself wearing out the one tiny section of the cassette which contained the piece used in the film titles themselves without bothering with the rest.

So for me, in the end, orchestral music only belongs alongside the visual. I can adore soundtracks, but I lack the discipline or the concentration or the subtlety of soul needed to love classical music for and of itself. Bernard Hermann's haunting love theme from Hitchcock's *Vertigo*, for instance, speaks far more powerfully and movingly to me about loss and yearning than Wagner's *Tristan and Isolde*, which is its very thinly disguised source. Perhaps that's a part of why I find myself reflecting and meandering at such length on the subject of old horror double bills rather than Mozart or Michelangelo. Popular culture speaks to me in a profound and immediate way which high culture only rarely manages. Pleb to my very core, I take lowbrow to new heights.

The opening of *The Mummy* remains very impressive. There's a sonorous beauty to the opening title – *Oh! Amon-Ra – Oh! God of Gods— Death is but the doorway to new life —We live today-we shall live again—In many forms shall we return- Oh, mighty one.* The opening sequence in the tomb boasts some very atmospheric lighting, and a palpable sense of tension as Bramwell Fletcher yields to temptation and ignores the ubiquitous Edward Van Sloan's stern warning not to touch that casket. The whole sequence seems paradigmatic of the horror film's unfortunate tendency to wish to punish the crime of intellectual curiosity – witness Dr Frankenstein, who sought to create life 'without reckoning on God', or Jack Griffin in *The Invisible Man* who 'meddled in things that man should leave alone.'

The cutaway close-up of Karloff's heavy-lidded eyes fluttering open is among the greatest moments in all horror cinema – although it owes a lot to a similar moment with Conrad Veidt in *The Cabinet of Dr Caligari* – and the long-nailed hand edging slowly into the corner of the frame, hovering above the life-restoring scroll for a moment before the unfortunate archaeologist becomes aware of it is no less impressive. And Bramwell Fletcher knocks it out of the park with his reaction. A short, but properly terrified male scream of shock, followed quickly by the genre's greatest mad giggle, rivalled only by Dwight Frye's similarly unsettling cackle as the crazed Renfield in *Dracula*. I'm afraid that a bit of experimenting has revealed I can't do it anymore – though the attempt has, I believe, led to me getting a few odd looks from the neighbours.

Time passes, and we're introduced to David Manners as our square-jawed hero. Manners is worthy of note as Universal's preferred hero of the period, and it says something about the way a fan consumes a horror film that rather than the empathy or identification that the hero role typically requires of the audience, the actor has always generated a profound antipathy in me. He is an insipid and unpleasant Harker in *Dracula;* the apparently preferred audience response seeming to suggest that we should be in sympathy with Harker's snootily xenophobic – and subjectively causeless – suspicion and assumption of superiority over Lugosi's much more interesting and attractive 'foreigner'.

Manners is equally colourless and bland in essentially the same role in *The Mummy* and later in *The Black Cat* where his arrogant misreading of Lugosi's entirely sympathetic Vitus Werdegast as 'creepy' and his willingness to shoot first and establish the situation later in the film's denouement render his 'hero' utterly inadequate and ham-fisted. Snobbish, dull, unimaginative and uninteresting was Manners' stock in trade and the fan of these films is always engaged by the monster rather than the tedious hero, though to be fair to the actor, it is Universal's take on the role which is more at fault than his perfectly competent performances.

That said, I've never been quite certain whether the production teams skilfully and deliberately rendered their 'goodies' completely colourless so as to make the true stars of the show more vivid by contrast, or whether it was an accidental by-product of poorly underwritten characterisation at the script stage. Collusion or incompetence: either way, it remains galling to me that Manners was paid twice Lugosi's salary for his role in *Dracula*.

Karloff reappears, and I'm reminded once more, if I needed reminding, of what an incomparably skilled physical actor he was.

Bandages gone, his desiccated Ardath Bey moves as though only an effort of will keeps him from disintegrating into dust. Equally remarkable is Karloff's first vocal performance of note for Universal – both *Frankenstein* and *The Old Dark House* which had preceded his work here render him mute bar the odd grunt and whimper. Those sonorous, cadaverous, lisping tones are almost as distinctive and imitable as Lugosi's and have been forever immortalised for every Halloween-loving child by Bobby 'Boris' Pickett's charming impersonation on the novelty single 'The Monster Mash.' It's an exceptional performance, once again.

On re-viewing however, I'm particularly struck, by a different, no less exceptional, performance: that of Zita Johann as the heroine, Helen Grosvenor, who is both the 1930s girl next door and the enigmatic reincarnation of Imhotep's long dead love.

Predominantly a stage actress who appeared in only a handful of films, Johann offers an extraordinary subtlety, endowing the traditional heroine role with a rare degree of maturity and independence, while simultaneously able with the slightest shift of the body or drift in the eyes to suggest a yearning, timeless, mysterious soul out of time. She embodies both the ordinary and the exotic with equal conviction and grace. A multi-layered performance of great shade and complexity, it passed me by completely as a twelve-year-old but now would rank for me as among the very best of the period.

Less dynamic than the drawing room confrontation of Lugosi and Van Sloan in *Dracula* there is a virtual re-staging of that iconic clash, with Van Sloan this time facing off against Karloff's Ardath Bey in Lugosi's stead. Despite Van Sloan being offered dialogue as juicy as his 'If I could get my hands on you, I'd break your dried flesh to pieces' the scene never escapes from the shadow of its more intense predecessor, although it is enriched by one extraordinary close up in which Karloff's face seems almost to glow from within, an effect much more brilliantly achieved than *Dracula*'s pinpoints of light which were designed to sparkle in Lugosi's eyes but tended to miss rather too often.

Another point which strikes me now, to stir up the Boris versus Bela debate a little further, is the method Karloff chooses to convey his character's sinister intensity as he looms over the water in his mystical chalice. Isn't the gesture he adopts – a tautened hand, fingers rigid, clawing the air – a straight lift from Lugosi? Hindsight has long recorded the different fates of the two stars, Karloff's versatility and range and shrewd professional choices contrasting with Lugosi's car-crash of a career which led rapidly into bankruptcy, alcoholism and drug addiction, but of course at this very early point in each actor's path that future was not yet written.

At this point Karloff, like Chaney before him, was a specialist in 'extraordinary characterisation', but when it came to screen *malice* Lugosi was the supreme model, established not only by *Dracula* but by his stellar performances in Robert Florey's visually remarkable *Murders in the Rue Morgue*, also in 1931, and perhaps most of all in the cheap but incomparably stylish and massively profitable *White Zombie*. Doesn't Karloff's conscious or unconscious borrowing from his rival suggest a degree of uncertainty, an uncharacteristic lack of confidence, when, as here, stepping for the first time into more overtly 'Lugosi territory'? Perhaps this was what Karloff had in mind when, interviewed in later years, he made his otherwise puzzling comment that Lugosi, or 'poor Bela' as he tended to refer to him, was 'a great technician.'

There's an accidental comedy for me in the way in which Manners' hero springs to life in the immediate aftermath of his screen father's horrible death. 'Do you really think I have a chance with her?' he cheerfully intones, the prospect of a quick bit of spooning with Zita Johann's Helen sufficient to shift the clouds of grief for his noble father in an instant. Had David Manners been the Globe's leading actor in 1605, *Hamlet* might have been a rather shorter play.

It occurs to me in fact just how limited grief is in the world of popular film and television. Outside the arthouse or the literary novel it's still quite rare to find something like Ricky Gervais's *After Life* which is specifically *about* grief, and elsewhere in popular culture an experience so desperately, overwhelmingly spirit-sapping in the real world that it can hollow all meaning out of existence is almost invariably shrugged off in a few minutes of screen time. The only notable exception of which I'm aware, and which in its absolute bleakness comes close to approaching the numbing awfulness of the actual experience is 'The Body', the brilliantly written and directed episode of *Buffy the Vampire Slayer* which follows the death of Buffy's mother, the impact of which is allowed to continue to resonate throughout the rest of the show's run.

As *The Mummy* draws to its impressively staged conclusion, Eros and Thanatos battling it out behind Zita Johann's enigmatic eyes, I'm forced to admit that the film is wonderful; a much more complete, fully realised and memorable work than my twelve-year-old self was able to appreciate. It's beautifully acted, sombre rather than sensational, and marvellously atmospheric, showing the benefit of all of director Karl 'Papa' Freund's previous experience and talent as a cinematographer – a role he had fulfilled, let's not forget, on Browning's *Dracula* as well as on much better respected 1920s classics of German expressionism. Above all, perhaps, it's an object lesson in subtlety and restraint, rather than the clumsy stalk and strangle narratives I more typically associate with the mummy sub-genre.

All of which leads me to wonder why it is that tastes blur and shift so substantially as time passes. Back in 1977 I read *The Mummy* described as the most 'poetic' of the classics in Carlos Clarens' seminal study of the genre. Setting aside false modesty, I think I was probably a bit more literate than the average twelve-year-old, but at the time I simply didn't understand what he meant. Somewhere else I think I remember hearing the children's writer Michael Rosen talking about showing Oliver Postgate's beautiful *Bagpuss* to a group of children and realising from their negative reactions that children don't really respond to or understand the quality of melancholy. Perhaps that is the essential difference between the twelve-year-old me who found *The Mummy* a slow and turgid experience, and the fifty-year-old who finds it oddly moving.

There's something in Karloff's three-thousand-year devotion to a lost ideal that touches me now and passed me by then, some ache, or loss, or nostalgia that can only be felt by looking back rather than forward.

It's an echo perhaps of the relationships among cast and crew which find their way somehow, subtly, onto the screen. Director Karl Freund was corpulent, middle-aged and unattractive; an autocratic, domineering presence on set and, according to Zita Johann's account, rather brutal, and perhaps more than a little prurient, in his approach to his female star, demanding (in vain, as it happened) that she film the flashback scenes topless despite the obvious impossibility of getting such material past the censors. Like Hitchcock's well-documented mistreatment of Tippi Hedren some thirty years later, one can't help but feel the malice and rage of the ageing director's response to the youth and beauty of his leading lady to be a mark of his own sense of loss and yearning – entirely justifying the #MeToo generation's outrage, but perhaps worthy of a degree of pity as well as anger.

I can't help but see those emotions mirrored and heightened in the narrative of *The Mummy*. In the face of his own unspoken desire, and of the simultaneous longing and resentment the old and unattractive often feel for the young and the beautiful, perhaps Freund was investing something of himself into the on-screen story of Karloff as Imhotep, a man yearning to recapture a long-lost, long-dead love and his inability to see the living, breathing Helen Grosvenor beneath the image of Princess Anck-es-en-Amon which he carries with him.

It's this desperate, helpless quest which drives the narrative, this baffled, even tragic sense of entitlement – this love was mine once, why should it not be so now? – which makes the story truly 'poetic', and melancholic. In the end it's a wistful and bleak meditation on the cruelties of time and age.

We've all seen it in life in some variation, if not in ourselves then in others: a desperate, increasingly absurd and pathos-inspiring attempt to cling to past glories, to a sense of ourselves as we once were, of the things we missed out on or once saw as our right but which are so no longer.

I've known a man – I couldn't call him a friend, but I've known him for more than twenty years – who for much of that time, and even before it, found his pleasure and focus and sense of self in displaying his considerable degree of talent and charisma in amateur theatrical productions. They afforded him the opportunity to socialise, and flirt, and perform and direct others and to have his pick of young women overawed by what they saw as his sophistication. To assume centre-stage, in other words, and let those younger and more naïve be won by his cleverness and charm, and to bask with narcissistic abandon in the image of himself he saw reflected in their too-easily-impressed eyes.

During the course of those twenty something years, however, time has done its inevitable work. A good-looking older man has become simply an old man. The room in which he works is covered in old photographs of those productions, frozen images of past glories and past conquests. The young girls in those pictures are now middle-aged mothers, and the young girls who have replaced them in his day to day life no longer give him a second glance. The room, and the man, have a strange, haunted quality, and in his eyes you see a bafflement that none of it works any longer. 'How did I get here?' they seem to ask. 'Where did the real me go?'

The answer being, of course, that he went for a little walk, but unlike Imhotep, he isn't coming back. There's a hint of Hitchcock, and Freund, and Ardath Bey in those eyes. Uncomfortably, I would also have to concede there's a hint of me too, with my greying hair and my guitars I never play anymore but cling onto anyway and my 'look I used to be cool' Rae-Bans.

Maybe, in the end, that's the answer. At twelve, my dream selves could be the vampire count, aloof and brooding and dangerous, the Monster, isolated and outcast and misunderstood, or the Wolf Man, battling his own inner turmoil. In my fifties, however, the inexpressible longing of a man out of time for a never to be recaptured past makes Imhotep a figure I finally understand.

# 7. THE WAY YOU WALKED WAS THORNY

### The Wolf Man (Universal, 1941, George Waggner)

*'Even a man who is pure in heart and says his prayers by night, may become a wolf when the wolfbane blooms and the Autumn moon is bright.'*
**Gwen Conliffe (Evelyn Ankers), Sir John Talbot (Claude Rains) and various villagers.**

*The Wolf Man* was the film that introduced the final addition to Universal's roster of A-list monsters from the Golden Age, and also the film that marked the emergence of Lon Chaney junior as a major horror star, in the role – that of Lawrence Stewart Talbot, the eponymous Wolf Man – that he remained fondest of for the rest of his career. So influential was this taut, economical 1941 masterpiece that many people assume it to have been the first werewolf film, but in fact this is not the case. There was a now lost 1913 silent film called *The Werewolf*, and there was also Universal's surprisingly turgid *Werewolf of London* in 1935 which, although better known amongst horror fans than the lost silent, remains entirely obscure among everyday non-horror folk – or Huggles, as I'm determined to start calling them.

So it is *The Wolf Man* that is the true progenitor of the werewolf sub-genre, and it is such an impressive piece of work that it fully deserves that plaudit. Fast-paced, punchy and moody, the film had everything my twelve-year-old self, who had just yawned a bit through the earlier screening of *The Mummy*, could have wanted, and I loved it accordingly. I still do, come to that.

The script by Curt Siodmak, who was to become one of the key players in the second phase Universal horrors of the 1940s, is a masterclass in tight yet ambitious storytelling, maintaining every iota of tension throughout the film's pared-to-the-bone 70-minute running time, and also incorporating some beautifully resonant folk poetry which is so effective that it is hard to believe it isn't authentic. It's not only the 'Even a man who is pure in heart..' rhyme which Siodmak's script passes from cast member to cast member in what must surely be the most 'werewolf-aware' village in the world, but also Marya Ouspenskaya's beautiful lament:
*The way you walked was thorny, through no fault of your own. But as the rain enters the soil and the river enters the sea, so tears run to a predestined end. Your suffering is over. Now find peace for eternity.*

I don't expect to see it cropping up in a poetry module on a Literature syllabus anytime soon, but for me that's more lyrical and profound than a lot of the stuff that does.

Also remarkable about Siodmak's contribution is just how much of what we think we know about werewolves in fact originates with his screenplay. From the transformative power of the full moon to the fatal qualities of silver to the mystical pentagram, Siodmak conjures the feeling of long-established folklore so successfully that it feels entirely convincing and traditional. The achievement is all the more remarkable for the lack of a recognised literary classic on which to hang it all. There's no equivalent to a Stoker or a Stevenson, a Shelley or a Poe, for the werewolf movie. Perhaps a consciousness of this lies behind one of the film's few flaws – unable to rely on the kind of foreknowledge an audience might have for the vampire or the man-made monster the script falls back occasionally on bursts of rather awkward exposition. It's a pardonable inelegance, however, when set against the powerful sense of doom which Siodmak layers moodily over the narrative from the word go.

He's ably assisted in this by some of the most atmospheric fog-enshrouded visuals Universal ever achieved and by the briskly imaginative direction of George Waggner, alongside another triumphant Jack Pierce makeup design.

Also worthy of attention are some subtly affecting supporting performances. There's Bela Lugosi, squeezing everything he can from the seven lines the script offers him, as the lycanthropic fortune teller who passes on the curse to Chaney's Talbot. As Larry's concerned father, there's one of Hollywood's most reliably terrific supporting actors, Claude Rains, who horror fans will forever remember for his exceptional performance as the lead in *The Invisible Man*, and who was shortly to come as close as humanly possible to stealing *Casablanca* from Bogart and Bergman. There's the consistently excellent Evelyn Ankers as Gwen Conliffe, and also more appealing takes than usual on the square jawed hero from both Ralph Bellamy and Patrick Knowles.

Most of all, there is Marya Ouspenskaya as Maleva, the gypsy woman. She carries an extraordinary dignity, tenderness and power, dominating the screen in every moment in which she appears and making so striking an impression that she was recalled for the sequel, *Frankenstein meets the Wolf Man*.

On re-watching the film, however, almost as striking as just how much of the now-established werewolf mythos springs from this single text, is how many of the conventions of the genre are nowhere to be seen. For one thing, there is no facial transformation scene. Chaney's change from man to beast is indicated through a series of dissolves between close ups of his increasingly hairy feet, before said feet start to stomp across his room with a further dissolve showing us those feet now stalking across the misty forest floor.

The sequence actually works very well, in context, if you are able to ignore the fact that before sitting down in the chair in which the metamorphosis takes place Chaney pulls off his shirt and tie to reveal a white vest, but when he's out in the forest in the full wolf man regalia he's in a dark shirt and a different pair of trousers. Ever since noticing this glitch, I've longed for someone somewhere to come across a long-forgotten deleted scene in which a fully Wolfied Chaney rifles through his wardrobe to pick out the perfect outfit for the sophisticated lupine about town to wear while popping out to kill a handy gravedigger in the woods.

More significantly, the mid-section of the film resembles a psychological thriller much more than a conventional monster movie. The possibility that the supernatural trappings of the story are merely a reflection of Chaney's increasingly hysterical perspective is left open until more than half way through the film's narrative. At one point Chaney's tortured face is freeze-framed and there's an effective, but quite unexpected kaleidoscopic swirl of distorted faces, silver canes and wolfbane which reminds me most strongly of the jarring animated montage with which Hitchcock surrounds Jimmy Stewart's face to signal his character's mental disintegration in *Vertigo*.

Perhaps it is partly this emphasis on the psychological over the physical which has led some viewers to dislike the film, often pouring scorn on the cod psycho-philosophical nature of some of the dialogue as unconvincing and pretentious in what is essentially a cheapy monster B movie. Rather more fairly, these poor deluded souls may also point to the incontrovertible fact that, though it may be *just* possible to suspend disbelief far enough to accept that even a man who is pure in heart may become a wolf when the Autumn moon is bright, it is completely *impossible* to believe that Lon Chaney Jr. is Claude Rains' son. Or a member of the British aristocracy.

*"Let's just agree to be the least likely father and son in cinema history."*

But all of these ideas about the film, the good and the bad, are missing the point in the end. Because *The Wolf Man* is not actually about poor, doomed Lawrence Stewart Talbot's tragic downward spiral into despair, lycanthropy and yak hair. This may seem to be the film's subject to most people admittedly. But most people are wrong.

*The Wolf Man* is about Mark Welch.

Fandom, you see, can be a lonely, isolated and isolating business. Or, on reflection, perhaps there is a distinction to be made here. Maybe *fandom* is essentially social: all those football fans or Trekkies or death metal enthusiasts finding community and identity and camaraderie and self-definition through their shared costumes at large scale, communal events – games or gigs or conventions. But I'm no joiner. Gangs and groups and clubs, whether physical or virtual, fill me with an almost existential terror. I try (or I used to try, until I decided to write a book about it) not to reveal my ludicrous enthusiasms to people I meet, at work or in the wild social whirl of my everyday life – although the attempt at concealment is always doomed to fail in the end, some chance remark or association which I can't bite back always leaping out to leave me revealed as the helplessly absurd creature I am.

I prefer to watch horror films alone, my choice of only Lugosi or Cushing or Price for company made easier by my childrens' tender age and my wife's deep dislike of 'scary' as a concept. It seems to me that many of the activities which best define us – in which we are most truly ourselves – are essentially solitary. Like masturbation. All of which perhaps suggests that maybe I'm not a fan so much as an obsessive.

Nonetheless, my love of these old films grants me automatic membership of an unassuming, unthreatening and largely anonymous community of a kind; one in which I take a quiet pleasure and which exists only because of the context surrounding broadcast television and the screening of these double bills in the 1970s.

People of a certain age – myself among them – will grow slightly dewy-eyed talking about the golden age of British television, and the way in which the entire country would gather around the Morecambe and Wise show, huddled together in the flickering light like mediaeval villagers held rapt around the fire by a lone storyteller. A single, shared, simultaneous experience, almost like an act of worship.

It's true, and nice, that for a young horror fan today with some curiosity about the classics there's ready availability for everything. Never seen *Dracula*? A quick scan of Netflix, or You Tube, or if you're really committed a fiver on Amazon and it's yours. Even so, there's a certain magic about having to see something at the time it's actually on, screened for an audience *by someone else*, a commonality of experience vital to the proper enjoyment of event TV.

In 1977 there were only three television channels in Britain, and that lack of choice produced real quality and a truly shared culture, in stark contrast to today's broadcasting world, in which more and more choice usually means an ever widening proliferation of channels all broadcasting the same depressing rubbish.

At the time, the TV broadcast of feature films was no different: shared, specific and single. No VCRs then, no DVD or blu-ray release, no streaming on demand. If you hadn't seen a Bond film at the cinema, that Bank Holiday Monday night on ITV became a vast, communal premiere for two thirds of the country.

So it was with these horror double bills. Of course the audience was smaller, though at 6.5 million or so it was still large enough to regularly top BBC2s Saturday night ratings, but for those of us who were there, for a whole generation of spotty schoolchildren, otherwise geographically scattered, lonely and isolated, they were a desperately important formative experience. And I can very quickly recognise it in other people.

It's a source of real pleasure to me to see a common grounding in the works of writers and artists I admire, because it suggests not only a shared sensibility but a strange kind of intimacy. I can watch an episode of *League of Gentlemen,* or read or see anything else in which Mark Gatiss, Reece Shearsmith, Steve Pemberton or Jeremy Dyson have been involved and I know pretty much where they were, what they were doing, and how they were feeling on specific Saturday nights in Summer between the mid-70s and the early 80s.

Steven Moffatt, Mark Kermode, Matthew Sweet, Jane Goldman and Andy Nyman are other names I'd throw into the mix, alongside specialists in the darker end of teenage fiction like Anthony Horowitz, Marcus Sedgwick and Charlie Higson, and, although they may be a couple of years older and therefore likely to have started with the ITV Friday night *Appointment with Fear* seasons which preceded the BBC2 double bills, Neil Gaiman and Kim Newman too.

More surprisingly, I'd hazard a guess at Jonathan Coe. Most of his witty and profound work, with its deft intermingling of the comic, the poignant and the socially conscious seems about as far from old horror as you're likely to get, but the influence of films like *The Cat and the Canary* and *The Old Dark House* are plain to see in his wonderful novel *What a Carve Up,* and there's hardly another of his works that doesn't boast some sly reference to Universal B movies, Vincent Price or Boris Karloff.

I'd even place an outside bet on the wonderful J.K. Rowling, defying gender stereotyping and lapping up all those gothic castles and haunted palaces.

I'm not a stalker – honest guv – and I will never write a fan letter, or tweet or Twitter or poke (are those the phrases? Somebody young let me know) any of the much more talented writers and creators I've name-checked. Even so, these double bills were sufficiently central to my own development, my own interests and my own sense of self that I can – I think – recognise their place in the hearts and minds of others when I see it reflected through the filter of their own work, especially if, like me, they were born in the 60s.

At the time, it never really occurred to me that there was anybody else feeling the same joy in the macabre visions being spun out before my eyes on a Saturday night. The films seemed, almost by definition, to belong to the isolated, and to the outsider. To me, in other words.

In *Fever Pitch* Nick Hornby nails the heart of football fandom beautifully as being accepted into a new, and enormous family 'except in this family, you care about the same people and hope for the same things.' Back then though, as now, everybody was a football fan – or at least all of the everybodies that seemed to count.

Horror was OK – it had the tang of transgression to make it credible in the playground and the classroom, and so it wasn't like being obsessed with Disney or musicals or bird watching or trains, but it was also more than a little odd and out of the way.

There *was* the equivalent of Hornby's 'family' as it turned out, but it was a family that consisted of just one or two of us skulking in the corner of every playground or quadrangle (no class distinctions here) across the country, all feeling as if we were pretty much on our own in those pre-Facebook and fan forum days. A family which only existed with the benefit of hindsight. In this regard I was lucky. I was not alone, not quite.

When it came to horror, Mark Welch was my significant other.

Although obsession is essentially private and inward, conversation fans its flames, and Mark Welch was the only other person in my school who knew who Jack Pierce was, or who was prepared to endlessly debate the Boris vs. Bela question. He himself was a Lon Chaney junior man as it turned out, and you don't meet too many of those around. The Wolf Man was always his monster of choice, just as Dracula was always mine.

Why his preference for lycanthropic Larry? Well, Welch (it was always surnames back then) was a hairy kid, his longish curls always unkempt and straggly and seeming to crave the epithet 'mop' in a way that nobody else's hair has ever quite managed, while whiskers appeared desperately keen to spring out of him, erupting with fecund abandon in apparently random patterns across his face. Swimming lessons and post-PE showers revealed pubes that would have decorously graced Bruce Forsyth's scalp, even back in '77.

Of course the brotherhood of the hirsute is more than skin deep. There's a clearly identifiable parable of adolescence at work in the werewolf mythos, which was evident long before 50s exploitation cinema gave us *I Was a Teenage Werewolf* (bizarrely starring Michael Landon, later to find international fame as the world's third most reassuring father in the saccharine 70s TV hit *Little House on the Prairie* – coming in just after John Walton from the equally saccharine 70s TV hit *The Waltons,* and my dad*)*. From the sudden physical changes, the strange nocturnal impulses, the animal urges and the wildly sprouting body hair, to the less easily definable sense of a body, and even a soul, accelerating away from itself, wild and out of control, the werewolf is really just puberty writ large.

And it was not only in the hairy sense that Mark Welch got adolescence bad. Like me, he longed for Shirley Chambers, though he never told me so, any more than I would have dreamed of mentioning the fact to him, or to anyone else, BECAUSE I DEFINITELY DIDN'T LIKE HER AT ALL ACTUALLY. No, the reason I knew of his desire for the divine Shirley was because it overcame him so completely that he lost control of his reason and actually did something about it.

I at least knew my place. I would keep my longing quiet and deniable, because I could see that Shirley Chambers was a celestial creature from beyond my sphere. She later went out with the captain of the football team, in true *David Watts* style. She was the most popular girl in the history of the universe ever. Mark Welch, on the other hand, was a spotty git, and no more popular than the likes of me. Nevertheless, in spite of this undeniable truth his inner Wolf Man overtook him utterly. He left a secret note in Shirley Chambers' desk, inviting her for a romantic weekend bike ride, the big mistake lying in how instantly recognisable his handwriting was.

It even had sketch maps.

I wish, I honestly, honestly wish, that we lived in an American high school comedy world and I could tell you that, against all odds, the ruse worked, she saw the inner value of the apparently nerdy no-hoper, and they strolled hand in hand to a happy future. But we don't. The only truth to be revealed by American high school comedies is that apparently nerdy no-hopers later end up making wish-fulfilling American high school comedies. In the real world, Mark Welch's humiliation was immediate and horrible to behold, giving new meaning to the word 'crestfallen'.

I don't know if Welch had drawn inspiration for his sadly ineffective seduction technique from his hero Larry Talbot but it's not impossible given the extraordinarily adolescent and immature – not to say creepy – nature of Chaney's courting of Evelyn Ankers' Gwen Conliffe in the film. To begin with, he eagerly spies on her in her bedroom through a long-range telescope. If that weren't bad enough – and it is – he then tracks her down and jovially reports his voyeurism to her, even down to identifying the earrings she has on her dressing table, all with a grin that suggests he thinks he's being a charming smoothy rather than a pervert. He then exacerbates all this further by blithely refusing to accept Gwen's repeated 'No' when he asks her for a date, and seems equally unconcerned by the fact that she is already engaged.

Perhaps in fairness however, I should point out that, while my feminist modern-day self recoils in horror from the film's blissfully unknowing sexual politics, back in 1977 if I had had a long range telescope and a nice vantage point from which to spy on any of the objects of my desire – Shirley herself, or Rachael Fahey or Kerren Punton or Karen who lived over the road or any of a hundred others – I would have been fiddling with my focus in a heartbeat, without a moment's consideration or guilt. Even a man who is pure in heart may become a wolf…

Such is adolescent maleness; pumped full of hormones that you know only too well what to do with but lacking the social or emotional or empathetic qualities required to actually connect or communicate with another human being, or even to really recognise that other human beings actually exist.

That's the twisted logic of objectification, and the instinct of the adolescent, which needs to be worked and matured through, and it's plainly there to see in the image of Larry Talbot grinning excitedly through his telescope. It works, interestingly, to position even the unhairy version of the character as, despite his age and appearance, essentially a teenage boy.

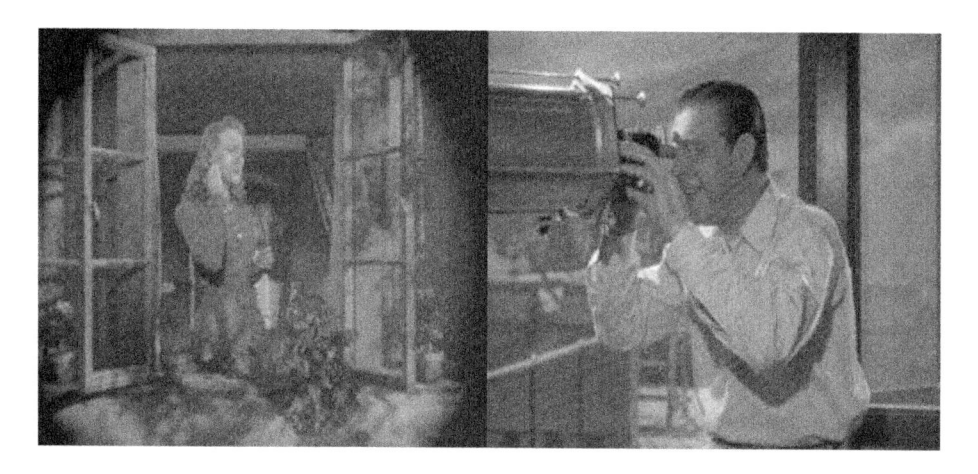

It also, perhaps, helps to explain Mark Welch's catastrophic attempt to get off with Shirley Chambers.

They were hard times, and those schools were hard places. Even so, it's not the undeniable misery which I now find most memorable, but the uncontrollable laughter. It is a strange fact, I think, that once you leave school you will never laugh so long and so hard and so hysterically again. Stuff just isn't that funny later on. Actually, in retrospect, it's quite difficult to determine what was so funny *then*, but somehow it was.

One of my most vivid memories of the time, and of Mark Welch in particular, is of spending the best part of a full day doubled up, helplessly giggling like a loon, tears squirting from my eyes, gasping for breath, sides aching and, despite the escalating threats from successive teachers, no more capable of stopping than of chewing off my own hand. The cause of this shared hilarity? The equivalent of the Monty Python sketch about the wittiest joke in the history of the world; a joke so funny it is instantly fatal to the hearer and becomes the Allies secret weapon to win the war? The cause, ladies and gentlemen, was Mark Welch and I occasionally whispering to one another at the very moment the last paroxysm of laughter had subsided, the words 'Stravinsky, Kaminski, Violinski'. Talk about you had to be there. For the uninitiated – though I don't think the knowledge will add much to anyone's sense of why this was so agonizingly hilarious – Mik Kaminski was the name of the violinist in ELO, and Violinski the name of his one-hit wonder spin-off band. Apart from the handy rhyme, I don't think Stravinsky had anything to do with it.

As the Kaminski reference might suggest, horror films were not our first, or only, shared interest. Alongside a joint and oddly specific sense of humour, music represented another mutual passion. Through 1976 and early '77 I had a real but relatively casual interest in the softer, poppier end of prog-rock. ELO themselves, Manfred Mann's Earthband, a hint of Genesis. It was Welch who converted me to punk. The persuasion wasn't subtle. There was no lending of albums – not when you only had about three – and no compilation tapes, since C90s weren't cheap either. He just banged on about it so long and so often that in the end I gave in and started to pay attention.

Like the rest of the country, reports of the notorious Pistols Bill Grundy interview had been what first brought punk to my attention, but I hadn't regarded it as anything more significant than a bunch of yobs hilariously swearing a lot on telly. Without Welch's endless droning about this single or album track he'd heard on John Peel I probably wouldn't have ever got any further than finding the whole thing a bit of a joke. But eventually I caved in, and everything was suddenly new.

I was too young to know what it was like in the 60s, with that extraordinary outpouring of talent and energy, each new single or album by The Beatles and The Stones and The Kinks and Dylan and The Who and The Beach Boys and The Byrds seeming better than the last, with that incredible sense of musical discovery being possible every time you switched on the radio. By the time that shining moment was palely reflected once more in the beautiful Britpop bubble of the mid 90s, much as I loved those bands, I was too old for them to *really* get to me, in the way that can only happen when you're fourteen or fifteen and music is the centre of everything.

So for me it was the golden years of '77 and '78 that were truly to define my musical tastes most indelibly and completely, and again it was that wonderful sense that each time you listened to Peel, or Luxembourg, or Annie Nightingale or Kid Jensen, some new Undertones or Buzzcocks or X Ray Spex or Members track would be the best thing ever. And for us suburban boys all around the country it was the radio and the music that drove the punk movement, not the fashion and not the trendy London art school gimmickry.

Despite Jimmy Pursey's best endeavours, however, us kids still weren't quite united. On the one hand there was the snarlingly threatening presence of the teds and greasers, always ready to bash a grammar school punk while weirdly acclaiming the sugar-coated retro 50s stylings of Showaddywaddy and Darts as the authentic voice of disenfranchised youth and even striking up a bizarre alliance with a nation of pre-pubescent schoolgirls in worship of Travolta and Newton-John's seemingly endless string of *Grease* soundtrack number ones.

On the other, even within our own ranks there was little unity. For the first few months, there was only punk. But then someone noticed that *My Aim is True* didn't really sound much like *Rattus Norvegicus* which in turn didn't sound all that similar to *Never Mind The Bollocks*, and so was born the concept of New Wave and we all started judging one another on how credible our tastes were. A new single by The Rats? They're shit compared to The Clash.

Wolf Man Welch and Dracula Galley were at loggerheads once more. He was for The Jam, hook, line and Rickenbacker, while I worshipped Elvis Costello, patron saint of NHS glasses-wearing 9 stone weaklings everywhere. As a result, though he also liked Costello and I also liked The Jam, we had to argue about who was best and could only do so by pretending that the other's preference was total crap.

With musical differences already in place, of course it was inevitable that we should form a band. Punk's famous 'this is a G chord, this is a C, this is a D, now release a single' DIY aesthetic notwithstanding, we found it hard to get past the 'having no instruments and not being able to play them even if we did' phase of our musical development.

What we did have was the ability to endlessly debate the best name for the band. My initial suggestion was The Fucking Cuntybollocks, which I thought at the time – and rather shamefully have to admit, still think – the most hilariously in your face band name ever. I loved the idea that, rather than wild eyed Rottenesque snarling, we might step onstage in sober fashion, taking a Beatlesy bow, and then gently announce 'Good evening ladies and gentlemen. We're The Fucking Cuntybollocks'. Wedding bookings might have been few and far between, but artistic integrity has to come first, doesn't it?

In any case, Welch was not so keen on the suggestion, and countered with the rather more sonorous 'Yesterday's Outcasts'. There was even a poem, briefly, intended for the sleeve notes, to which I believe I contributed the immortal couplet 'Went to a party, stole some streamers/Yesterday's Outcasts, tomorrow's dreamers.'

With that kind of profundity, it's little wonder that I quickly became the band's lyricist in chief. I wrote a song called *Brain Surgery*, intended as our debut single (*Anywhere around this great blue globe/ If you have a frontal lobe/ They're gonna get ya for/ Brain surgery/ Maybe a brain cell or two/ The government back it to avoid a coup/ All of society makes a moron of you/ They don't admit it but they know that it's true*), added the B-side *The Evolutionary Scale* (*Man is on the bottom rung/ Though he thinks he can get no higher/ Compared to us he's a load of dung/ Don't think that I'm a liar*) and quickly began work on my punk rock opera and concept album *Jesus Christ: Punk Rocker*.

I intended something a little less blandly respectful than Rice and Lloyd Webber – in fact *Jesus Christ: Lust for Glory,* Eric Idle's original title suggestion for what became *Life of Brian,* catches some of the spirit of what I hoped to achieve. My artistic vision was restricted, however, by having too much Chemistry homework, and I never got any further than a single song, called *Crucified* (the lyrics escape me now, but it's a safe bet it wasn't a gigantic developmental leap on from the searing social critique of *Brain Surgery*) and a proposed cast list for the film. Elvis Costello was to be Christ, of course, with Paul Weller as John the Baptist and Johnny Rotten as Pilate. Even now, I rather wish someone with a modicum of talent had stumbled on the idea and made it happen. Not to be, sadly.

Still grappling with the name which might best represent us – I had an inkling Yesterday's Outcasts might have just the tiniest whiff of the pretentious about it, and wasn't altogether in keeping with our stripped down Punk credentials – we eventually settled on The Superboes. That's pronounced Superb-oes, not Super-boes, for those few of you miraculously retaining any interest whatsoever in my doomed tilt at rock stardom.

We invented a few album titles, like *Sombrero Fallout* (don't ask me why – I've still never read the novel) and *The Superboes Live (Almost)* – a title I found funny because it dispensed with the requirement to actually be live, but I think on reflection may have owed slightly too significant a conceptual debt to a 1976 episode of The Goodies called *The Goodies Almost Live.*

Welch was also in the habit of creating his own weekly top 30 listings consisting of entirely fictitious singles, designed either to reflect events at school or to just have funny titles. Oddly, despite the questionable independence of these chart placings given Welch's heavy influence on his own self-penned hit parade, our band only ever made number 1 once, with *I Remember Nicky Goodwin* (sung to the tune of Danny Mirror's jaw-droppingly bad tribute single *I remember Elvis Presley*) and replacing The King with the name of an odd little boy in the year below us who once fervently berated me in the school canteen for using my fingers to eat a doughnut with the plaintively repeated lament "A spoon! You're supposed to eat it with a spoon! A spoon! You're supposed to eat it with a spoon!" Nowadays he would be diagnosed with Asperger's or OCD. Back then he was just a nutter who made excellent comedy fodder for invented novelty singles.

Although one Christmas around this time I did get a three quarter size guitar and a four page 'how to play' manual which came with it, we never got as far as recording. Or gigging. Or rehearsing. In fact, disconsolately following around a fourth year boy who was rumoured to own a drum kit and never having the nerve to speak to him was as close to getting together a proper band as we ever got. Somehow, the very slow acoustic version of *The Drunken Sailor* which, thanks to a combination of the manual's limited repertoire and my own sticky-fingered incompetence (a quality that continues to haunt my guitar playing to this day), was the best we could do never seemed to quite cut it in the 'let's stop coming up with names and song titles and actually do something' stakes.

It didn't seem so to me at the time, but with the scintilla of hindsight that a passing decade or four tends to bring, I'd say that forming a punk band that did absolutely nothing and played not so much as a single note was a very punk thing to do. The Superboes nailed the zeitgeist – not a sentence I'd ever have imagined myself writing.

Of course, even music had not been the first of our joint passions. Unlike most of the friendships in the first year of secondary school, ours had not been formed at primary level. We'd been to different schools, but an exceptional commonality of interest and experience formed an early and tight bond.

It was *Who* initially – avidly watching and sharing our impressions of the preceding Saturday's episode on a Monday morning. My scumbag 1970s comp did not possess a water cooler, but Welch and I shared plenty of those moments, swapping Target novelisations and our own ideas for brilliant sci-fi stories which were always unacknowledged but unabashed rip-offs of already existing brilliant sci-fi stories.

As the years went slowly by, our reviews became less breathlessly enthusiastic and more smugly sardonic and sneering. Each adolescent schoolboy kills the things he loves, and like a teenager inflicting some deliberate cruelty on an old, once much-loved teddy bear to prove how far from childhood he has grown (and all the time crying inwardly over Twee-Twee's sorry fate), we moved steadily further and further away from the show.

In truth our early years had been spoilt; the UNIT family Pertwee era of 1970-74 followed by Tom Baker's glorious first three years still represent the show's golden age for me, and many of the later Tom Baker stories were indeed hard to love.

The show's demographic shift away from dark, gothic-influenced teen-friendly stories towards more overtly comedic, primary school devices like the cute robot dog K9 left us out in the cold – or perhaps the shift was more in ourselves than in the show. Whichever it was, the more determinedly bleak and pessimistic *Blake's 7* began to fill the grown up sci-fi shaped hole in our hearts, sharing as we did the almost universal adolescent conviction that dark and gloomy is somehow intrinsically more 'adult' than positive and upbeat.

In its subject matter and some of its dialogue, as well as its doom-laden mood and atmosphere, *The Wolf Man* itself might seem to fulfil that requirement for gloom. Indeed, some of Claude Rains' Jekyll and Hyde style philosophising that the wolf is simply an expression of the dark side of the human personality, along with Larry's more than a little dubious pre-werewolf way with the ladies, suggests to me that perhaps Larry Talbot might have been originally intended to be a rather darker character than the one who finally emerged on screen.

Lon Chaney Jr. is probably the least highly rated of the great horror stars amongst fans of the genre, but I don't accept the charge in some quarters that he was a bad actor. He wasn't. In fact, he was a very good actor, but within a comparatively limited range. When called on to do dark and sinister – as in *Son of Dracula* say – he floundered. But he could do affable Everyman, and alongside it turmoil and torment, extraordinarily well, and this is what he gives to Lawrence Talbot.

Rather than his performance suggesting a dark underside, which the character's behaviour and some of the dialogue might easily have supported, he takes the opposite tack, and as a result his character's descent into despair and monstrosity is rooted in compassion and generates enormous sympathy. I think Chaney's very touching and effective performance, so ripe for empathy in its *ordinariness*, is a major part of the reason *The Wolf Man* resonated so strongly with me, and even more so with Mark Welch.

There's an extraordinary level of dependence that forms in those adolescent relationships. As in so many things, it's only in absence that that level of dependence becomes fully realised. On the odd occasions Welch was off sick the days stretched out like funeral bells, and I'd wander the school grounds miserably, on the assumption that it was better to present a moving target, glumly searching in vain for whatever dark corner seemed least obtrusive to hide away for the endless lunch hours.

I remember the fear and desolation which ate away at me like the gnawing wolf within poor old Larry Talbot over the course of one long summer holiday when it seemed likely that a change in his dad's job would mean Welch had to change schools and wouldn't be back the following September. Even that year's set of Saturday double bills only provided a temporary respite from the nagging unease – particularly since there was a hint of bottom barrel scraping about the 1979 offerings, which included lowlights like *Night Monster* and *Black Friday*. No mobiles, no texting or Facebooking back then. It wasn't until that September morning when he walked in again that I knew the outcome, and there have been few occasions in my life when I've been more pleased and relieved to see anybody.

There was nothing physical about the relationship, and I don't think I'm in any kind of denial when I say that there was no undercurrent of repressed sexual feeling about it either, despite the sneering insult 'you bears' hurled like confetti at the happy couple about a hundred times a day. 'Bear' incidentally was a strange, and, given that I've never met anyone since who knows the phrase, probably school-specific piece of slang meaning 'bender' or 'bum bandit', themselves terms of endearment to which I was no stranger. Nonetheless, the intensity of the connection could hardly have been heightened if there had been. And yet…

Mark Welch was my best friend from some point in late 1976 to the end of June 1981. I can be that precise not because of any sudden death or other such dramatic incident, but because at the age of 16 I scraped enough O levels to get me into Sixth Form. Welch only got two, which didn't do the same for him. He phoned me on results day and told me. That was the last time we ever spoke. We had no reason to after that. School had been the only context for us, and he wasn't at school anymore. Without the context, there was no relationship.

It leads me to wonder about myself a little. I've never lived alone, and in my forties became what people still refer to as a 'family man', and yet in many ways I think I'm self-contained almost to the point of neurosis. I take real pleasure in my own company, and have always had the capacity to shrug off friendships like a snake shedding skin. Welch may have been the first, but he certainly wasn't the last.

There was Paul, a childhood playmate with whom I spent the bulk of my Saturdays for more than a decade, while drifting further and further apart the whole time. I passed the 11+ and he didn't, so Grammar school and Secondary Modern made for the first separation. I grew increasingly bookish and nerdish, and our mutual frames of reference receded as our teenage years rolled by. At sixteen he got a job at a carpentry business making doors, and although I continued to see him on the occasional Saturday, it was more out of habit than anything else. When I left for university I failed to get in touch when I came home for holidays and the friendship was over. I later heard he'd lost part of his hand in an accident at work, and feeling guilty, met up briefly over the space of an awkward couple of pints, but, duty done, I allowed the relationship to lapse, permanently this time.

At university there were long, desperately earnest and intense nights of conversation and bottled pretension which came to a similarly abrupt end. I think it's normal, isn't it, to form intense relationships through the crucible of flat sharing and wild living in your university years and then gradually lose touch as a decent period elapses? I managed to lose touch with my college friends while I was still sharing flats with them.

A little later as a trainee teacher I formed a tight-knit group of friends, and discovered for the first time as the earnest 80s gave way to the laddish 90s that I could make people laugh around a pub table and that to do so wasn't necessarily reactionary and oppressive. As a result, that year remains one of the most enjoyable and uncomplicated periods of my life, and I still think very fondly of the people who shared it with me, but no more than a couple of years after it was over I couldn't have given you addresses or phone numbers for any of them, which was entirely down to me.

Over the years since then there have been bandmates and song writing partnerships, drinking buddies and football fan friends, stag dos and weddings and births and dinner parties, but it makes me strangely comfortable to note that with the fortunate exception of my wife, my family and the odd work-based friendship, I'm not in touch with anyone I've known for longer than about five years. I'm not absolutely sure what the slight tingle of pleasure I get from shedding people, from moving on and avoiding intimacy or lasting entanglements, says about me, except that the anonymity that comes with being known only partially and fleetingly by anyone except those very closest to me feels right and true and secure.

An introvert and an obsessive. Like poor old Larry Talbot, I really am a lone wolf, in the end.

*Mark and Shirley*

# DOUBLE BILL FOUR

## Saturday July 23rd 1977

SON OF FRANKENSTEIN                22.10 – 23.45

KISS OF THE VAMPIRE                23.45 – 01.10

> **10.5 News on 2**
> Weather
>
> **10.10-1.10 am**
> **Dracula, Frankenstein—and Friends!**
>
> **Son of Frankenstein**
> starring Basil Rathbone
> Boris Karloff, Bela Lugosi
> Twenty-five years after his father's death, Frankenstein's son arrives to occupy the ancestral castle...
> Baron Wolf von Frankenstein
>                             BASIL RATHBONE
> The Monster..........BORIS KARLOFF
> Ygor......................BELA LUGOSI
> Krogh....................LIONEL ATWILL
> Elsa..........JOSEPHINE HUTCHINSON
> Peter....................DONNIE DUNAGAN
> Amelia..................EMMA DUNN
> Director ROWLAND V. LEE. (Black and white)
>
> **11.45**
> **Kiss of the Vampire**
> starring
> Clifford Evans, Noel Willman
> Edward De Souza, Jennifer Daniel
> A honeymoon couple in peril among vampires in Bavaria.
> Professor Zimmer..CLIFFORD EVANS
> Ravna....................NOEL WILLMAN
> Gerald Harcourt..EDWARD DE SOUZA
> Marianne..............JENNIFER DANIEL
> Carl........................BARRY WARREN
> Sabena................JACQUIE WALLIS
> Tania....................ISOBEL BLACK
> Director DON SHARP. Films / page 10

# 8. BUTLER-EATING BABIES AND HEAD-TO-HEAD BEDS!

## Son of Frankenstein (1939, Universal, Rowland V. Lee)

*'When the house is filled with dread, place the beds at head to head.'*
**Amelia (Emma Dunne)**

I have a hard time with favourites.

When people find out you like films – or books, or music – they'll almost inevitably ask you what your favourite is. It's a well-meant attempt to engage you in conversation on a subject they know you're interested in, but the downside of course is that it reveals them to be somewhat lacking in what Renfield, in between gobbling flies and spiders, called 'the aerial powers of the psychic faculties'.

After all, given the wealth of delights which the history of cinema, or even just the horror genre, has to offer, anyone with half a brain cell should know it's impossible to pick a single favourite. Depends what you mean ... Depends what for ... Depends what mood I'm in ... I went through a phase of rather wearily trying to explain all this to them. Then I went through a phase of replying by asking them to tell me which of their children was their favourite. Then I didn't have any friends and no-one wanted to talk to me anymore. So now I say *"Son of Frankenstein."*

The film holds a very specific place in the Universal cycle. It's the first film in the second wave of Universal horror, appearing after an almost three year break in the production of monster movies which had come about partly as a result of the virtual ban on the genre in Britain. The British market served as a lucrative source of extra income for the Hollywood studios, and so the embargo which held sway in this country after the perceived sadism of the 1935 Karloff/Lugosi vehicle *The Raven* made the American studios abandon the genre in favour of safer stuff which could still generate decent audiences in Tunbridge Wells.

It was only the vastly profitable reissue of the original *Dracula* and *Frankenstein* in 1938 which, taking Universal entirely by surprise, convinced the studio that there was life in the old ghouls yet, and prompted *Son of Frankenstein* into production.

*Son of Frankenstein*, however, is not only, or even primarily, the first of the new cycle, but rather the last of the old. In its casting, in its set design, in its budget, *Son* is the last of the glossy, high profile Universal horrors. From here on, they were essentially B movies, made fast and efficiently on slender budgets to play as the second feature – often very imaginatively and effectively, but very different in tone to the prestige horror productions which characterised Universal's early thirties output.

Florid, lush, rich and stylised, *Son of Frankenstein* is both a culmination and a summation of all that came before, and although its very healthy profits were sufficient to launch a new, rather less ambitious cycle, it represents the end of the true Golden age of classic horror, somehow seeming to embody and encapsulate all the different and apparently disparate strands of the earlier films.

The set design is wildly expressionistic, but seems to draw not only on the *Caligari* flavoured visual style of Robert Florey's *Murders in the Rue Morgue,* but also encapsulates the more full-blooded gothic of *Dracula* and *Frankenstein* while even somehow maintaining a kinship with the ultra-modern Bauhaus of Ulmer's *The Black Cat.*

There is a heightened, baroque quality to every aspect of the film which steps precipitously close to parody, without ever quite tripping over the edge. It's no co-incidence that this is the film Mel Brooks draws on most heavily for *Young Frankenstein.*

The film even boasts a wonderful line which suggests of Benson the butler that he 'went up to the nursery with the baby's supper dish ... we haven't seen him since,' enabling a whole generation of horror fans to dreamily envisage the monstrous butler-gobbling baby. It's a testament to the lavish, delirious atmosphere the film creates from the first frame to the last that it wouldn't have seemed entirely out of place.

*"Now nobody's going to be cross. Just tell us the truth. Did you eat Benson?"*

I have a similar feeling for *Son of Frankenstein* as I do for Sergio Leone's *The Good, The Bad, and the Ugly* – it's my favourite of all the spaghetti westerns, taking many of the stylistic tics which characterised the early, more prosaic versions and pushing them almost to breaking point. The result is an extreme, vertiginous experience: breath-taking, operatic and epic, but just one step further would bring the whole edifice crashing down in a puff of bathos. Both films are a joyous summation of, and progression from, past glories, but leave nowhere to go for their respective cycles. The enjoyable, briskly pedestrian Universal horrors that came later were perhaps the only direction the studio could have taken after the wild excesses on display here. In every way, *Son of Frankenstein* feels like a wonderful ending.

The acting too is beautifully judged, played to the absolute hilt but somehow – just – never quite slipping into the overripe or hammy, and *Son of Frankenstein* boasts probably the finest cast ever assembled for a horror film. Karloff and Lugosi and Basil Rathbone and Lionel Atwill, and all of them at the top of their game. It's a true ensemble piece, beautifully and diversely played by each of them.

It's Karloff's swansong as the monster, and although he's given rather less to do here than in the first two films, the howl of anguish he delivers over Lugosi's dead body is right up there with the 'catching the sunbeams' moment from the original and stands unabashed alongside the brilliance with which he endowed every moment of *Bride of Frankenstein*.

Rathbone too is a delight, his Wolf Frankenstein operating at a deliciously sustained pitch of barely contained hysteria. His scenes verbally fencing with Lionel Atwill's equally impressive turn as the shrewd Inspector Krogh are a pure joy, anticipating their return battle as Holmes and Moriarty in *Sherlock Holmes and the Secret Weapon* a couple of years later.

Atwill himself deserves special mention here I think. Less well-known today than the first rank monsters, he sits alongside George Zucco in the pantheon of horror stars, never quite hitting the heights of a Lugosi or a Karloff, but always effective, always reliable, never giving a bad performance and at times giving a great one.

A few years earlier, in *Mystery of the Wax Museum,* Atwill had been – alongside the ubiquitous and wonderful Fay Wray – part of one of the great monster reveals of all time when his 'face' is beaten away to reveal a genuinely hideous makeup job beneath. It's a film, remade very well in the 50s as a 3D Vincent Price vehicle called *House of Wax* and remade again, appallingly, as a vehicle for Paris Hilton in 2005, which remains one of my very favourites from the golden age of the early thirties, not least because of Atwill's fantastic performance.

Here, in *Son of Frankenstein,* his Inspector Krogh is a minor gem. He's complex and believable, with the blackly comic bits of business Atwill lends to the character's false arm – the *Strangelove*-anticipating salutes, the monocle-cleaning – proving an endless source of pleasure and suggesting the actor's wickedly dark sense of humour.

If horror has a first eleven Atwill deserves a place. Chaney, Lugosi, Karloff, Chaney Jr., Carradine, Lorre, Rathbone, Price, Cushing, Lee, Atwill. That's eleven. Poor George Zucco will have to make do with twelfth madman.

My fondness for Atwill was only increased by my later discovery of the career-threatening sex scandal which engulfed him in 1940, revealing the clipped and rather portly actor as the unlikely wet-lipped host of a string of wild and frenzied orgies and as the owner of an unrivalled collection of pornographic films. In fact, it was only the loyalty shown to Atwill by Universal which enabled his career to survive the scandal – a fact I've always found a little odd given how shamefully the same company misused, mistreated, and ultimately ignored Lugosi, whose exhilarating but dreadfully underpaid performance in the massively profitable *Dracula* in 1931 had effectively saved the company from ruin.

As a dyed in the wool Lugosi worshipper, it's also a source of enormous pleasure and pride to see my favourite so charmingly and effortlessly stealing the film from actors with the power and presence of Rathbone, Karloff and Atwill. His Ygor in *Son of Frankenstein* is very possibly the greatest single performance in the history of the horror film, filled with charm and menace, cunning and sly humour, pathos and passion, and all underscored by an exceptional degree of – for want of a better term – twinkle.

There is a critical consensus which, on the back of his early thirties films, regards Lugosi as a limited ham capable only of a series of stylised, theatrical variations on his version of the immortal Count. There's far less tendency to aim the same kind of charge at other stars of the era who explored a similarly limited palette – Bogart, or Gable, or Cary Grant or Jimmy Stewart for instance. To my mind though, it's a source of great regret that Lugosi was given too few, rather than too many, chances to explore those variations on the silky menace of his era-defining performance – just look at *White Zombie* and imagine a world in which he'd been granted more roles affording him those kind of opportunities.

However, even if you momentarily concede their wrongheaded point, then it's still only fair to remark that those critics who adopt this dismissive view tend to conveniently forget Lugosi's performance as Ygor, possibly because he is so completely subsumed into the character that he is virtually unrecognisable.

Perhaps a part of the sense of mischief, of sheer delightful play, at work in Lugosi here is as a result of the enormous relief he must have felt to be in the film at all. He had been virtually unemployed for the previous two years, production on horror films having been effectively ended in Hollywood, with no American producers able to see that Lugosi could be accepted by audiences as anything other than the 'horror man'.

As it was, Lugosi was initially only hired for a few days' work in a minor role on a minimal wage – the studio knew of his desperate financial straits as well as the potential marquee value of his name and shamefully used his desperation to hire him on the cheap. It was only the innate decency of the film's director, Rowland V. Lee (alongside his bloody-minded willingness to defy the studio executives), that led him to expand Lugosi's role and keep him employed throughout the shoot. In return Lugosi's performance delivered Lee a piece of film history.

It could and should have been enough to offer Lugosi a second shot at major film stardom, at least as a talented and versatile character actor, and it very nearly was. Impressed despite themselves with what Lugosi had delivered, Universal placed him under non-exclusive contract, brought him back to reprise Ygor almost as effectively in *Ghost of Frankenstein* and considered him for the lead in *The Wolf Man*.

For the second time in his career, however, Lugosi was supplanted by the appearance of a new rival for the horror crown. First it had been Karloff, now it was Lon Chaney junior, who over the next few years was to play not only the Wolf Man but *all* of the classic Universal monsters including – worst insult of all – Dracula.

Nevertheless, whatever sorrows and disappointments and humiliations laid in wait for Lugosi, Ygor remains a performance to be relished and appreciated for all time. Given immortality by the magic of celluloid and the charisma of the actor, the role is a powerful and enduring testimony to Lugosi's talent and grace, however much that talent may have been wasted by the limited opportunities he was to be given later.

Perhaps it was not only that sense of relief which injects something extra into the performance, and into the feeling of the film as a whole. Never really friends, but never the daggers-drawn rivals they have sometimes been portrayed as either, the teaming of Lugosi and Karloff here seems genuinely close. At the time of the filming of *Son of Frankenstein* both men had recently become first time fathers, and perhaps it was this bond that leant the on-screen chemistry a sense of warmth and camaraderie that is never suggested elsewhere in the many collaborations of horror cinema's greatest double act.

*Boris Karloff on set with Bela Lugosi junior*

    The power of the new father bond should never be underestimated. Something in the heady cocktail of delight and fear and dad-shock opens one up emotionally. I once had an extra phone line installed unofficially and without charge by a telecom engineer simply because a conversation over the obligatory cuppa revealed his girlfriend had just given birth to their first child while my own daughter was only a few months old.
    This was a notable exception to the normal pattern of such encounters for me, incidentally. Does anybody else find workmen in the house as awkward as I do? There's the whole 'do I leave them to it and read a book in the living room or do I stand around awkwardly while they work in case they want to talk?' debate. Then, assuming I've made the latter choice, there's the whole 'assumption that I know something about plumbing/ electrics/ windows/ phones/ wireless connections/ <u>*insert relevant trade here*</u>' thing. An assumption that, for whatever pathetic reason, I feel as if I can't contradict without having to add shamefacedly 'I've no willy', like Eoin McLove in *Father Ted*. Thus lots of knowing 'mms' and

'yeahs' and informed nodding, interspersed with a few well-placed 'mates' added in an accent a bit more rough and ready than my own, none of which makes me look like an idiot at all.

I don't know why I should feel as if I need to maintain some vague semblance of manliness in those situations – or why it should be 'manly' to know about combi boilers anyway. When talking to me, no-one feels the least need to fake a knowledge of assessing pupil progress in the Key Stage 3 English Curriculum for fear of appearing to be a bit of a jessie.

Whatever the reasons – new fatherhood, the return from the grave of an apparently deceased genre, the personality of Rowland Lee – the film has a golden, late summer feeling to it, and contemporary accounts suggest that the shoot was indeed a very happy one. In large part it may be the faint, insubstantial traces of this joy in the making which transmits itself to me and renders it, though I would readily admit it may not be the best film ever made, my favourite.

In fact, a bit like John Lennon being asked if Ringo Starr was really the best rock drummer in the world and laconically replying 'He's not even the best drummer in The Beatles', I'd be quite prepared to concede *Son of Frankenstein* is not even the best film in this season. Certainly *The Premature Burial* and *The Fall of the House of Usher* are more eerie and unsettling. *Frankenstein* is darker and bleaker and *The Black Cat* more strikingly original. *Dracula* is more ground breaking, while *Brides of Dracula*, *Plague of the Zombies* and *The Reptile* are faster-paced and more dramatic. *Bride of Frankenstein* is wittier and more moving. I think those things are undeniable, objective truth. But then, pleasure is essentially *subjective*, isn't it?

Of course Shakespeare is a greater dramatist than Dennis Potter, but *The Singing Detective* moves and impresses me more deeply than *Hamlet*, *King Lear*, *Othello* and *Macbeth* put together. The 'me' is the key element in that heretical statement. It goes without saying that Potter's masterpiece isn't 'better' than Shakespeare's tragedies, but it moves *me* more. An accidental co-incidence of elements in my history, my background, and my personality make me more receptive to the lesser work than to the greater.

It's in this sense that, with a polite raise of the hat to Christopher Ricks, it's perfectly fair to investigate the question of whether or not Bob Dylan should be spoken of in the same breath as Keats, and why I will always love old horror movies and TV fantasy more than Greek tragedy or the nineteenth century novel. Joss Whedon is not a better writer than Thackeray, I just happen to *like* his work more, and there's nothing wrong with that. Art is not a competition: my unique, entirely subjective appreciation of *Firefly* and *Buffy the Vampire Slayer* does not wipe *Vanity Fair* out of existence, any more than my love for Norwich City makes them in any objective sense a better team than Liverpool.

Even more than this defence of subjectivity, however, and rather less often commented on, I'd argue that our responses are much more a part of the specific circumstances surrounding our encounter with the artistic work than is often allowed for.

Our *personal* context, in other words. In an extended interview with Chris Rodley my favourite director, David Lynch, described one specific viewing of his own film *Eraserhead,* in which it appeared to him 'perfect'. Lynch has never struck me as especially arrogant or self-satisfied, and *Eraserhead* is not a film I particularly enjoy, and yet I know exactly what he was driving at. Lynch wasn't suggesting he had made a perfect film; only that on that one particular day, in that one particular set of screening circumstances, the film had felt that way to him.

On the Saturday I most recently re-watched *Son of Frankenstein*, I went to see Norwich City, despite an unprecedented injury crisis which looked likely to see them served up like sacrificial lambs to the Premier League champions, produce a dizzyingly good performance to beat the mighty Manchester City 3-2. It was a blissful Saturday afternoon fit to convince me that my club were on the verge of taking the Premier League by storm[2], and the surge of disproportionate joy I felt carried me over into the film later that night, which presented itself to me as absolutely perfect.

There was not a single flaw, not a moment of *Son of Frankenstein* I would have wished any different; an uncharacteristic generosity of spirit I even extended to the presence of Donnie Dunagan (later to be the voice of Bambi) as Basil Rathbone's teeny tot son Peter. Under normal circumstances the appearance of a child actor in any film is enough to make me wish to immediately call upon the combined services of the childcatcher from *Chitty Chitty Bang Bang* and Joan Crawford armed with a wire coat hanger.

More than forty years previously on the 23rd of July 1977, when I settled down to watch *Son of Frankenstein* for the first time, the Summer holidays, and an escape from all the miseries of school, were properly underway. The England cricket team, boasting the elegance of the late Bob Woolmer and the nervous energy of Derek Randall in its batting line up, a bowling attack including Bob Willis, John Lever, Chris Old and 'deadly' Derek Underwood, Tony Greig's gangly all-round brilliance and Alan Knott, still the finest wicketkeeper ever to pull on the gloves, had recently beaten Australia by 9 wickets and were well on the way to regaining the Ashes.

A couple of weeks earlier had seen what may well have been the greatest Wimbledon men's singles tournament ever, back at a time when I

---

[2] Our humiliating relegation later in the season, losing every one of the final ten games, helps to demonstrate the reasons my career in football punditry never quite kicked off.

had become almost obsessed by the sport, perhaps because in the 70s and early 80s the players' games seemed to be somehow an expression of personality as much as ability, a pleasure that the modern game, for all the exceptional talents which grace it, no longer seems to offer spectators. The semi-finals that year saw brash slugger Jimmy Connors win, but in the process, almost unbelievably, lose a set to an unknown teenager who had come to play in the junior tournament but progressed all the way through the *qualifying* rounds of the real thing, before beating seasoned pro after seasoned pro to reach the semis of the main event. The upstart's name was John McEnroe. In the other half of the draw the semi was between the iceman and the rock star, Bjorn Borg against his practice partner Vitus Gerulaitus, and the pairing produced an epic five-set battle which eventually went to Borg 9-7 in the fifth and remains for me perhaps the greatest, most enthralling tennis match I've ever seen, rivalled for skill and drama only by the two finals Borg contested with McEnroe in 1980 and 1981 respectively. The final in '77 was no let-down either, Connors beginning like an express train and Borg only gradually finding a way back into the match to take it in another gruelling five sets.

The pop charts across that July included The Pistols with both *Pretty Vacant* and *God Save the Queen* (of course it was number 1 in the week of the silver jubilee, even if the BBC pretended it wasn't, just as surely as *Ding Dong The Witch is Dead* dominated the charts in the week of Margaret Thatcher's funeral), ELO's *Telephone Line,* The Stranglers' *Peaches/Go Buddy Go,* The Ramones' *Sheena is a Punk Rocker* and *Halfway Down the Stairs* by The Muppets.

*The Spy Who Loved Me* was in cinemas and I'd been to see it with my mum (how cool was I?), probably this very week. Still my favourite of the Bond films, this one is more familiar to non-Bondians as 'the one with the underwater car' – a white Lotus Esprit – or 'the one with Jaws'. Even though we initiates know that in fact there are two 'ones with Jaws' because the steel-toothed henchman played by Richard Kiel was popular enough to be brought back in *Moonraker*, the next, considerably less effective, entry in the series. *The Spy Who Loved Me* was the last Bond movie for many years to achieve a fully successful balance between humour, entertainment and excitement, many of the later films teetering over either into self-parody or, in reaction, a determined po-facedness, and I continue to love the film to this day.

But perhaps most significant of all in influencing my mood as *Son of Frankenstein* began was that this was probably the point when my love of the horror double bill became secure. I'd settled in, in other words. This was the fourth week and I was no longer *finding out*, or *realising*. By now I *knew* how much I was going to love each three hours or so in front of the

TV late on a Saturday night and there was an extra dimension of cosiness, pleasure and joy in that foreknowledge.

All of these things together combined, mystically, in front of this particular screening to create a sense, of living, however briefly, in the best of all possible worlds. It couldn't happen independently of the film of course. No amount of summer holidays or sporting or musical excellence could have made, say, *Night of the Lepus* into an all-time favourite for me, but when those personal, contextual intangibles combined with the intrinsic quality of a film as good as *Son of Frankenstein* I was sold for all time. Which is why it's my favourite. Even though I don't have a favourite because the idea of having just one favourite is … etc.

Whether it's a film or a book, a band, an album, a football team or a life partner, we love the things and the people we love for a reason – or reasons – and our response in the end is our own, unique and sovereign and irreducible: a fact that, in this world of ever more received opinions and ever more skilled and insidious methods of infiltrating and colonising the insides of our heads, we should kick and scream and fight and scratch to defend.

# 9. BLOOD! MORE BLOOD!

## Kiss of the Vampire (1963, Hammer, Don Sharp)

*'She has, as you may put it, grown up - tasted the more sophisticated, more exotic, fruits of life.'*
**Dr Ravna (Noel Willman)**

When I think back to the BBC2 horror double bills of the 1970s (and by now it may be becoming apparent that that's something I do quite a lot), there are two specific images which remain frozen onto my inner eyelids more vividly than any others, and it's interesting to me that both are from this 1977 season, *Dracula, Frankenstein – and Friends!* and both are from Hammer films.

One is a moment from *The Reptile* in which John Laurie's mad Peter sprawls into close up, framed through a window, eyes blank and staring, his neck black and crusty from the reptile's bite and white foam bubbling from his lips, and the other is this one, from the opening of *Kiss of the Vampire*.

The mournful toll of a funeral bell. A gnarled tree, leafless and twisted, occupies the foreground of a gloomy, shadowed graveyard. A sombre, muted gaggle of mourners. A grim-faced, black-clad figure appears at the brow of a hill, approaches the graveside and suddenly launches the gravedigger's spade through the splintering wood of the coffin. Ear-splitting scream. Close up of coffin lid. Bright red blood wells and pulses around the spade, before the camera glides through the coffin lid to reveal the face of the woman within, fangs bared, and we crash into the opening titles.

It's archetypal Hammer, the same conscious 'shock 'em quick' strategy which governs the opening of their majestic 1958 *Dracula* and the same copious use of that oddly lurid approximation of human blood which has become immortalised as 'Kensington gore'. It was always too startlingly crimson for any undue realism to intrude, but also the perfect shade to make the most striking use of Hammer's lush Eastman colour stock, as much a part of the production designs as the red-painted berries foregrounded in *Curse of Frankenstein,* or the scarlet of Christopher Lee's eyeballs.

The image has remained with me forever, and I'm led to wonder why. It's not the film itself I remember so vividly, and in fact there are many of the films I first saw in these horror double bill seasons which I remember better, as whole texts. And although naturally I've seen *Kiss of the Vampire* many times since (or perhaps that's not so natural if viewed with any degree of rationality), it's still that specific moment, captured in mental freeze frame like some internal PrtScr technology, which sticks with me, rather than the film as a whole. And of course, it's the gore, isn't it?

Gore holds a curious place in the history of the genre, and also in my relationship with it. To a contemporary generation of fright fans for whom the question 'how good is the film?' is almost directly synonymous with the question 'how gory is it?' this may seem unbelievable, but blood and guts have not always been a convention of the genre. The golden age of black and white offered a pinprick of dark grey blood on Renfield's fingertip, and that was about it. No lingering close-ups of death and mutilation. No body parts. Suspense, malice, and sub-textual perversity, yes, but gore had no role to play. Shadowplay, off-screen stakings and out-of-shot screams. That was horror. Until Hammer. Until colour. Until the gunshot to Christopher Lee's face in *Curse of Frankenstein*.

As the vividness of my memory of *Kiss of the Vampire*'s plunging spade suggests, in the first flush of my horror film enthusiasm I responded to the visceral impact (or perhaps more literally, the viscera) of Hammer's gore revolution in a way both powerful and direct, just as 1950s cinema audiences, faced with a startlingly new and bloody take on the gothic, had done before me.

The most immediate and obvious evidence of my response was confronted by my English teachers in those early years of secondary school. After having spent a futile year of pleading with me to write stories about something other than *Doctor Who*-influenced alien invasion, they were suddenly presented with a seemingly endless succession of severed limbs and buckets of blood. No amount of healthy, clean cut role model types in the books on the required reading lists could stem the blood-dimmed tide; no suggested story title was sufficiently innocuous to avoid a set-piece dismemberment. Picasso had his blue period (don't trouble to check it out, art philistines, it's not nearly as interesting as the name suggests); this was certainly my red one.

Looking back, I regard this first prelapsarian flush of gory enthusiasm as roughly analogous to the utter, cheery brutality and innocence of the childhood id. I see it again now, in my own children's hysterical laughter when a squabbly tug of war over a plastic baby results in each of them suddenly gazing in surprise at a severed leg clutched tightly in their hand while the torso flops disconsolately onto the carpet. Either I've bred two prospective serial killers, or children have an instinctive sense of the absurd comedy inherent in the body's brutalisation.

It was a relatively brief interlude for me, however, before the intervention of the disapproving superego. As I increasingly began to value the subtlety and restraint of the 'old ones', I came to reject and undervalue the newer, bloodier aesthetic with ever more censorious fervour. I became that rarest of horror fan animals, the anti-gore purist.

While the heightened gothic atmosphere, the literary respectability, the high production values and the distinguished acting chops of Cushing, Price and Lee allowed me to – a little bit guiltily – continue to adore the Hammers, the Amicus anthologies and Corman's AIP Poe Pictures, the 70s new wave was too much for me.

Despite the gore I continued to find perfectly acceptable in my own essays I reacted with genuine anger and disgust to the gritty and disturbing realism of the blood and entrails on offer when the 1978 season of BBC2 horror double bills included a screening of George A. Romero's *The Crazies*. It took many years before I was able to see the satiric genius in Romero's magnificent, gore-fixated oeuvre, or any merit whatsoever in the likes of Tobe Hooper's *Texas Chainsaw Massacre,* John Carpenter's *Halloween* or anything with Wes Craven's name attached.

Of course artists are always gradually pushing boundaries, and the 70s new wave of horror films – almost all remade in the last decade or so – now themselves seem tame to the *Saw* and *Hostel* generation, but for me the brutal pessimism and nihilism I first encountered in Romero's dystopian visions continues to make for slightly queasy and uncomfortable viewing.

Pleasure or objection: either reaction to the gore which has become so established a convention of the genre stems ultimately from the same source, which is a profound sense of transgression. The gore movie revels in its ability to display the forbidden and the taboo. In the real world we're not supposed to see the insides of another human being, unless we're a surgeon or a soldier. I remember a friend of mine trying to describe to me what his experience of being in the operating theatre for his wife's caesarean had been like, and, growing slightly wide-eyed, he whispered conspiratorially 'I've seen Kate's spleen.'

Some of us are drawn to the transgressive and the forbidden, others are terrified and disapproving; most of us are a bit of both. I don't pretend to be Richard Dawkins (or not since receiving that 'Cease and Desist' order from his solicitors anyway - sorry again about that, Richard) but I wonder if there may be a biological, evolutionary imperative at work here. Many of the deepest fears on which the horror film works have a buried, ancient, primeval quality – the darkness beyond the circle of fire, the monster lurking in the woods. To the hunters of the ancient past the sudden startling exposure of the body's interior could mean urgent, life-threatening danger but might equally be the precursor to food. Blood serves as a warning but also an appetiser. Somewhere in the primordial swamp of the collective unconscious, I think we're still responding to the same stimuli.

I may be – yet again – merely revealing my own intense philistinism, but I strongly suspect that it's a similar response at work in my love of the art of Francis Bacon. For others there may be an altogether more refined aesthetic in play, but I fear there's something rubberneckingly voyeuristic about my appreciation of all those twisted bodies, all that semi human roadkill somehow always caught in a moment of agonised transformation. We are all raw meat for Bacon. See what I did there?

There are many and varied reasons why David Lynch is my favourite filmmaker – not least his ability to capture an extraordinarily beautiful, poignant and romantic sense of yearning and a deeply felt humanity which is often overlooked by those who see only the nightmarish and absurdist qualities in his work. Alongside those qualities though, a further key to my love of his films lies in his Baconian morbidity, on display in the various gunshots to the head taken by Frank Booth in *Blue Velvet*, Deputy Cliff in *Twin Peaks Fire Walk With Me* and Bobby Peru in *Wild at Heart*; in his love of giants and little men; in the half glimpsed anguish of Bill Pullman's transformation into Balthazar Getty in *Lost Highway*; in the loving way his camera enfolds and caresses Spike, the baby ('they don't know if it *is* a baby') in *Eraserhead*; and of course in John Hurt's heartbreakingly moving turn as John Merrick in *The Elephant Man*.

There's always a sense of the physical in flux: Bacon's paintings and Lynch's films share a preoccupation with the wild, excessive possibilities that may befall the body, both as a source of horror and as a sensual indulgence of the act of looking. If Bacon and Lynch stand at the artier end of the spectrum, then amongst more lowbrow horror fare, Tod Browning's notorious *Freaks* occupies similar territory of course, and whether through disease, deformity or the trauma of sudden and bloody violence – a spade through the coffin lid, for instance – the brutalisation of the body is perhaps the dark subtext of all horror stories.

Beyond the impact of *Kiss of the Vampire*'s memorably bloody opening, for me the film is one of the best of Hammer's vampire pictures. Like *Brides of Dracula* – which it closely resembles in a number of ways – it remains partly defined by its christopherleelessness, but I find the icy detachment of Noel Willman as Dr Ravna, the lofty patriarch of a perverse vampire family an interesting variation on the theme. Hammer's Dracula also carried a coldly autocratic manner with him, but coupled it with an animalistic ferocity and sensuality. Lee's sinewy physicality is replaced here by Willman's remote, cerebral quality – he reportedly informed his fellow cast members that he intended never to vary his facial expression in playing the part – which seems to suggest distaste, rather than desire, for his victims.

Willman is introduced immediately post-credits as a sinister observer; with the economy and tautness of narrative approach I was beginning to recognise as characteristic of the Hammer style he is established for the audience as the source of danger and threat from the off.

If Willman's Dr Ravna is an interesting variation on Lee's Dracula, then the contrast offered by Clifford Evans' Professor Zimmer to Cushing's Van Helsing is even more startling. Fulfilling essentially the same role, Evans brings a fiery, even frightening quality to the part. 'This time it's personal', his tagline might have run, because it emerges that it is Zimmer's own daughter, corrupted by the decadent vampire cult (in this film vampirism seems to be more like a lifestyle choice than a supernatural affliction) whose body he has defiled with the gravedigger's spade in the opening sequence. He is harsh and unapproachable in a way that was never true of Cushing's at times frosty, but ultimately warm and humane vampire hunter. He is a broken down drunk at the beginning of the film – in a scene which echoes Cushing's burning out of Meinster's bite in *Brides of Dracula* Zimmer tellingly uses alcohol rather than holy water to cauterise his wound. By the film's conclusion, he is prepared to use an occult ritual to turn all the powers of Hell (summoned in the slightly less than impressive form of plastic toy bats Hammer bought in from Woolworths) against the vampires in a 'by any means necessary' manner which would have been quite alien to Van Helsing.

*Fear the toy bats of the apocalypse!*

Don Sharp, the director of *Kiss of the Vampire,* was new to Hammer and to the horror genre, which perhaps accounts for the very interesting variations he works on the established Lee/Cushing/Terence Fisher formula. Perhaps the most notable of all these innovations, however, is the way he reconfigures the Hammer film as something more akin to the paranoid thriller.

Paranoia is key to *Kiss of the Vampire,* and it is perhaps inevitable therefore that of all Hammer's gothics the film owes the biggest debt to Hitchcock. Hammer had enjoyed some minor success in the wake of the master's 1960 low budget box office bonanza *Psycho* with a short series of black and white contemporary thrillers which wore the influence unashamedly on their sleeves; *Taste of Fear* in 1961, *Maniac* and *Paranoiac* in 1963, and *Nightmare i*n 1964, now often grouped together under the everything you need to know label of 'mini Hitchcocks'.

Under Sharp's able direction however, *Kiss of the Vampire* was a much more original homage to the master in its fascinating combination of Hitchcockian paranoia with Hammer's more familiar gothic period milieu. When Edward de Souza and Jennifer Daniels' newlyweds finally arrive at the local inn, the quirkily friendly innkeeper and his close-lipped, tearful wife, apparently welcoming but clearly harbouring dark, tormented secrets of their own, seem to have stepped straight from *The 39 Steps* or *The Man Who Knew Too Much.*

An extended sequence of classic paranoid cinema develops when de Souza awakes after a ball at Ravna's chateau to find his wife missing and no-one willing to admit that she has ever existed. It is the dilemma straight out of Hitchcock's *The Lady Vanishes* (itself reworked in a little known early Terence Fisher movie called *So Long at the Fair)* but as befits a frantic search for a spouse rather than a stranger, it is played at an even higher pitch, and de Souza's rising panic and desperation is palpable. The failure to convince, or to be believed, or even to get anyone to listen, is the key to Hitchcock classics like *North by North West* and *The Wrong Man.* It's essentially a childhood fear, isn't it? That sense of panic, and injustice, and the horror that a cold and smugly complacent adult world will judge us and condemn us and simply refuse to listen because, of course, it knows best.

This fear of voicelessness is surely a troubling part of everyone's childhood. It's made strikingly literal in the most visceral moment in the Wachowski's *The Matrix,* when Neo is apparently under FBI interrogation and the mysterious Agent Smith somehow, impossibly, seals up his mouth. It is a universal fear which Hitchcock – and Don Sharp here – nags away at remorselessly, like scratching a scab.

There's another, and perhaps an even deeper, kind of paranoia at work in *Kiss of the Vampire* though. It's no coincidence that the young couple at the heart of the narrative are honeymooners, a recurrent motif in the horror film.

What is it about young honeymooners or nearly weds? Why should they so often be at the head of the queue for persecution from vampires and villains of all persuasions? What makes them so vulnerable? It's true of quality genre fare like *Kiss of the Vampire*, *White Zombie* and Edgar Ulmer's *The Black Cat*, but also abysmal schlock titles like 1964's *Honeymoon of Horror* or 1982's *Horror Honeymoon*. I suppose again it is a vulnerability associated with transition – with the uncertainty inherent in moving from one stage to another.

The general assumption would have been that the young couple on screen were sexually inexperienced, certainly for 1930s audiences faced with *The Black Cat*, and in the main for those of the 1960s, particularly when the film has a period setting like *Kiss of the Vampire*. Indeed, one way of seeing the film, with its decadent cult of hedonistic vampires, is as a puritanical rejection of the permissive values which were transforming the sixties. The threat then derives from placing the honeymooners' naivety in conflict with a more experienced, perverse version of adult sexuality – whether Ravna and his 'family' in *Kiss of the Vampire*, Murder Legendre and Beaumont in *White Zombie* or Karloff's Hjalmar Poelzig in *The Black Cat*.

Stepping over the threshold of adult sexuality is often seen only in terms of its pleasures and its excitements, but it has its terrors and anxieties too, of which 'will I be any good?' is only the most obvious. Ian McEwan dissects the psychology of nervous young newlyweds with the precision of a surgeon in his novel *On Chesil Beach*, but the paranoia was there for all to see writ large in the subtext of classic horror many years before that.

Gerald and Marianne Harcourt are introduced to us as the conventional 'happy couple', utilising all the period's stock devices, including a very chaste sort of suggestiveness to establish the idea that they are 'in love.' Alongside it though is a strange, rather stiff, unnatural and colourless quality, a forced jollity which feels curiously uncomfortable and artificial. De Souza's Gerald and Daniels' Marianne seem to represent neither wild young lust nor cosy domesticity, but a tense and uneasy hinterland between the two.

The tension is subtly but unmistakeably exploited when the pair accept an apparently innocuous invitation to dinner at the Ravna chateau. While a complacently oblivious Gerald looks on, his wife is entranced, enraptured and comprehensively seduced by the piano playing of Ravna's 'son' Carl – the only member of the 'family' to incongruously adopt a cod German accent.

Jennifer Daniels plays this almost dialogue-free scene exceptionally well, her face, framed in tight close up, registering at first merely polite interest, which quickly shades into something altogether more burning and intense, into sensual pleasure and an overt sexual attraction. As the intensity of Carl's playing increases, she begins to rock backward and forward, entirely overpowered by the strength of her own response, and it is only at this point that de Souza's Gerald notices something may be wrong.

'Are you alright?' he asks, quite uncomprehending of the nature of the scene which has unfolded and fearing merely that the little lady may feel a trifle faint. Marianne's eyes never flicker however, the desperate urgency of her attention still fixed unwaveringly on Carl as she gasps 'please...please don't stop' like many an actress before and since in a quite different kind of movie. The contrast between the sexual power and potency of the Ravna household and the dull stolidity of Gerald could hardly be more overt.

The power of the scene is heightened further by the fact that it is cross cut with the sequence in which Zimmer – in slow motion at the crucial moment – burns out the vampiric poison from the bite inflicted earlier on his hand by Tanya, the teenage temptress of Ravna's pseudo family who is later revealed to be the missing daughter of the innkeeper and his wife. The parallel editing brilliantly draws out the contrast between the alluring and decadent temptations the cult offers and the true horror the film posits as lying poisonously beneath its seductive surface. In this it taps neatly into the anxieties of a generation of 1963 parents watching aghast as their children grew their hair, discovered the pill, invented sex, and simultaneously dropped acid and their aitches.

The editing, incidentally, supervised like all the great Hammer films by the unsung James Needs is magnificent throughout. So, come to that, is the cinematography, here handed to Alan Hume, rather than the brilliant Jack Asher, now deemed 'too slow' by Hammer's economy-conscious producers despite the fact that his wonderful work on the earlier films had, alongside Bernard Robinson's exceptional production designs, done so much to establish the characteristic 'Hammer look'.

Regardless of anyone's opinion of the genre, the technical accomplishment of Hammer's best films, all achieved on the slenderest of budgets, is exemplary and unquestionable, and it's a crime that the BAFTAs and Oscars that the craftsmen responsible so emphatically deserved were never bestowed on them by a shamefully sniffy film establishment. The quality of their work was so high it's little wonder to find the finest cinematographer Britain has ever produced, Freddie Francis, becoming one of Hammer's most reliable directors, or so sophisticated a film stylist as Martin Scorsese quite happy to describe the influence and inspiration he derived from the studio's output.

The masked ball sequence, particularly, is perhaps the finest example in the Hammer canon of all the technical elements working perfectly together. The lushness of the costumes and the masks, both sinister and beautiful. The sumptuous colour palette – particularly the rich scarlet of Marianne's gown set against a sea of black tailcoats and, perhaps surprisingly, Ravna's pure white robe. The sensual and haunting music of James Bernard, composer of nearly all of the very finest and most distinctive Hammer soundtracks. The ballroom set itself, which, like all Bernard Robinson's work, offers luxury on a shoestring. The prowling, sinuous camerawork, and the exceptional fluidity of the edit which glides us seamlessly from a swirling, crowded dance floor to a sinister tableau in which only Carl and an apparently oblivious Marianne occupy the floor while a still and silent crowd of masked figures observe impassively from the sidelines. It moves the narrative of Marianne's seduction forward with a beautiful visual economy, and like so much of Hammer's best work it's simultaneously sexy and scary.

Alongside this lush, exotic, sinister and sumptuous eroticism, stumbles poor Gerald. He is absurdly flattered by the apparent interest of the beautiful Sabena, and indulges in some awkward drunken flirting while paying a clumsy lip service to fidelity of the grinning and finger wagging 'I'm a married man' variety, completely oblivious to the schemes that are working on and around him.

Rear-grounded by the framing of the earlier piano scene and rendered ridiculous in the ballroom sequence, poor Gerald is utterly inadequate and uncomprehending. How could he ever hope to provoke or understand, let alone fulfil, the intensity of desire the vampire cult seems to unleash in his young bride? There's a terrible inevitability to her succumbing. Later, entirely subsumed into Ravna's dark subversion of the nuclear family, a sultry and contemptuous Marianne spits into the face of the husband who has finally tracked her down.

This ultimate male paranoia is the fear played on at the heart of the film. Gerald's failure to recognise or satisfy a female sensuality which lies always beyond his reach leads to Marianne eagerly submitting to the temptations of a fuller, richer, more mysterious and powerful version of sexuality than he could ever be capable of awakening. It's a vivid embodiment of a universal male fear, and one that Edward de Souza's rather charmingly effective performance as the rather charmingly ineffectual Gerald makes all the more ripe for empathy.

After all, isn't it true that for most of us male desire seems somehow single and clear, easily defined and measurable in inches and fluid ounces? Female sexuality, on the other hand, seems shifting, looser and deeper, more subtle and ephemeral, amorphous, ambiguous and crucially, impossible for a man to truly grasp or control.

The same dilemma underscores Hitchcock's *Vertigo,* and David Lynch's extraordinary *Lost Highway,* perhaps most of all in the sequence in which Balthazar Getty's Pete and Patricia Arquette's Alice make love in the desert. Pete's yearning and the brilliance of the headlights bleach the frame to almost white, accompanied by This Mortal Coil's haunting cover of Tim Buckley's *Song to the Siren.* What might, in a more conventional and less honest film, have served as the culmination of the couple's longing is here concluded by Arquette leaning in to whisper 'You'll *never* have me', before walking out of the hapless Getty's reach, and clean out of Lynch's narrative itself.

Male anxiety in the face of female desire is archetypal. It's this anxiety which accounts for a great deal of *Kiss of the Vampire's* undeniable power, but in a much more genuinely sinister way this same anxiety is at the heart of much that is repressive and brutal in male mistreatment of women through the ages and around the world. It's at the root of witch trials and the burka; of female circumcision and the story of the Fall; of chastity belts, bible belts and the degradations of pornography; of honour killings and twitter rape threats. The male will to power is always ugly, but in this fearful and psychotic determination to control that which it both fears and desires it is ugliest of all. Horror movies are often described as misogynistic, not least because they play on exactly this kind of male anxiety, but for me films like *Kiss of the Vampire* suggest that it's more complex than that.

I recognise that this is hopelessly, naively, fatuously optimistic, but I sometimes dare to dream that my daughters could grow up in a world which has no further place for male aggression against women, where opportunities are equal and freedom real. A world where individual men and the twisted male dominated societies they create no longer feel the need to control and punish women for their own panicked sense of inadequacy, impotence and longing.

I'm afraid I have to admit, reluctantly, that I don't really believe such a world will ever come to pass, but if it does, the work will be done in part by stories like *Kiss of the Vampire,* which allow the roots of male fear and envy and resentment to be embodied, and explored, and, like the vampires in the final reel, dragged screaming and shrivelling into the daylight, rather than repressed and distorted and turned viciously outward against the innocent.

# DOUBLE BILL FIVE

## Saturday July 30th 1977

DRACULA'S DAUGHTER					22.35 – 00.05

PLAGUE OF THE ZOMBIES				00.05 – 01.30

---

As the élite football nations of the world prepare for next year's World Championship in Argentina, tonight's film presentation recalls the memories of three tense weeks of competition in a wet and stormy German summer: Franz Beckenbauer and Johan Cruyff; tiny Haiti who scored the first goal against Italy for two years; the decline of mighty Brazil, three times World Champions; Scotland, unbeaten and yet eliminated; Poland, who knocked out England in qualifying and became the surprise packet of the tournament; the inventive flowing football of Holland; and the Final itself in the Munich Olympic Stadium, with two penalties awarded by English referee Jack Taylor, ultimate disappointment for the Dutch, and triumph for the hosts, West Germany.

Producer MORTON M. LEWIS
Director MICHAEL SAMUELSON

### 10.25
### Cricket: Third Test
England v Australia from Trent Bridge. RICHIE BENAUD introduces highlights of the third day's play.

### 10.55–1.30 am
### Dracula, Frankenstein – and Friends!

A season of *Midnight Movie* double bills of fantasy and horror.

---

Triumph for West Germany

### Dracula's Daughter
starring **Otto Kruger**
**Marguerite Churchill, Gloria Holden**
A chip off the old block, Miss Dracula – or rather the Countess Marya Zaleska – manages to be lovely and deadly at the same time.

Jeffrey Garth............OTTO KRUGER
Countess Marya Zaleska
................GLORIA HOLDEN
Janet Blake..MARGUERITE CHURCHILL
Sandor................IRVING PICHEL
Dr Von Helsing.EDWARD VAN SLOAN
Lili....................NAN GRAY
Lady Esmé Hammond.HEDDA HOPPER
Sir Basil Humphrey.GILBERT EMERY
Sir Aubrey Vail...CLAUDE ALLISTER
Sergeant Wilkes...........E. E. CLIVE
Based on *Dracula's Guest* by BRAM STOKER
Director LAMBERT HILLYER
*(Black and white)*

### 12.5 am
### Plague of the Zombies
starring **André Morell**
**Diane Clare, Brook Williams**
**Jacqueline Pearce, John Carson**
When a strange malady strikes a small Cornish village, the local doctor enlists the aid of eminent specialist Sir James Forbes to try and solve the mystery...

Sir James Forbes....ANDRÉ MORELL
Sylvia................DIANE CLARE
Dr Peter Tompson.BROOK WILLIAMS
Alice...........JACQUELINE PEARCE
Clive Hamilton........JOHN CARSON
Denver..............ALEX DAVION
Sergeant Swift......MICHAEL RIPPER
Martinus..........MARCUS HAMMOND
Constable Christian
................DENNIS CHINNERY
Coloured servant....LOUIS MAHONEY
Vicar................ROY ROYSTON
Director JOHN GILLING. *Films*: page 11

# 10. MAD? OR UNBELIEVABLE?

## Dracula's Daughter (Universal, 1936, Lambert Hillyer)

*'Possibly there are more things in heaven and Earth than are dreamed of in your psychiatry, Mr. Garth.'*
**Marya Zaleska (Gloria Holden)**

*Dracula's Daughter* is, let's face it, bonkers. Not to say that it's a bad film. It isn't. In fact, it's a neglected and underrated little gem of a movie, but there's no getting away from the fact that the weirdly perverse wrong-headedness permeating almost every decision Universal made about the project gives a kind of barmy quality to the finished film that is probably the reason why it's so often overlooked and undervalued.

The thought processes of Hollywood producers frequently passeth all understanding, even setting aside probably apocryphal stories like the one about the studio exec with an eye on the main chance who, in 1990, after hearing that the then box office hot Mel Gibson had signed up for the lead in Franco Zeffirelli's *Hamlet*, responded by copyrighting the title *Hamlet 2: The Return*.

With all due apologies to the spirit of Bob Newhart, and involving considerably less exaggeration than you might suspect, I'd like you to imagine this telephone call taking place in an office on the Universal lot some time in 1935:

*'Hello Mr Laemmle ... what a pleasure ... yes, yes Bride of Frankenstein is still packing them in ... oh, what do I think has made it such a big hit? ... well, er, Mr Laemmle, if I knew for sure what makes a hit I'd probably be sitting in your chair instead of mine ... but I guess I'd say audiences just wanted to see more of the monster ... and we got back Karloff and Colin Clive from Frankenstein, and the same director, and carried on the story of the monster everybody loved from the first film ... what's that sir? It's funny I should say that, because you've got a great idea of how to top it ... I see ... a sequel to Dracula ... yes sir, I agree that sounds fantastic ... would you like me to get Tod Browning and Lugosi on the phone ... you wouldn't ... no sir, but I was just assuming that if we were following the formula that made Bride of Frankenstein so great we might want to carry on with Browning and Lugosi and the monster everyone loved from the first movie ... oh ... oh I see ... Browning and Lugosi are already working together ... oh, at MGM? ... on a film called Mark of the Vampire where Lugosi plays a count who's a vampire ... but he's not called Dracula because we own the rights to Dracula not MGM ... but it doesn't matter because you've already got a better idea ... oh, not technically your idea ... David Selznick's idea ... the David Selznick who runs a unit at MGM? ... no sir, I'm not aware of another David*

Selznick sir, but I just wasn't ... oh, you've already bought the rights from Selznick ... for $12,500 plus a 5% share ... I see ... no, no sir, I'm sure it's a great deal ... it's just that ... well, don't we already own the rights to Dracula? ... we do ... that's what I thought ... but we don't want to come up with the idea for a sequel ourselves because ... because you like Selznick's title ... OK ... what title is that? ... Dracula's Daughter ... no, no, it's fine sir ... it's just ... well ... I think maybe someone here could have thought of the title Dracula's Daughter for a bit less than $12,500 and a 5% share ... oh, yes I see ... you didn't just buy the title ... no, of course you're not sir, I certainly didn't mean to suggest that you were ... you bought the screenplay from Selznick too ... and it's by who? ... oh, Balderstone ... who wrote the original film ... no, no sir, genuinely, great choice ... now we're getting somewhere ... so when do we start shooting? ... oh I see ... some problems with Balderstone's screenplay ... just teething problems, I hope sir ... no, no teething ... teething ... you know, like vampires, and fangs ... no, no sir, I won't try to be funny again. So what kind of problems are there with the script? ... I see ... whips, you say ... and chains ... and she ties them up ... and then they ... yes, sir, I can certainly see that the Production Code Office might not appreciate that ... yes ... but it's not a problem because ... because you hired someone else to write a new screenplay ... really? R.C Sherriff, who wrote The Invisible Man script for Whale ... yes, well, he's certainly good ... no sir, I don't have a problem with that ... it's just ... well ... couldn't we have just hired Sherriff to write a script in the first place instead of paying Selznick ... no, I understand, we've already been over that ... and Whale's agreed to direct? That's fantastic news sir ... but he wants what? ... he wants us to buy the rights to a novel called The Hangover Murders for him to direct first ... yes, well, I can certainly see how that would give us time to fix Sherriff's script before we start shooting, so every cloud has a ... wait a second, sorry ... we need to fix <u>Sherriff's</u> script too? ... more whips ... and more chains ... and he touches her with what? ... with her husband's severed arm ... well yes, I can certainly see that we might need to tweak that just a tad ... well, thank goodness for The Hangover Murders then ... oh, it's not going to be called that ... because the Production Code won't let us say 'hangover'... well, yes, I can certainly see that if they don't like the word 'hangover' than they might have an issue with the whips ... and the chains ... and the severed arms ... excuse me for saying this sir, but we are sure Whale and his friend Sherriff actually want to make this movie ... no, no, it's just I heard Whale really wants to get away from horror movies to do musicals ... Showboat, yes ... well, you don't think he might be just making the Dracula script unworkable so he can do Showboat instead ... yes, of course, much too cynical ... I'm terribly sorry sir ... of course ... so ... we've hired another scriptwriter to fix it ... and we've paid Sherriff ... really? ... yes I'm sure $17,000 is cheap at the price for a writer like Sherriff, but if we can't actually use his script at all ... money well spent, I see sir ... no, it's not that ... it's just ... well, it's just that some people might see it as ... not me, you understand, but some people might suggest that what we've done so far is spend $30,000 and all we've got to show for it is a two-word title the janitor could have come up with on his coffee break ... that's not all we've got ... Really? Lugosi is in ... no, no sir, I take it all back, that is truly wonderful news ... yes sir, I'd go so far as to say so long as we have Lugosi for this then we can't lose ... yes, yes, I know he was the reason Dracula made all that money for us in the first place ... yes, so long as we have Lugosi ... and you've fixed the script by? ... by hiring another writer ... yes I see ... Peter who? ... for another $2000 ... but it hasn't worked out because ... because of the whips, of course ... yes at least we have Lugosi, and Whale ... and who? ... Karloff too, you're kidding ... that's wonderful ... except ... I see. Whale doesn't want to direct it after all ... no, no I see ... doing Showboat instead ... no, not completely surprised sir, just call me Sherlock I guess ... so now Karloff doesn't want to do it after all ... but it's OK because ... because you hired another scriptwriter ... Garrett Fort ... yes, yes, he's good ... but there's still a problem with Fort's screenplay because the Production Code Office don't like the ... the what, sir? ... oh ... the 'perverse sexual desire'... they think Dracula's daughter is a what? ... no, well, I can see why they're not keen in that case ... but you think we can make Fort's script work anyway if we can get her to look at the girl's neck instead of her what? ... oh, those ... yes, I can see that would be better ... so you've paid Fort $6,500 ... no that's fine, we've got a script now ... no, sir, it's just that ... well sir, it occurs to me that we've paid about five times more for scripts we can't use than for the one we can ... No Sir! No, I'm emphatically not saying you need to pay Fort more ... no, no sir ... shouldn't be focussing on the negatives, no sir ... absolutely sir, at least we have Lugosi ... and a script ... and you hired a new director? That's great sir ... A. Edward Sutherland and ... yes that's good ... except ... except you've paid him off again for $17,500 ... after he'd shot? ... after he'd shot nothing at all ... well, yes, at least we have Lugosi, and a script ... and a new director ... that's great ... Lambert Hillyer? ... no, no, it's just that ... well, doesn't he make Westerns? ... well, it's just that, well, Transylvania isn't Texas you know sir ... no, sir, that's true, I was forgetting about that armadillo in Dracula's castle ... so now we have Hillyer ... and we're paying him how much? ... a third of what we gave Sutherland for not directing the film, of course we are ... and Sutherland went off to do a picture with W.C Fields ... yes sir I believe it was Fields who said never give a sucker an even break ... no sir, I absolutely did not mean to imply that you were a sucker ... although, sucker, you know, bloodsucker, as in vampire ... yes sir, I really will stop trying to be funny. So we've got a script, and the director, and at least we still have Lugosi ... what's that sir? You've decided you don't actually want Lugosi after all? Even though he was the reason everyone went to see Dracula in the first place ... but you don't want Lugosi because ... oh, the element of surprise ... yes, well, I can certainly see that that would be surprising ... and you've paid Lugosi $4000 for not being in the film ... no, I'm not crying sir ... no, it's just ... well, we've paid him a lot more for not being in the sequel than we paid him for being the star of the original ... I'm not seeing the big picture, yes sir... I see, we don't need Lugosi, because Dracula is still going to be in the movie ... and Dracula's going to be ... he's going to be made out of wax ... of course he is ... and does the wax dummy look like Lugosi? ... not even a little bit ... and ... what's that sir ... bankruptcy you say? ... you've got to sell the company? ... no Mr Laemmle, not totally surprised, no...'

Of all the logically-challenged decisions Universal took concerning the project, the biggest one of course centred around the role – or lack of it – of Bela Lugosi. That Universal habitually undervalued and underused him almost goes without saying. That his performance in the 1931 original had pretty much single-handedly launched the Universal monster cycle and saved the company from liquidation is beyond question.

Even assuming the studio judged the quality of his performances in the early 1930s as too theatrical for modern audiences, the profits generated by not only *Dracula*, but *White Zombie, The Black Cat* and *Mark of the Vampire*, for instance, might seem to suggest that the modern audience in question disagreed. Lugosi was a bankable horror star, so it would seem odd for Universal to be placing aesthetic considerations above commercial ones. He was most bankable of all in the role with which he would be forever most associated, and yet over and over again Universal went to extraordinary lengths to avoid doing the obvious thing.

*What might have been...*

*...and what was.*

They preferred the clearly miscast Lon Chaney junior when they finally re-introduced the immortal Count in *Son of Dracula*. They used the – admittedly much better cast – John Carradine for Dracula in their two *House of...* monster rallies. At least in the case of those films there were mitigating circumstances. Lugosi was visibly older by the mid-1940s, and involved in touring productions of *Arsenic and Old Lace*. In fact, Lugosi didn't get a chance to reprise his most famous role on screen until he met Abbott and Costello in the very last gasp of the Golden Age.

In the case of *Dracula's Daughter* however, Lugosi was still physically much the same man he had been in 1931. He was keen to be involved. The script was written to include a lengthy prologue featuring Lugosi as Dracula. And then not only did Universal decide not to cast Lugosi, they removed the character of Dracula entirely from his own sequel, the only case in movie history of the most important character in a film hitting the cutting room floor before a frame had been shot. And yet he remains in some ways the most important character, because his absence casts a pervasive influence over the film which means it is impossible to watch it, for all its many strengths, without a wistful sense of missed opportunities.

The bizarre decision-making process behind the production blends rather happily with the emphasis on barminess in the story itself. We begin, with a pleasing respect for the original, in the moments immediately following the end of the first film, as two of Universal's stock company of comedy coppers discover the bodies of Renfield and Dracula, with Van Helsing (now rather oddly re-christened Von Helsing) still lurking in the crypt. Not unreasonably, they assume Von Helsing is barking mad, and a murderer to boot.

Banged up for homicide, the fearless vampire killer faces either the rope or a lifetime in a hospital for the criminally insane. To help him out of this mess, does he turn to a crack team of the finest legal brains in the country? Rumpole of the Bailey? Atticus Finch? Perry Mason? Ally McBeal? Alicia from *The Good Wife* and Harvey from *Suits*? *Petrocelli?* No, Von Helsing places the whole of his legal defence in the hands of a psychiatrist he happens to know. Not because he's angling pragmatically for an insanity defence, but because he thinks the headshrinker is best placed to demonstrate his innocence by proving the existence of vampires. In which the psychiatrist in question doesn't believe. It's like *Miracle on 34th Street* with haemoglobin.

All in all then, it's remarkable how well the whole thing hangs together. The narrative is taut and pacy, and the acting excellent for the most part. I'll admit to being ambivalent about Otto Kruger's at times wooden and at times gratingly smug psychiatrist Jeffrey Garth, but Marguerite Churchill as Janet puts an appealing enough spin on the 30s and 40s trope of the independent, capable and confident 'fast-talking dame' seen elsewhere in films like *His Girl Friday* and also in genre fare such as *Dr X*.

Irving Pichel's Sandor is effectively menacing, and best of all, Gloria Holden lends a sombre, enigmatic power and poetry to the title role. Perhaps she was aided in this by her evident distaste for a type of material she felt was beneath her, which, paradoxically, imbues her performance with a strangely potent sense of icy detachment.

In fact, given the staginess which many critics feel mars the original Lugosi film, the unbearable cop-out ending which destroys the otherwise atmospheric *Mark of the Vampire*, and the miscasting of Lon Chaney Jr. which ruins *Son of Dracula*, some have even argued that *Dracula's Daughter* has a strong claim to being the very best vampire film of the golden age.

There are certainly wonderful scenes and standout moments. Unconvincing wax dummy of the Count notwithstanding, the scene in which Zaleska lights Dracula's funeral pyre, shielding her face from the cross and solemnly intoning a eulogy, is exceptionally beautiful and among the most atmospheric sequences in all of 30s horror. In its doom-laden melancholy and wonderful chiaroscuro lighting I think it's possible to trace a direct line from this sequence to the visual baroque of Mario Bava's critically lauded 1960s Italian horror film *Black Sunday* in which Barbara Steele gives a haunting performance with strong echoes of Gloria Holden's Marya Zaleska.

There is a later, equally effective scene in which Holden, hoping that Dracula's death has liberated her from the curse of vampirism, begins to play the piano as an expression of her new-found freedom, only to find herself becoming seduced by 'the darkness' once more. The dialogue moves between Holden's increasingly ineffectual attempts to cling to the light, and her darker impulses which are voiced through her servant Sandor's expression of morbid dread. 'Evil shadows ... bats wings...' he intones, as though giving on-screen advice to Universal's set dressers. Their conversation is underscored by Zaleska's increasingly schizophrenic piano playing in order to suggest both her desperation and her helpless inability to escape her own essential nature.

The scene creates a new and highly influential sense of vampirism as addiction, or mental illness, an idea developed through Zaleska's later hope that Jeffrey's psychiatry may offer her a cure. The diegetic music proves very effective in embodying the character's conflicted nature – using music from within the world of the film to anchor the emotions of the characters in this way is rare outside the conscious artifice of musicals, but it's a technique horror has frequently used to great effect. There are comparable scenes in *Kiss of the Vampire*, *The Reptile* and *House of Dracula* from this season alone, for instance.

However, the best-known moment in the film, and the most controversial, is the one played between Holden and Nan Grey as the artist's model and soon-to-be victim. In itself, the scene plays very powerfully, as an increasingly intense Zaleska persuades the young girl to remove her blouse to pose for a portrait, and is then unable to control her rising blood lust, moving ever closer as she hypnotises the terrified Grey until the scene culminates in an off-screen scream.

As a straightforward scene of vampiric predation, it works very well, and could be seen as no more than an echo of the earlier moment in which Zaleska entrances and drains dry a mute, top-hatted city gent. More troublingly, however, the very very thinly disguised subtext here is to see lesbianism as the 'addiction' with which Zaleska is struggling.

Perhaps it's unreasonable to expect anything else in the context of the 30s Hollywood studio system, and it's true that Zaleska is portrayed sympathetically for the most part, but even so I still find it a tad uncomfortable to see, fairly overtly, homosexuality being represented as mental illness.

*Dracula's Daughter* is not the only film of the period to create this image of the threatening, dark-clad lesbian, of course. Think no further than Judith Anderson as Mrs Danvers in Hitchcock's *Rebecca*, terrifying Joan Fontaine's second Mrs De Winter while lingeringly caressing her predecessor's underwear. Subtlemuch.

If you've never read Vito Russo's book, or seen the documentary film based on it by Rob Epstein and Jeffrey Friedman, I'd heartily recommend *The Celluloid Closet* for a thoughtful, informative and moving exploration of the representation of homosexuality in classic Hollywood cinema.

Perhaps it would be easier to tolerate depictions of homosexuality as a mental disorder which might be 'cured' in screen fiction, were it not for the horrible and tragic reality of the 'treatments' and 'cures' that were actually inflicted upon so many gay victims of societally-approved oppression through much of the twentieth century. The Alan Turing story, recently filmed as *The Imitation Game*, is probably the most high-profile example of such state-authorised torture, but is in fact only one of many such shameful case histories.

At the time Gloria Holden was making her advances towards Nan Grey, homosexuality was widely seen as a disease. It would not have been too much of an imaginative leap from actual, everyday reality to have her see in Jeffrey's psychiatry the possibility of a cure for the 'sickness' which is weighing on her, nor to have the voice of twentieth century science confidently assert the idea that such a disease exists, and that it can indeed provide such a cure.

It's more than fifty years since Thomas Szasz published *The Myth of Mental Illness* and drew attention to society's tendency to label anything it finds uncomfortable as a disease (in Soviet Russia any form of political unorthodoxy was a diagnosable symptom of mental illness, just as was homosexuality in the West), but there are cultures and communities around the world in which to be gay is still seen in the same twisted light. Even in the liberal West, where there have undeniably been enormous advances in attitudes and legislation over the past twenty or thirty years, homophobia continues to blight the lives and the development of thousands of innocent people, and those advances, if not fought for, will be all too easily eroded as a newly illiberal wind begins to blow.

Turing himself received a posthumous Royal Pardon, which was described as a 'fitting tribute to an exceptional man', rather than, more appropriately, as a recognition that he did nothing wrong in the first place. It was the rest of us who did something wrong. Like countless *un*exceptional, entirely ordinary and anonymous men and women, Turing suffered horribly purely because an entirely natural sexuality was seen as sickness or sin, often diagnosed by prejudice masquerading as science or faith.

Understandably, given the repression and oppression they have faced, many in the gay community eagerly embraced the idea of the 'gay gene'. Turns out it's a DNA thing, with no element of choice attached. While I understand the impulse, I don't feel the end to prejudice lies in so deterministic a direction. Whatever the truth of the scientific evidence, it's the interpretation of it that troubles me. It can move so quickly from a 'fact of biology' to 'Don't blame me. It's not my fault', the problem there being the underlying acceptance that there is a 'blame' or 'fault' to begin with. And there simply isn't.

For me, the only real 'fact of biology' at work here is that sexuality – yours, mine, Marya Zaleska's – is not about categories and labels and boxes. Sex is much more joyous and fluid and slippery than that – or at least it is if you're doing it right. If we truly want to move beyond prejudice, I think we need to break the boxes, and remove the labels. Sexuality is a spectrum. A continuum, not a fixed point. And terms like 'gay' or 'straight' or 'lesbian' would be better and more progressively seen as adjectives describing a preferred activity than nouns denoting a single, separate category or identity. I believe it may have been Gore Vidal I remember saying that human beings are not 'homosexual' or 'heterosexual', they are merely 'sexual'. It seems to me that kind of recognition of a common identity points to a much more positive way forwards than we have found so far. Certainly a much more positive one than Dracula's daughter was able to find with Jeffrey.

Predictably, the conclusion of the narrative sees the Countess destroyed. Accepting that there can be no release from her own nature, she kidnaps Janet and returns to Castle Dracula, an interior equally impressive here as it was in the original film. Leaning lasciviously over the supine heroine, she is interrupted by the intervention of Garth, and then gets an arrow through the heart courtesy of a jealous and fatally wounded Sandor. Yes, she is penetrated by his shaft. Sigh. Cue Janet waking, Jeffrey realising his true feelings for her, and the heterosexual norm being reasserted once more.

In fairness to *Dracula's Daughter* however, at least Zaleska's subtextual lesbianism is treated seriously and with some degree of empathy, rather than objectified for the male gaze as would be the case by the time Hammer got its hands on the literary wellspring for lesbian vampires, Sheridan LeFanu's novella *Carmilla*. Hammer's early 70s Karnstein trilogy (*The Vampire Lovers, Lust for a Vampire* and *Twins of Evil*) was very much a case of 'Fangs for the Mammaries' I'm afraid, and a clear indication that attitudes to sexuality had added titillation to the mix without shifting far from the central view of lesbianism as a perversion or a disease.

We've thankfully moved on since then, but there is still much further to go in finally abolishing the damaging and degrading myth that there is such a thing as 'normal'.

Perhaps this is why, as the film's tagline, now rather poignantly, suggests of Marya Zaleska 'She Gives You That Weird Feeling.'

# 11. ZOMBIE!

## Plague of the Zombies (1966, Hammer, John Gilling)

*'I find all kinds of witchcraft slightly nauseating and this I find absolutely disgusting.'*
**Sir James Forbes (Andre Morell)**

There is a well-established and widely-accepted version of the story of Hammer Films into which *Plague of the Zombies,* filmed on the cheap alongside *The Reptile* in 1966 as a cost-cutting experiment in reducing Hammer's shoestring budgets still further, might seem to fit nicely. The standard – and to me rather annoying- line goes something like this: Hammer burst onto the scene in the late 1950s with a new, fast-paced and dynamic approach to Gothic horror. There was a brief run of very polished productions (*Curse of Frankenstein, Dracula, The Mummy, Brides of Dracula* and *The Hound of the Baskervilles*) before trouble with the censors and increasing difficulty in attracting American finance meant a quick descent into uninspired and cash-strapped sequels, often featuring a visibly disinterested and disapproving Christopher Lee. The 1960s for Hammer was one long exercise in diminishing returns until the company disintegrated into bankruptcy and irrelevance by the early 70s.

    The truth however, as always, is rather more complex than the 30-second soundbite news agenda version might suggest. Yes, Hammer made some shockingly bad films in the 1970s, but they also made some very good ones such as *Captain Kronos Vampire Hunter* and the 'so much better than its title might give you any reason to expect' *Dr Jekyll and Sister Hyde.* And actually, at least for me, Hammer's 1960s output, despite the occasional misfire, includes the very best films the company ever made. From that point of view, whoever selected the films for transmission in the 1977 season of BBC2 horror double bills demonstrated a quality of judgement bordering on genius. Not so much in the choice of the Universals, which, once you start with *Dracula* and *Frankenstein* pretty much select themselves, but in approaching the AIP and the Hammer movies the level of critical discernment is extraordinary.

    *The Premature Burial* and *The Fall of the House of Usher,* both of which I first saw as part of the 1977 season remain, for me, the most powerful and absorbing of Roger Corman's AIP Poe films. The others are all great; the more critically lauded *Masque of the Red Death* including some breath-taking cinematography by Nicholas Roeg; *Tomb of Ligeia* making full use of the opportunity to break out of the series' claustrophobic, studio-bound conventions in its beautiful deployment of the Norfolk landscape, and *The Pit and the Pendulum* featuring some more overtly frightening imagery. Even so, if I were given a choice of only two for my desert island film season it would always be the two shown on BBC2 in the Summer of 77.

The same holds true for Hammer. The studio was so extraordinarily prolific that there is a wealth of wonders for the programmer to select from, but the decision to largely steer away from the more obvious selections – *Dracula*, *The Curse of Frankenstein*, *Dracula Prince of Darkness* – meant the inclusion of some of the less well-known gems which, for me at least, are the best things that Hammer ever did.

*Brides of Dracula*, *Kiss of the Vampire*, *The Reptile* and *Plague of the Zombies*. It's an inspired selection – to this day they would probably occupy slots one, two, three and four in my list of favourite Hammer films (think I don't spend my idle evenings making and remaking that particular list, even though it never really changes? Ha!). Of all Hammer's films the only others that would ever edge close to that top four would be *The Devil Rides Out* and *Quatermass and the Pit* (both also from the company's mid 60s period and both of which I saw first in a subsequent season of BBC2 horror double bills in 1979).

Thank you, anonymous acquisitions and scheduling genius of the airwaves, for bringing me *Plague of the Zombies* and the others in such quick succession. I can never repay you.

For one thing, *Plague of the Zombies* is still a very effective shocker, in the good old-fashioned sense of the word. Borrowing most of its plot points and characterisation from a combination of Stoker and Conan-Doyle, the literary pedigree was a promising one.

One of the features that moves *Plague of the Zombies* beyond its unacknowledged source material, however, is a real *nastiness* in many of its key moments which is quite 'modern' in sensibility. I mean nastiness as a compliment; there's a harder, edgier quality to the film than is often associated with Hammer in the 1960s.

The most obvious example is the genuine brutality with which the film disposes of Jacqueline Pearce's Alice, one of the films' female leads. Ben Aris, in a zombie makeup which would hold its own in a gruesomeness competition with anything in *The Walking Dead,* appears at the crest of a hill, emits a gleefully inhuman cackle of delight and hurls Alice's broken body down the rocky slope, her neck horribly and unnaturally twisted.

It may be the best-known single image from the film, but it's by no means an isolated moment.

There's a truly disturbing sequence in which Squire Hamilton's red-jacketed, fox-hunting posh-boy henchmen kidnap Diane Clare's Sylvia in a scene – virtually a restaging of the opening of Hammer's *Hound of the Baskervilles* – which is quite overtly leading towards gang rape, with only the intervention of the squire himself preventing the action becoming even more horrifying.

There is also a fantastic scene in which the zombified Alice rises from her grave, while a horrified Andre Morell murmurs 'Zombie..!' before striking off her head with a handy shovel.

That scene in turn prompts an equally gripping dream sequence – a very rare storytelling device for Hammer – in which a whole array of zombies struggle out of the earth to menace Alice's horrified husband. Perhaps a response to the success of the dream sequences being so effectively deployed by Roger Corman in the Poe cycle for AIP, Doctor Thompson's nightmare actually illustrates the *differences* between the approaches of the two companies far more than the similarities.

As befits the more psychological terrors the Poe films exploit, Corman's frequent and brilliantly imaginative dream sequences feel vague, formless, hallucinogenic and genuinely dream-like. By contrast there is something hideously *concrete* about the dream scene in *Plague of the Zombies*, a sense that the undeniably nightmarish imagery is also solid, remorselessly physical and corporeal.

Perhaps the most remarkable thing of all, however, is the sheer pace of the storytelling. For illustration, consider the fact that all of the scenes I've just described occur, virtually one after another, in the space of about fifteen minutes of screen time. The sheer velocity of the narrative is exceptional, even by the adrenaline-packed standards of Hammer's scriptwriters.

The performances are also worthy of attention. Andre Morell – previously a very effective Watson to Cushing's Holmes in *The Hound of the Baskervilles* – is on top form as Professor Forbes. Crusty and irascible, he's introduced to us treating his daughter as though she were an idiot and observing that he 'should have drowned her at birth' – to which our preferred response is clearly intended to be 'what a lovable old curmudgeon', which is, bizarrely, exactly what Diane Clare as his daughter seems to feel about it.

*'You lovable old curmudgeon you.'*

Morell is skilled enough to lend Forbes a considerable degree of charm alongside the grumpiness however, and he inhabits the role of upper class scientific hero adventurer convincingly.

John Carson is an equally effective antagonist, doing suave aristocratic villainy to the hilt in a highly impressive performance aided by his uncanny ability to channel the voice of James Mason and thus echo all those cold-hearted blackguards Mason delivered in a series of Gainsborough melodramas of the 1940s.

Also worthy of note, lending a genuine depth and sincerity to the limited screen time she is allowed, is Jacqueline Pearce, later to help a whole generation of schoolboys through their difficult teenage years in her role as Supreme Commander Servalan in the BBC's *Blake's Seven*. Her Alice Thompson is a subtle, affecting performance which helps give the horror of the character's ghastly demise a far greater impact than it might have had were the part to have been played by a less skilled actress. Although only appearing in a handful of scenes, Pearce is responsible for much of what is best in *Plague of the Zombies*, and she was given a further chance to display her considerable talent for Hammer in *The Reptile*.

One further mention seems appropriate. Roy Ashton's grisly makeup designs are genuinely terrific – the undead monsters here are the first screen zombies to actually look like rotting corpses, as opposed to the wide-eyed somnambulists seen earlier in films like the Halperins' 1932 *White Zombie* and Val Lewton's *I Walked With a Zombie* for RKO.

I think I may be right in boldly asserting that *Plague of the Zombies* also represents the last major cinematic outing of the original Voodoo version of the zombie which had been introduced to the movie-going public in Lugosi's *White Zombie*. Only a couple of years after the release of *Plague of the Zombies,* George A Romero's seminal 1968 *Night of the Living Dead* stripped away all the magic and exoticism, re-imagining the zombie as a grimly non-supernatural creature lurching much more uncomfortably close to home in quasi-documentary form.

Given the seemingly endless proliferation of its hellish progeny, Romero's masterpiece has a fair claim (at least alongside *Psycho*) of being the movie that spawned the contemporary horror film. It is, without question, one of the most influential films of the past fifty years, a movie of undeniable power, not least in its scathing social commentary, but also in its approach to narrative resolution. For me it is *Night of the Living Dead* which made the downbeat ending almost compulsory for the horror genre, at the time subverting the convention so strikingly that it has itself *become* the convention, to the extent that Hammer's narratives, with their ultimate triumphs of the forces of good, now seem more than a little quaint.

For all that, however, I rather like a touch of the supernatural in my monsters, and respond if anything even more deeply to the old-school zombie than to the thinly disguised satirical purpose of Romero's gut-gobbling head-splatterers and their descendants, in movies like Danny Boyle's *28 Days Later* or the brilliant TV series *The Walking Dead*. There's a satirical purpose in the old-school *Plague of the Zombies* too, of course, but it's less overt and specific than, say, *Dawn of the Dead's* pleasing 'zombies as consumers' shopping mall conceit which feels so on the nose as to be, in the end, a little trite, and for me the older film is ultimately more subtle and powerful as a result.

Class politics lie at the centre of *Plague of the Zombies*, but they remain the sub-text of a rattling good horror yarn, rather than giving the impression that the neat intellectual metaphor came first and the plot second. Consequently, the Hammer film, like *White Zombie* before it, has much more of what is sometimes referred to as 'heart'.

The zombie workforce operating the abandoned Cornish tin mine under the control of the aristocratic Squire Hamilton makes the metaphor of the zombie as exploited proletariat fairly self-evident. What is altogether less evident is *why* Hamilton feels it necessary to go to such lengths to run a tin mine – as George Warleggan could have told him, it's possible to pay your workers a pittance without necessitating the use of voodoo.

Marxist theory would see nothing strange in this however. The logic of ownership and acquisition always has an unacknowledged absurdity at its heart which makes the – in this case quite literal – objectification of the workforce an inevitable corollary of capitalist economics. Marx used the analogy of vampirism to describe the relationship between Capital and Labour, but the zombie as a living (no, sorry, *not* living) embodiment of the process of reification is perhaps an even more potent symbol. Even death is not an escape from economic slavery.

The class conflicts simmering through *Plague of the Zombies* are not restricted to this central metaphor though. The villainous squire, and even more overtly the gang of posh 'young bloods' who he controls, demonstrate a sense of total entitlement which is deeply unpleasant. When their fox hunt takes a wrong turn – deliberately misled by Sylvia, an early hunt-saboteur – they are quite prepared to disrupt a funeral procession, and utterly unconcerned when they cause the coffin to be overturned and the unfortunate corpse to tumble out. This sense of entitlement is pushed to its logical extreme as a kind of communal *droit de seigneur* when they kidnap Diane Clare and hurl her from man to man, before cutting a pack of cards to see who gets first go.

Although clearly the hero of the film, Andre Morell's Sir James is able to take a similarly high handed and self-assured approach to such matters as the law – which is clearly meant for men of lower status than himself. Indulging in a spot of unauthorised grave robbing, he is caught in the act by (who else?) Michael Ripper as the local copper, but takes less than a minute to have Ripper on-side and helping out by volunteering to fill in the grave himself while Sir James takes a breather.

This sense of assurance, and entitlement, is what Sir James and Clive Hamilton share, and it makes the conflict between them an engrossing one, shown best in the one icy face to face confrontation the script allows them, as it is the only conflict between equals we see throughout the film.

Elsewhere, the conflicts are all about *inequalities* in status and authority, all about hierarchy. For instance, the working class villagers lucky enough to still be breathing are bitterly resentful of Doctor Thompson, the middle class professional unable to explain or prevent whatever is causing the flurry of mysterious deaths which have afflicted the village. In a confrontation between Thompson and the villagers in the local pub the brother of the most recent victim snarls 'Oh, so we're not good enough for you…', voicing the source of the villagers' resentment. They feel it is Thompson's disdain, regarding them as a bunch of backwards peasants, that means he believes it is not worth his time to discover why they are dying.

The confrontation is only defused by the arrival of the genuinely upper-crust Sir James, who is granted a natural authority as a 'proper gentleman', dealing with the locals with an aristocratic grandeur and insouciance which Thompson, educated but lacking in confidence, at times self-pitying and wheedling, at times almost aggressive, is unable to assume.

Brooke Williams' Thompson is not particularly likeable, and certainly has none of the charisma of Andre Morell's hero or John Carson's villain, but I find myself sympathising with him more than the on-screen representation might suggest, because I understand a little bit about class insecurity myself. While I'd like to see myself as the assertively assured Sir John, or as one of the salt-of-the-earth loyal-as-they-come villagers, the truth is that I'm much closer to Thompson.

Perhaps it is a certain uncomfortable awareness of the ambivalences and insecurities of my own class position that means I respond so strongly to the symbolically heightened class conflicts that form the sub-textual heart of *Plague of the Zombies*. Even as early as that first horror double bill screening back in 1977 I'd already passed what was then called the eleven plus exam and was well aware that I was on the path to being educated away from my roots and into a different order of life, a process that solidified and accelerated as the years went by.

As I type these lines, I'm drinking a glass of St Emilion, from a bottle I bought nipping out to Waitrose just prior to my wife hosting a dinner party for her book group friends – teachers for the most part, though one of them has a touch of blue blood. Sinatra, Astaire, Bowlly, Crosby and Billie Holiday are crooning, Django is burning up the fretboard and Satch is tootling incomparably from my ipod dock; shelf upon shelf of books – nice copies for the most part, Folio and the like – surround me. And I'm writing by scented candlelight. In other words, I'm undeniably, irredeemably and inescapably middle class.

It wasn't always so. Dad was an electrician by trade, blue overalls never mind blue collar. Mum worked on the factory floor. Wine was only for Christmas, and it meant Asti Spumante, or, for a touch of extra sophistication, Blue Nun. Books only came on loan from a library (except for Christmas annuals and my Target novelisations), and candles were only for keeping in a drawer as an emergency measure for the power cuts with which the miners brought down Ted Heath's government.

Moving *between* classes makes you more acutely aware of the betrayals and the unexamined hypocrisies inherent in the system than belonging in an unmediated, uncomplicated way to one class or the other, and guilt is an inescapable part of the process. It's lodged somewhere deep down in my psyche, nagging away at me whenever I write a cheque for the cleaning lady.

Resentment and bitterness are just as inescapable, however, surfacing every time one or other of our friends, many of whom are teachers in state schools, pack their kids off into the independent sector and perpetuate the inequalities at the heart of our society. And voting

Labour once every five years does very little to alleviate either the guilt or the anger, even in these post-Corbyn days.

Perhaps that's why, in some viewings of the film, I like those Cornish tin mining zombies much more than the young doctor who puts them up in flames in the final reel, and why in others I respond to the insecurity and uncertainty of the young middle class doctor himself more than the patrician authority of his old professor or the aristocratic entitlement of the villainous squire.

Incidentally, those 1970s power cuts may have brought the Tories low and inspiringly asserted the collective strength of the proletariat, but they also had the unfortunate side effect of making me miss Jon Pertwee's Doctor sorting out Aggedor of Peladon. I cried for hours.

# 12. THE FANDOM MENACE

I've always been a fan, I think. It makes me wonder about the difference between being a fan and just *liking things*. My wife, for instance, is not a fan. This doesn't mean there aren't books or films or telly programmes she loves. There are. She will happily gobble down a TV box set beside me, and there are many cult shows she likes more than I do – *Game of Thrones* and *Mad Men* for example. She can disappear into a novel more fully than anyone else I've ever met, so much so that conversation becomes impossible. As, with a troubling degree of convenience, does the possibility that she might help with the kids, the laundry or the washing up.

The difference is that, while she may be just as completely absorbed as me by one of these things when she's reading, or watching, or listening, she doesn't feel compelled to expend much time or energy on it the rest of the time. She doesn't crave the action figure, or read the Official Guide to Season Two. Nor the unofficial one. She doesn't scour the internet for interviews with the showrunner/ director/ novelist/ singer-songwriter in question. She doesn't allow it to colour the way she looks or dresses or feels or views other people or the world around her.

In the end, the difference between the fan and the non-fan is in the degree to which you allow the thing you love to occupy the inside of your head when you're not actually in its company.

To offer just one small example, I'm a fan of the American band the Mountain Goats. It's a fairly recent fixation, and it's probably all too predictable for me to say that it's one that began when their song *Up the Wolves* cropped up on the soundtrack at the end of one of my favourite episodes of the brilliant AMC zombie series *The Walking Dead*. I adored the song at first listen – quite an unusual thing for me, perhaps driven by the way this first encounter was tied up in my mind already with the backstory of Daryl Dixon, my favourite character from the show – and was immediately and fannishly unable to leave that adoration at the casual enjoyment level of most viewers.

I didn't recognise the song, and the credits offered no title or band name, but a Googling of the chorus lyric meant I could source it without much difficulty. Persistent as the true fan, this one hearing was enough for me get hold of the album *The Sunset Tree* which a quick run through of track lists on Amazon told me was the album which featured the song. A more sensible approach might have been to simply download the one track I knew I liked, but, as I said, I'm a fan, not a sensible person. And the album was extraordinary; a breathless, fragile, beautiful song cycle full of beauty and hope and pain and survival.

Again, the casual fan – I've seen it suggested that there is no such thing as a casual Mountain Goats fan – might have stopped at that point. Oh no. Not me. More research. I find that the band is essentially the vehicle of the singer-songwriter and novelist John Darnielle, whose first novel, *Wolf in White Van* I immediately order and blissfully devour over a couple of days. I hunt you tube, and find interviews and concerts galore. On one of these online forays I come across a song that speaks to me as instantly as had *Up the Wolves*. This one is called *Animal Mask*.

It's the beautiful clarity and simplicity of the chord pattern which attracts me first. I play a little guitar myself and have written a few songs from time to time, one or two of which I would proudly claim even begin to stumble awkwardly from the barren valleys of Appalling Incompetence to almost attain the distant peaks of Borderline Mediocrity, and that limited little bit of ability and experience is enough for me to recognise and admire that beautiful finger walk from G to an unusual C shape – it may be a C9, I've never been completely sure. It's a chord move which I also knew from a few Oasis tracks and Tracey Chapman's *Talking Bout a Revolution* as well as a song I'd written called *Grains* which used the same two chord step.

That was a love song I'd written about my wife, and at first a straightforward love song was what I heard in *Animal Mask* too. But quickly, as I listened and re-listened obsessively, I came to know the lyrics as well as the chord structure, and it didn't seem to fit. Darnielle appeared to be singing, tenderly and lovingly, about *wrestling*. That's *actual* wrestling, costumes and tag teams and half-nelsons and all that, not wrestling as some kind of double entendre.

Fan fan fan, I had to know more. Yes, I discovered, the song was indeed about a cage fight and was actually a track from *Beat the Champ*, which was – and get this – *a concept album about the world of professional wrestling*. And not today's big budget Hollywood-star- producing corporate version, but the low end pre-WWF world of pro wrestling which Darnielle remembered from his 70s childhood.

I immediately fall even more deeply in love with John Darnielle. It's not that I've ever liked, or had any interest in wrestling whatsoever, but the sheer chutzpah of insisting on a much derided childish obsession as worthy of an album of songs made me – perhaps wish-fulfillingly – recognise a kindred spirit, thousands of words as I am into a study of the deep philosophical significance of a season of horror double bills I saw forty years ago when I was nearly twelve.

But still I hear a gentleness, a vulnerability in the words which call me back to my original sense of *Animal Mask* as a love song. *Some things you will remember,* he sings, slightly tremulous, completely heartfelt, *Some things stay sweet forever...* Ostensibly, the song is about the formation of a wrestling tag team in the heat of battle, but now I'm hearing, in the singing, in the delivery of the lines, the power of metaphor. It's a song about forming bonds, about trust and hope, about what we get from and give to relationships and friendships and love.

I don't think I'm an exceptionally gifted or astute listener or critic, and I don't kid myself that anything I've described so far about my evolving relationship with the song is anything which an average, reasonably motivated listener might not have got to. What happens next though, is different, and it's the true mark of the fan.

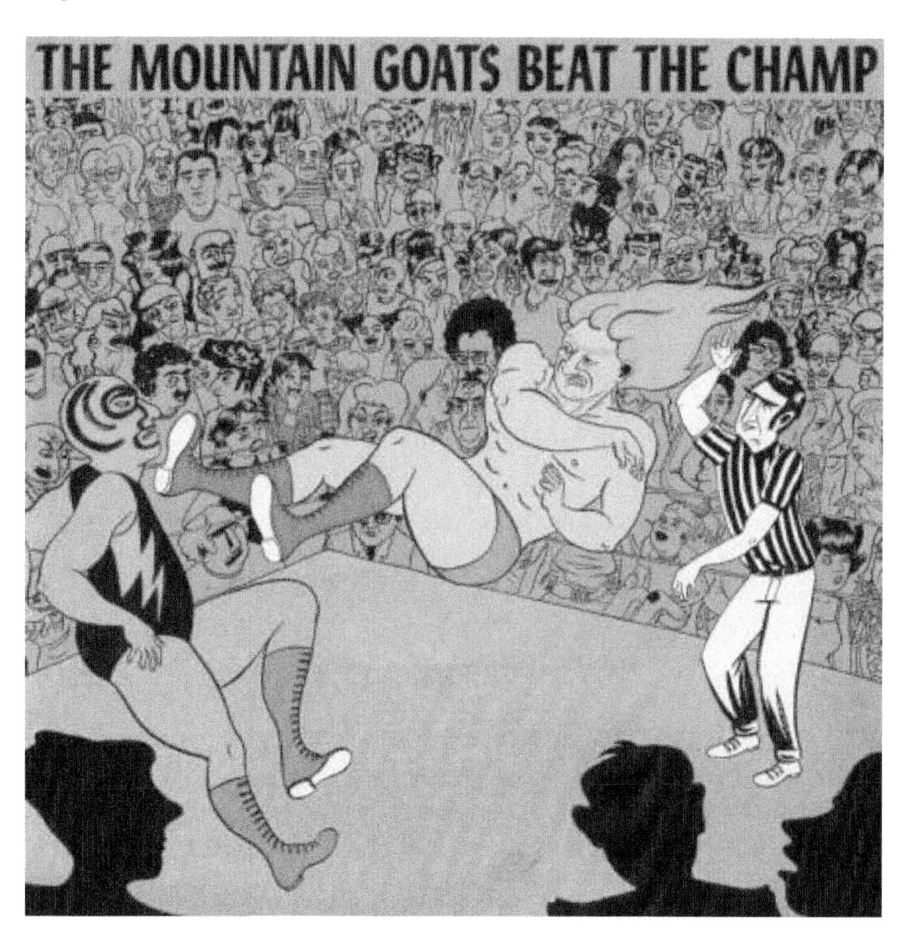

I keep digging. I listen, and I listen – at this point the Mountain Goats seem to have erased the whole of the rest of my record collection. I can't listen to anything else without thinking 'Why am I listening to this when I could be listening to the Mountain Goats?' and quickly rectifying the mistake by listening to the Mountain Goats instead. So I listen, and I listen, and I listen. And something else seems to begin to work its way mysteriously through the song's central metaphor.

*They won't see you,* he sings, *Not until you want them to,* with an extraordinary, tender *protectiveness* that doesn't quite sit with a sense of the song as either a straightforward wrestling ballad or as love affair metaphor.

So I dig deeper. Interviews, live clips. And there it is, eventually. A live performance from the Newport folk festival, and Darnielle introduces *Animal Mask* with a funny and self-deprecating explanation of the song's wrestling background, and just at the end, a throwaway line just before those beautiful chords kick in. 'And it's also about the delivery room,' he says.

And now the song reveals itself to me so purely, so openly and entirely that I can no longer listen to it without tears stinging my eyes. I don't think I would ever have reached that reading of the song without that throwaway line, and without hearing an interview subsequently in which Darnielle elaborates a little, movingly, on the relationship which forms so immediately as your child is presented to you in the delivery room, that moment in which you form your own specific tag team, passionately and protectively.

And now the song makes me cry, because I'm connected to it on an intensely personal level which would never have happened without the obsessive dedication that sent me though hours of songs and interviews and youtube footage. I don't think anyone would pick up on the parent and child bond theme of the song from a casual listen, or even a few casual listens. The lyric is so oblique, so indirect, I don't think that immediate connection is possible. It could be argued, I suppose, that this is a weakness in the songwriting; that if the song relies on a level of metaphor that requires a fannishly obsessive response, then the song doesn't stand on its own two feet – a metaphor needs to be readily understandable and general to really resonate, rather than specific and cloaked. But, needless to say, I don't agree.

This last, most specific level to the song doesn't narrow the power of the metaphor; it deepens it. I don't share Darnielle's ability as a songwriter, sadly, but I do share the experience of the intensity of those moments in a delivery room. His experience and mine become one, because that last, half hidden and very specific and personal level of the song is general in a deeper sense, and the fact that like a true fan he wraps up his most profoundly personal and emotional moments in the language of his own fannish obsessions means even more to me. It is, partly, because of this shared journey that I love the song so much. I cry with joy and tenderness and recognition.

And this is the gift of the fan.

As a very small child I loved *Watch With Mother,* which English people of a certain age will remember was the umbrella title (and one which makes me smile now, not only for what it says about the blithely unknowing sexism of the time, but also because today it would be called *Watch on Your Own while your parents check Facebook*) for a lunchtime children's TV slot which showed a different programme each day – many of them now among the most fondly remembered shows of the period – things like *Camberwick Green, Trumpton* and *Pogle's Wood*. Although I loved all of these, my own favourite was *The Herbs*.

Just in case anyone under forty-five or who isn't from the UK is reading, *The Herbs* told gentle, sweetly song-punctuated stories about the adventures of Parsley, the lion ('I'm a very friendly lion called Parsley/And you must never speak to me harshly…') and his friend Dill the Dog. 'I'm Dill the Dog, I'm a Dog called Dill' Dill used to sing, with emphatic if rather circular logic. There were a number of other eccentric herb-related characters such as the aristocratic Sir Basil and Lady Rosemary, and the ruggedly proletarian Bayleaf the Gardener ('I'm Bayleaf I'm the Gardener, I work from early dawn/You'll find me sweeping up the leaves and tidying the lawn'). The witch Belladonna, or Deadly Nightshade, gave just the hint of threat so beloved of toddlers everywhere in this otherwise bucolic garden world, while Sage the owl provided some grumpy comic relief ('I'm a rather fat feathery owl named Sage/ I'm not very happy in fact in a rage'). It might help explain some of the show's gentle, good-hearted charm to know that it was written by Michael Bond, the creator of Paddington Bear.

For those of you by now not unreasonably wondering why, in a book supposedly about horror movies, you seem to be surrounded by almost unbearably cute friendly green lions waving at you instead of reading about Hammer's gruesome *Plague of the Zombies*, the point is that even as a pre-schooler I was recognisably a fan. It wasn't enough to simply watch the show. I drew Parsley the lion repeatedly, with the relentless resistance to boredom of the true obsessive. I had to have the annual every year. If there'd been the T shirt to have got back then, I'd never have taken it off. And perhaps most significantly, I made up continuing stories about Parsley and the gang when *The Herbs* wasn't on.

I think this, for me, is the redemptive quality at the heart of fandom, in all its otherwise pointless nostalgia and adolescent self-indulgence, and this is why I refuse to feel any further shame or embarrassment about the fact that, when alone, I'll often find my hand curling, ring and index finger splayed in a passable imitation of the Lugosi claw, before it reaches out to pick up my *Curse of Frankenstein* mug for a swig of coffee, which I started drinking black twenty five years ago because that's how Agent Cooper liked it.

Whatever else it may or may not have done, my enslavement to the fan gene has been the spark to ignite any capacity for creativity or imagination I possess. My lifelong love of fantasy, and storytelling, and the pleasant tingle of suspense, can be traced back in a line through Joss Whedon and Neil Gaiman and David Lynch, and Philip Pullman and Hitchcock and *Star Wars,* and the glorious fifty year history of the Doctor, through Conan Doyle, and horror double bills, and on back through Stan Lee and Spider-Man comics, through *The Hobbit* and *Stig of the Dump* and Narnia's wintry landscapes, and on, further and further back, through Mole and Ratty, through the Moomins and their apocalyptic comet, to the gentle garden adventures of a rag taggle gang of condiment-christened animals and cultural stereotypes in *The Herbs*.

Without the trigger that comes from obsession, rather than mere enjoyment, I may never have found my love of story; may never have tried writing my own; may never have shone in English lessons; may never have gone to university. Who knows, in other words, how different, and how spiritually impoverished, my life might have been. The things that allow, or even demand, fandom as a response are precisely those which enlighten or enliven the creative process, by making the audience or reader active, rather than passive.

Social realism, soap opera, the kitchen sink – these things have their place, but it's hard to see them inspiring fan fiction, or any sort of response beyond an admiring recognition of a certain kind of verisimilitude. Judy Blume, Jan Mark, Melvyn Burgess, others of their kind – these are wonderful children's writers, but I don't think they inspired many of their readers into writing themselves. J. K. Rowling on the other hand, will almost certainly be responsible for the next generation of storytellers, just as *Doctor Who* script editor and noveliser extraordinaire Terrance Dicks begat Russell T. Davies, Steven Moffatt, Mark Gatiss and all. I feel incredibly lucky to have stumbled upon so many stories and writers that made a fan of me, because in doing so they widened the doors of perception for me much more truly and lastingly than any drug. They made me who I am.

Inheriting the pattern from Parsley, and *Doctor Who,* it was *Plague of the Zombies* which prompted my first foray into horror film fan fiction. Strange in a way that it hadn't happened earlier – but something in the way that *Plague* took place in Cornwall, rather than middle Europe, something about the rather sketchy backstory of its chief villain, triggered a response in me and at some point in the year that followed I attempted to write a full sequel – now sadly lost to the archives – called *Return of the Zombies.* The story was just a clumsy rehash, and the style – I'm guessing – was histrionic and forced, but it would also have shown the impact the horror double bill season had already had on my reading history.

I'd graduated directly from Doctor Who novelisations to Stoker, Mary Shelley, and Poe. At school, immediately prior to the swimming lesson which, in a fairly competitive field, marked my personal lowlight of the week, we had a blissful reading hour in the Library, allowing a final glorious escape before the humiliating watery plunge to follow. During one of these hours I came across an edition of Poe's *Tales of Mystery and Imagination,* which I devoured obsessively, and also of an anthology edited by Peter Haining called *The Monster Makers* which I read fervently and desperately, and returned to week after week after week, but most particularly to the extract from *Frankenstein* and to Poe's *The Facts of M. Valdemar's Case.* I have such fond memories of these old friends that it was a delight to me to come across the self-same editions of each of them together once more, and be able to rescue them from a purge of old stock in the library of the (different) school where I now work. Shelley, Poe, Stoker and Doyle became the models for my attempts to 'write like the nineteenth century' in my *Plague of the Zombies* sequel, and in almost everything else I wrote for the next three or four years.

Even later, as a supposedly more mature individual with more refined tastes, a student, rather than merely a reader, of Literature, the fan was never far away. As a nervous sixth former reading off-syllabus (always much more fun than on-syllabus) I discovered James Joyce, and immediately clutched him to my heart, but I did so as a fan, not as a student or critic. In the absence of a 'Joyce Rules' T shirt I carried around my copy of *Ulysses* ostentatiously, hoping someone might notice it, realise how clever and erudite I must be beneath the gawky awkward twitchiness of my everyday persona and therefore shag me. And I copied him. Embarrassingly badly, but I did.

I wrote stream of consciousness fan fiction.

Just as surely and appallingly as later I copied Dylan Thomas's poetry, and Orwell's prose.

Worse still, I responded to criticism of my literary heroes as a fan responds. There's nothing measured in my dislike of Virginia Woolf, for instance. She had the temerity to object to the coarse, Rabelaisian quality of *Ulysses* and dismissed the most important novel of the century as a 'queasy undergraduate squeezing his pimples', preferring her own predilection for minutely dissecting the oh so sensitive thought processes of over privileged well-to-do dilettantes as they arrange the lilies and mull over their dinner plans. I loathe her work accordingly, never really giving myself the chance to see anything of value in the output of a writer universally recognised as one of the most insightful and perfect prose stylists in all literary fiction.

It's the flaw of the fan; the total inability to see or accept anything from the other side. Someone telling me they like Woolf is a bit like them telling me they follow Ipswich Town – it may not be their fault, but it makes them Them rather than Us, and it's hard to forgive. I stopped just short of chanting 'You're shit, and you know you are' in lectures on Virginia Woolf, but it was only a small step away.

*Come and have a go if you think you're hard enough*

Football, incidentally, is fandom-lite. Most people experience it to some degree or other, and in many cases it can be all-consuming, but its place now is so mainstream that its eccentricities and idiosyncrasies pass relatively unnoticed, normalised by their generality.

I've been a fan of Norwich City since going to my first games at Carrow Road with my dad in the 1971-72 season – working class rites of passage tradition that it is, or rather was, before such a thing began to be priced out of possibility. I would have been six or seven. I can still name that squad from memory (Keelan, Paine, Black, Forbes, Stringer, Anderson, Briggs, Paddon, Livermore, Foggo, Sylvester, Cross, Bone…).

Again, the games themselves were never enough – I painted scenes from the matches, the most vivid image captured in this way being the strikingly blond hair of Mervyn Cawston, the reserve team goalkeeper (yes, we went to reserve games too), framed through the net in mid dive forever, frozen into immortality by the power of my art – until it was chucked in the bin a week later.

During long hours of back garden football with my dad I fantasised scenarios in which Sir Alf finally gave a long overdue callup to my hero, Kevin Keelan – the finest goalkeeper never to be capped by his country, his career coinciding with an embarrassment of English goalkeeping riches that included Banks, Shilton, Clemence, Stepney, Bonetti and Corrigan. I collected programmes and kept a scrapbook of match reports and features from the local paper.

All of this being completely normal, of course, except that a similar habit when applied to horror movies or sci-fi programmes has the perpetrator immediately delineated as 'sad', 'nerd', 'geek'. And the same people most likely to snigger up their sleeves at all those convention-goers dressing up as their favourite Doctor, or pretending to be Klingons, see nothing odd in pulling on their replica shirts to go to the game on a Saturday afternoon. What is a balding, overweight middle-aged man in a Manchester City shirt that says 'Aguero' on the back doing if not dressing up as his favourite character?

Ultimately the point is not whether football fandom is better or worse than horror fandom, or sci-fi geekery, or any of the other outposts of obsession to which the human being can fall victim. In one of the more wonderfully hilarious news stories of the past couple of years, the police were called to a sci-fi convention in my home city to break up a violent clash between the Whovians and the Trekkies.

In the end the point is *belonging*, and it's fundamentally tribal in instinct. We're all desperate to belong: to lose ourselves in the company of those who share our particular and absurd passion. On countless occasions I have threatened, raucously and tunelessly but in some imitation of song, to kick in the fucking heads of total strangers who happened to be sitting or standing in a different section of a football ground to me, not because I ever intended to do anything of the sort, but simply because I wanted to join in the song that everyone else around me wearing the same Canary-yellow shirt as me was singing.

A similar tribal instinct once found me, several pints down and in my local to watch an England game, joining in with a particularly catchy number which had begun to echo around the bar before I even recognised that I was singing *No Surrender,* and that, therefore, presumably, the BNP were in town. Interestingly, at the point I realised what was happening, my membership of a different, left-leaning, tribe led me to stop singing along and begin bellowing 'Shuttup you twats' at the top of my voice every time the chant began, and ultimately led to me being invited outside to settle our disagreements. An invitation which I readily accepted, one of my favourite maxims at the time being Trotsky's 'If you fail to persuade a fascist by argument, acquaint his head with the pavement'.

Rather more seriously, and perhaps one of the reasons I found ignorant hairy-knuckled Norfolk-dwelling Neanderthals chanting *No Surrender* so unacceptable; I spent most of the 1980s living in Northern Ireland (or 'war-torn Northern Ireland' as my Belfast-born friends of the time used to ironically introduce their homeland to anyone who came from anywhere else – 'Hello. I'm Janet from war-torn Northern Ireland.').

For the first part of that time I was a lapsed English Catholic living in a quiet but staunchly Protestant little triangle of coastal towns surrounding Coleraine, and hearing rumours about naïve English girls being punched in the face in pubs by locals for referring to the biggest local town as Derry rather than Londonderry.

For the latter part of the decade, just to really get to grips with the contradictions of my own position, I went to live in Belfast, just off the Antrim Road. For those unfamiliar with Belfast geography, that was, at the time, middle class enough for it to be – probably – safe to have an English accent without worrying, and religiously mixed enough to – probably – be OK whichever foot you kicked with. I lived in a house from which you could, very occasionally, hear the bombs and the bullets, but in which you could also blithely ignore them.

I loved Belfast, always feeling very comfortable with its warmth and vibrancy, and for years afterwards, now back home in England, would bore anyone unwise enough to ask for my impressions of my time living in the city with my startling and idiosyncratic insight that, like Newcastle or Liverpool or Manchester, it was really just a Northern Industrial Town. Then I bought a Billy Bragg album called *William Bloke,* which had a song about Belfast on it called *Northern Industrial Town* and realised my insights weren't quite as unique and startling as I'd hoped, so I decided to shut up about Northern Ireland. Until now.

Politicians and sociologists, intellectual commentators and tut-tutting figures of all descriptions have attempted to explain the 'Irish question' in any number of different ways, and all of them riddled with irreconcilable contradictions. The leftward radical slant of the Provos for instance, none of whom ever seemed to recognise that there was a somewhat ambivalent quality to spouting internationalist proletarian socialist solidarity while shooting 18-year-old working class squaddies. Sometimes while perched as snipers in the ironically named Friendly Street. The point, in the end, is tribal. Not religious. Not political. The point is *belonging*. The we and the not-we.

*A Northern Industrial Town, seen from the Cavehill*

There's a well-known story about a young American reporter caught up in a skirmish at the height of the Troubles being dragged round a corner by balaclavaed and kalashnikoved paramilitaries who hissed at him with a gun to his temple 'Are you a Protestant or a Catholic?' To which the hapless reporter replied 'I'm Jewish', only to be undone by the remorselessness of his interrogator's bigotry. 'Of course you are. But are you a Catholic Jew or a Protestant Jew?'

None of this is peculiar to Northern Ireland, admittedly, but I think it may be true that having spent most of the eighties across the water meant I was a little less baffled than some of my contemporaries by the kind of thought processes that could later lead to fatwas and the burning of *The Satanic Verses* on the streets of Britain. To the Taliban and the shooting of young girls who dared to want an education. To ethnic cleansing and collateral damage and friendly fire. To 9.11 and 7.7, and cars driven at pedestrians on Westminster Bridge. To the rise of UKIP and the wallbuilders and the populists who opportunistically prey on all our worst instincts. To Syria and Islamic State and online beheading videos which attract almost as many views as clips of cats doing the funniest things.

Ultimately the path to peace is in ourselves. It's a change of our own mental landscape we have to aim for. A revolution in the head. We need to stop judging and abandon our own sense of shame. Accept our absurdity, embrace the ridiculousness of our tribal fandoms and enthusiasms and faiths and beliefs alongside the ridiculousness and absurdity of everyone else's. We must truly and finally accept that our membership of this or that tribe is no sign of our greater moral worth or insight into the One Truth, but simply an accident of birth or circumstance. Born forty miles down the road, and, much though I shudder to admit it, I'd have been an Ipswich fan. Actually, Virginia Woolf can write a bit.

In the end, The Whovians shall lie down with the Trekkies, and their sonics and their phasers shall be beaten into ploughshares.

# DOUBLE BILL SIX

## Saturday August 6th 1977

THE GHOST OF FRANKENSTEIN    22.50 – 23.55

THE PREMATURE BURIAL               23.55 – 01.10

---

**10.45 News on 2**
Weather

**10.50-1.15 am**
**Dracula, Frankenstein – and Friends!**

### The Ghost of Frankenstein
starring
Lon Chaney Jr, Bela Lugosi
Cedric Hardwicke, Lionel Atwill
Further horrendous happenings in the Frankenstein saga...

| | |
|---|---|
| Dr Frankenstein | CEDRIC HARDWICKE |
| The Monster | LON CHANEY JR |
| Dr Bohmer | LIONEL ATWILL |
| Erik | RALPH BELLAMY |
| Ygor | BELA LUGOSI |
| Elsa | EVELYN ANKERS |
| Cloestine | JANET ANN GELLOW |
| Dr Kettering | BARTON YARBOROUGH |
| Martha | DORIS LLOYD |

Director ERLE C. KENTON
(Black and white)

**11.55**

### The Premature Burial
starring Ray Milland
with Hazel Court
Richard Ney, Heather Angel
Believing that his father had been buried alive while in a cataleptic trance, Guy Carrell is haunted by the fear that the disease may be hereditary.

| | |
|---|---|
| Guy Carrell | RAY MILLAND |
| Emily Gault | HAZEL COURT |
| Miles Archer | RICHARD NEY |
| Kate Carrell | HEATHER ANGEL |
| Dr Gideon Gault | ALAN NAPIER |
| Sweeney | JOHN DIERKES |
| Mole | RICHARD MILLER |

Director ROGER CORMAN. Films: page 19

# 13.   MY BRAIN AND HIS BODY…

## The Ghost of Frankenstein (1942, Universal, Erle C. Kenton)

*'You can make us one. We'll be together always. My brain and his body. Together.'*
**Ygor (Bela Lugosi)**

So after the enjoyable diversion into tortured lesbian vampires and Cornish zombies of the previous week, the following Saturday's BBC2 horror double bill returned to the central spine of the season, Universal's unfolding Frankenstein series, with the next entry: *The Ghost of Frankenstein*.

It's hard to argue too vigorously with the received wisdom that *The Ghost of Frankenstein* marks the beginning of the series' downturn in quality. It's an enjoyable, fast-paced and efficient little film, but it is a *little* film, both in the quite literal sense of its B movie-suitable 68-minute running time, making it the shortest film in the Frankenstein series, and in the evident lack of both the financial and the creative resources which had characterised the previous three films.

It's not only shorter than the other films; it's *flatter*. The set design, despite the presence of the brilliant middle European village which Universal was to use and re-use through its second wave 40s monster rallies, is neutral and anonymous when measured against the lavish production designs of the earlier Frankenstein movies. The lighting and cinematography are also somewhat bland, and to demonstrate that this is not merely a case of judging a cheaper B-movie by the standards of its more expensive A-feature predecessors, compare *Ghost of Frankenstein* with its equally cheap and cheerful but richly atmospheric near-contemporaries, *The Wolf Man* and *Frankenstein Meets the Wolf Man*.

The problems with *Ghost of Frankenstein* are due at least as much to a lack of imagination as a lack of cash, and they are thrown into even sharper relief by the inclusion of a flashback scene of footage from the original 1931 *Frankenstein*. It's a bad sign for a film when its most impressive sequence is actually taken from another film made eleven years earlier.

The rather more uninspired, formulaic approach extends to the narrative itself, which begins with a group of disgruntled torch-bearing villagers storming a castle and ends with a different group of disgruntled torch-bearing villagers storming a different castle.

It also infects some of the performances. No-one is dialling it in exactly, but with the exception of Lugosi no-one seems able to bring *more* to the script than it deserves. Cedric Hardwicke is perfectly effective and assured as Ludwig, Henry Frankenstein's other son, but his stolid respectability feels more than a little underwhelming when judged against the manic, hysterical qualities both Colin Clive and Basil Rathbone had previously brought to the surgical table.

The always reliable Lionel Atwill – yes, he's back again – lends some skilfully drawn elements of wounded pride, professional jealousy and low cunning to his role as Doctor Bohmer, but there is none of the wonderful inventiveness he leant to Inspector Krogh in the previous film. The equally reliable Evelyn Ankers is fine as Ludwig Frankenstein's daughter Elsa, but nothing like as affecting as she had been in *The Wolf Man*.

And crucially, of course, there is a Karloff-shaped hole at the centre of *The Ghost of Frankenstein* which, for all his considerable bulk, Lon Chaney junior is unable to fill. In my mind, the film is closely allied to *Dracula's Daughter* for the way in which both films, whatever strengths they may have to offer, are ultimately defined and dominated by the fact that their true leading men – Karloff and Lugosi respectively – are *missing* from the film.

Chaney's broader features present an immediate physical contrast to Karloff's gaunt, haunted visage, but his largely immobile face also lacks Karloff's expressiveness, and although I wouldn't go so far as to say Chaney gives a bad performance, the lack of Karloff's subtlety makes it an oddly hollow one. Chaney's is a monster emptied of character. Moments obviously intended to give opportunity for some Karloffian nuance and pathos fall strangely flat here – the tenderness between Ygor and the monster, the scene where Chaney encounters a little village girl and carries her to a rooftop to fetch her lost ball – and in these moments the absence of Karloff is a much more powerful impression than the presence of Chaney.

Not that the film has nothing to enjoy. There's a particular thrill for the sharp-eyed fanboy in noticing that the first set of villagers includes Dwight Frye, who had gabbled and giggled and chewed the scenery with the best of them as Renfield in *Dracula* and Fritz the hunchback in *Frankenstein* – his blink and you'll miss him appearance here ready testimony to a career fall even more precipitous than Lugosi's.

Lugosi himself, reprising his favourite role as Ygor, effortlessly dominates the opening and is by some margin the best thing in *Ghost of Frankenstein*. He's given some great lines. 'Your father was Frankenstein – but your mother was the lightning!' is a belter which Lugosi relishes to the full. Ygor's sly manipulation of the 'educated and cunning but not quite as cunning as the uneducated Ygor' Dr. Bohmer works wonderfully and is beautifully played by both Atwill and Lugosi. But even Lugosi, magnificent though he is here, does not quite reach the standard he set in *Son of Frankenstein,* at least partly because in the crucial interactions, Chaney's monster doesn't offer him the kind of subtlety and personality to play against which he was afforded by Karloff.

The return of Ygor is certainly the most enjoyable element of a film which, whatever its shortcomings, remains intensely watchable, but the *manner* in which *The Ghost of Frankenstein* accomplishes his return might itself be revealing. I must admit to loving the cheerfully slapdash speed with which Ygor's startling resurrection after being unequivocally shot to death by Basil Rathbone at the end of *Son of Frankenstein* is explained away with a portentous, and utterly nonsensical line of dialogue – 'Ygor does not die that easily…'.

Even so I can't help wondering if it isn't also the jump the shark point for the series; the moment where Universal begins to display a degree of contempt for its own output. How do you bring back a character from the dead? Who cares? Ygor's return from the undiscovered country from whose bourn only he, Jesus and Elvis (apparently) have ever made it back alive has more than a hint of Bobby Ewing suddenly appearing in the shower; some sense of the screenwriters holding up their hands in surrender as though a white towel were being hurled at the feet of any last vestiges of credibility. A sense, in other words, that any old rubbish will do for an audience stupid enough to like this sort of thing in the first place. Certainly my twelve-year-old self (who in many ways was so much older and more earnest than the middle-aged child writing these words today) was irritated by the lack of respect for continuity as he sat in front of the latest BBC2 horror double bill muttering his fanboy outrage about flagrant disregard for canon. He didn't mutter for long, however, because he loved *The Ghost of Frankenstein,* uncritically and entirely.

The young adolescent is a strange audience. At that age I could be peeved by the lack of realism in the continuity, even though the result of it was that I got another fantastic hour of Bela Lugosi's Ygor, but beyond that I simply did not register that, on the whole, the film just wasn't as good as the others.

The truth is that, watching in 1977, I didn't notice the flat, unimaginative sets. I didn't notice the lack of atmospheric, fog-enshrouded visuals once Ygor and the Monster had stumbled through a well-realised graveyard in the opening moments. I didn't notice the flatness of Chaney's performance. I didn't notice that the Monster's fondness for the little village girl here was any less convincing than Karloff's affection for Donnie Dunagan in *Son of Frankenstein.* I didn't notice that the narrative more or less went round in a circle, or that the ghost of Ludwig's father didn't look much – or at all – like Colin Clive. Perhaps above all, I just didn't notice how much less complex, demanding and grown-up this film was than its predecessors.

*Is this the beginning? Or is it the end?...... Both, actually.*

All I saw, watching wide-eyed as *The Ghost of Frankenstein* flickered across the TV screen back in 1977, was that this was the next Frankenstein film and that as such it was, by definition, utterly and completely brilliant. And some days, if I'm very lucky and the wind is in the right direction, there's just enough of that twelve-year-old left in me that I can, sometimes, manage to relish the uncomplicated, undemanding, ungrown-up things that can be a part of what makes life worth living without feeling the need to analyse and dissect and unpack them until all the joy and wonder slips away through my tightening fingers. On those rare days, I still love *The Ghost of Frankenstein* – amongst other things – enthusiastically and breathlessly and whole-heartedly, and although age and experience mean I can't be quite so blind to the flaws of the film or to the greyness of so much of existence as I once was, I can at least adjust the focus of my eyes a little to catch a fleeting glimpse of a film, and a world, that shines with child-like delight if viewed without cynicism.

Some of the best things of all in *The Ghost of Frankenstein* centre around the film's approach to personality, identity and psychology in the brilliantly bonkers brain-swapping shenanigans that form the climax of the narrative.

It started in the very first film of course, with Dwight Frye's butter-fingered Fritz dropping the handily labelled 'Normal Brain' intended for Henry Frankenstein's creation and rapidly substituting it with the jar marked 'Abnormal Brain'. Interestingly though, the original film doesn't submit to an idea as deterministic as the fact that the Monster is dangerous because of a simple and physiological question of brain tissue and brain chemistry. Rather, Whale's original 1931 masterpiece, like the novel on which it is loosely based, seems to suggest it is misunderstanding and mistreatment (as at the hands of the sadistic torch wielding Fritz himself, persecuting a cowering and whimpering Karloff) which prompts the Monster's ferocity, not the mere unalterable fact of him getting the brain stamped 'Abnormal.'

I was reminded of Fritz and his handy labels not long ago, when a colleague of mine came into the staff room clutching a 1960s teacher training text book which she had found in a clear-out of her stock cupboard. One chapter was titled *How to spot a Mental Defective* and was illustrated with a black and white photograph of an unfortunate child smiling at the camera accompanied by the helpful caption 'A Mental Defective.' As the father of a ten-year-old girl who is clever, kind, funny, and also autistic, thereby apparently qualifying for inclusion in that chapter if she had had the misfortune to have been born a comparatively short time ago, I'd like to take this opportunity to offer a copy of the book in question to anyone who finds themselves overusing the phrase 'Political Correctness Gone Mad' to give vent to their irritation at the modern world. It might serve as a gentle reminder that there are worse follies than well-meaning if a little over-earnest attempts to make some of the ways in which we use language a bit less offensive.

If the original *Frankenstein* lights a subtle Bunsen burner under the test-tube debate surrounding identity, mental illness and the physiological versus the psychological, *The Ghost of Frankenstein* turns up the heat and watches gleefully with a maniacal cackle as it bubbles out of the test tube, across the laboratory table and over the floor.

To begin with, Ludwig Frankenstein is not a research scientist in the vein of his father, but instead runs a hospital for Diseases of the Mind. The asylum is of course, one of the archetypal settings for horror – perhaps initiated as such in literature by Dr Seward's hospital in *Dracula*, though there may well be earlier examples I'm forgetting. Pre-dating what we now think of as the horror genre of course, the depiction of insanity as a source of simultaneous comedy and terror is one of the key conventions of Elizabethan and Jacobean tragedy, but in the horror film it is the madhouse itself, as much as its inhabitants, which carries the power.

As such, Ludwig Frankenstein's sun-drenched, rose-gardened hospital is considerably less overtly gothic than, say, Seward's asylum in Badham's 1978 *Dracula*, Boris Karloff's institution in the 1946 *Bedlam*, or the eponymous *Asylum* from one of the best of the Amicus portmanteau films. Even so, its brightly-lit upper levels and clinical laboratories conceal a network of stone dungeons in the basement which Ludwig uses to conceal the Monster, and it can fairly easily be read as a metaphor for the conscious, rational mind above and the dark primordial chaos of the unconscious mind beneath.

The metaphor might be extended by seeing Hardwicke's icily controlled Ludwig as the living embodiment of the disapproving Superego, facing down the wild aggression of Chaney's monster with no more than a stern look and a stiff upper lip. Atwill's Dr Bohmer then becomes walking Ego, serving his own ends through an entirely self-centred rationalism, with the Monster as pure Id, child-like in his appetites and instincts. Ygor, perhaps, sits somewhere between the two.

For many an English child of the 1970s though, the local mental hospital had attained a kind of mythic quality in real life rather than simply in old films. We all somehow seemed to live in the shadow of the 'looney bin' back then. Those old, often Victorian-built buildings lurked stonily in the corners of every major city, but they loomed just as large in the adolescent conversations and urban myths of the time as they did in the topography of the suburbs. Listening to our 'this really happened…true story…friend of a friend…' narratives back then anyone would have been convinced there was a wild-eyed knife-wielding escapee around every corner, even before John Carpenter rendered the trope immortal in *Halloween*.

The truth about our own local institution was more benign, as I had every reason to know, since that was where my dad worked. He'd moved between jobs a fair bit as a young man, from the navy to the railways to the prisons, but from the point I begin to have any really continuous memory up until his retirement, a period of about twenty years, he was a maintenance electrician at St Andrews Hospital, a fifteen-minute walk away from our house. For all our excitable adolescent urban myth whispering, there was never any real sense of threat about the place. It was a relatively open site, with voluntary and non-dangerous patients who were free, if they wished, to have a wander out of the grounds and up to the river or the local shops.

Mostly, there was just sadness. A sizeable number of the patients were Polish immigrants who had arrived during the war, some of them to fight against Hitler, and then, largely due to language difficulties and no-one really knowing where to put them when the war was over, they had been housed temporarily in the hospital, and twenty or thirty years later were too institutionalised to be anywhere else.

Occasionally, there was also laughter. I hope we weren't quite like the fashionable Georgian ladies and gentlemen whose idea of an entertaining afternoon out was to nip down to Bedlam to laugh at the loonies, but Dad would sometimes have us in stitches with his accounts of some of the more bizarre behaviours he'd come across in his time there.

There was the little old lady who pretended to be asleep in an armchair and then, as soon as dad's back was turned, leapt to her feet, scuttled across the ward, unplugged his drill from the wall, and then rushed back to the armchair and resumed snoring as though nothing had happened, repeating the whole exercise four or five times much to dad's bafflement before he finally spotted her in the act. There was the patient who registered his protest against the rather demeaning outfits the inmates were still being forced to wear in the early days of my dad's time in the hospital by solemnly removing the much hated straw boater from his head, placing it on the floor in front of him, urinating copiously into the offending headwear, and then returning it to its rightful position.

As time went on and I got a bit older – by now the BBC2 horror double bill fan with whom you've become all too familiar – dad used to take me down to the hospital most Sundays for us to take advantage of the full-sized snooker table in the recreation room, and on these jaunts I would often meet one or two of the patients whose personalities and peculiarities had assumed almost legendary status.

The one I remember best was a gentle giant of a man named Sid Stoneybroke, so called because whenever he saw any of the hospital workers he would stand stock still, arms outstretched like the crucified Christ and call out 'Stoney Broke' at which point my dad, or whoever happened to be on the receiving end of Sid's dignified demonstration of tragic impecuniosity, would hand him 10p or whatever small denomination coin they had on them. These Sid would put together to buy his favourite delicacy, tinned spam. He would then remove the spam from the tin, storing the meat in the pocket of his jacket until it attained just the degree of sweatiness he preferred.

*Then...*     *...and now*

I think it's a relatively typical sign of the times that 'Dad's hospital', as I always thought of and referred to it, is no longer there. The hospital itself has long since closed down, its sprawling grounds, its cricket pitch and its bowling green ploughed up and built over, most of the site now just an ugly conglomeration of office blocks and the remnants of the hospital building itself eerily abandoned and derelict. It leaves me with slightly mixed feelings I have to say. On the one hand, those vast old residential institutions were a ghastly throwback to a Bedlam model of mental illness, and their closure in favour of the much more right-on sounding 'Care in the Community' programmes a cause for nothing but celebration. Even so, a progressive phrase like 'Care in the Community' can actually be a mealy-mouthed euphemism for 'Close that expensive institution, sell the site off to private businesses in a thinly disguised land-grab swindle and dump the residents onto the street,' while Dad's hospital, and the men and women who worked there, did at least offer some kind of security and safety to the patients who had ended up there.

I wonder where Sid Stoneybroke would find himself in today's world.

I also wonder now, as I began to even then, what happens to explain how someone ends up slipping so far outside of society's norms. Is this a matter of tablets, and chemicals, and concrete physical abnormalities in the brain, or is it simply a question of what Thomas Szasz, dismissing the very idea of mental illness, insisted were merely 'difficulties in living?' Where does our personality, our identity, lie? Is there a mind which is somehow distinct from the simply physical brain? As Morrisey once elegantly had it – *Does the body rule the mind or does the mind rule the body? I dunno.*

The breathtakingly entertaining ending of *Ghost of Frankenstein* insists on a quite simple physiological resolution to the debate. Brain transplants. When Ygor's brain ends up inside the Monster's skull, the Monster speaks with Lugosi's instantly recognisable voice. It appears the brain even transcends an entirely different set of lungs and vocal cords. Of course, Ygor is not the only contender for transplant in a filmic climax that might be subtitled 'Whose Brain is It Anyway?'

Cedric Hardwicke's Ludwig Frankenstein is persuaded out of his initial plan to dissect the Monster by the appearance of the ghost of his father, an apparition who interestingly looks and sounds more like an out of focus Hardwicke himself than Colin Clive (who appears in flashback elsewhere in the film), seeming to momentarily suggest a subtler, more Freudian model of a multi-faceted psyche in which different parts of the self may find themselves talking to one another, rather than the speedy brain-swaps of the film's denouement.

Instead, Ludwig decides to replace the monster's brain with that of his kindly colleague, Dr Kettering, recently murdered by Lon Chaney on the rampage. In this way, he is convinced, the Monster's destructive tendencies, which are only there because of a diseased brain, will disappear.

The Monster himself, however, has a different candidate in mind. He fancies the brain of the little girl with whom he bonded over a ball on a rope, perhaps seeing in her grey matter the possibility of a return to a child-like innocence for himself. Karloff's Monster was already a child-like innocent, able to convey this movingly in a gesture or two. Chaney's Monster in *Ghost of Frankenstein* is essentially brutish, and can only aspire to innocence with the transplant of a handy child's brain. To this end he kidnaps the little girl, and when Ygor tries to persuade him to a different course he crushes his only friend behind a door.

Ygor has still other plans. As he tells Ludwig 'Ygor's body is no good. His neck is broken, crippled, and distorted. Lame and sick from the bullets your brother fired into me.' As a result, he fancies the kind of strength and power he could achieve with his 'sly and sinister' brain in the Monster's massive frame. Unsuccessful in his attempts to persuade Ludwig, he works smoothly on manipulating Atwill's Dr Bohmer, who surreptitiously substitutes Ygor's brain for Kettering's prior to Hardwicke transplanting it into the Monster.

In the end though, the film's relentlessly physiological approach to identity is the undoing of the Ygor Monster. A matter of blood incompatibility renders him blind. 'What good is a body without eyes?' he cries. Then the second group of villagers launch their attack and everything blows up. Again.

Not necessarily influenced by *The Ghost of Frankenstein*, nor by Sid Stoneybroke and my dad's place of work, nor even by my fear of becoming like Norman, the special boy in my primary school who used to do a strange dance and sometimes didn't make it to the toilet, I used to genuinely fear as a child that my brain would stop working properly and I would become a different person. At one point I learned a new long word and carefully consigned it to memory as a way of reassuring myself that so long as I could remember that special word I knew my brain was still working. I've actually included it in this chapter, and there's a special prize (not really) for anyone who wants to hazard a guess as to the identity of my talismanic 'still not mental' word. Sort of like the crappest DVD Easter egg ever.

Even today though, losing my mind is my greatest fear. There may, admittedly, be more immediate ones. Heights terrify me. So does change. And so do thick set men with sticks. That last one dates back to high school hockey – all the same people I was scared of in rugby lessons, but now they were heavily armed. So perhaps if a thick set man with a stick took me to a high place and forced me to change, it's conceivable that my fear of losing my mind might slip briefly onto the backburner, but in the ordinary run of things it's the biggie.

I'm far more frightened by Alzheimer's, for instance, than by cancer or heart disease. Don't get me wrong – I have plenty of fear to go round, and I can devote hours of terror to a twinge in my chest, or a dull ache in my left gonad but, for me at least, dementia tops the lot. A heart attack, an inoperable tumour – they just take your life. But Alzheimer's? It steals your soul and leaves you hanging around. That's the last and nastiest twist of the knife – it kills you, absolutely; it utterly annihilates everything that you are, or ever were, or ever could be, *but you're still here.*

That uncanny and problematic combination of absence and presence is right at the heart of horror, an insidious evil and a pervasive fear. The clown's frozen face; the zombie's shambling walking deadness. That which looks like us but isn't. In horror's animated corpses and doppelgangers, in its devil dolls and moving statues, we are trembling at an awful prefiguring of one possible future. That one day we will walk, and talk, and not be us at all: both present and finally, irrevocably absent.

An aunt of mine died recently, at the age of 91. No tragedy in that, certainly. It might almost be the definition of that proverbial 'good innings'. The only tragedy was that she didn't die three or four years sooner, before dementia had taken hold and siphoned her away in stages, leaving her an angry and increasingly emaciated zombie on a bed, shouting meaninglessly at the world around her. If I'd had the chance to offer her Ygor's brain I'd have done it quicker than you can say 'Hardwicke', but unfortunately brain transplants are not yet available on the NHS, even if one of the workers in her care home did bear more than a passing resemblance to Lionel Atwill.

# 14. DEATH IS THE MONSTER

## The Premature Burial (1962, AIP, Roger Corman)

*'I wasn't running from what was inside that coffin. I was running from what I knew to be inside me.'*
**Guy Carrell (Ray Milland)**

For me, Roger Corman's wonderful *The Premature Burial* provides the most profoundly unsettling experience of all the films across the entire run of BBC2 horror double bills. Undeniably a masterpiece, it is a disturbing, uncomfortable and haunting experience which perfectly captures the essence of Poe's peculiarly queasy tone while in its details not owing him much more than the title.

It's an often-told story that Corman had a difficult time trying to persuade his bosses at AIP that for the same money it would take to make yet another double bill of low budget black and white quickies he could instead give them a single, colour, 'proper' horror film to rival the Hammer product sweeping so profitably across the States. In particular, they objected to his proposal of an adaptation of Poe's *The Fall of the House of Usher* (of which more later) on the grounds that he'd be making a monster movie with no monster in it. 'The *house* is the monster' Corman quickly and successfully improvised.

Well, the *Usher* strategy was an enormously profitable one, launching an eventual eight films in the Corman AIP 'Poe Cycle' of which *The Premature Burial* was the third, though this time, uniquely, the starring role of Guy was taken by the accomplished Ray Milland when on every other occasion the lead was Vincent Price. And this time, the monsterless monster movie took on the biggest bogeyman of them all. In *The Premature Burial*, Corman might well have pointed out, *Death* is the monster.

The first and last shots in the film are of headstones. The most significant sequences unfold in a graveyard or in the mouldering family crypt, over which broods the pervasive presence of Milland's conviction that his father was buried alive. Succumbing ever deeper to the paranoid obsession that the same fate that befell his father now awaits him, Guy's imaginative 'mancave' solution is to build himself a homemade tomb studded with an endless succession of escape methods in the event that he wakes up after his own funeral, culminating in a draught of poison should all else fail. The twitching dead frogs and galvanic batteries with which Guy and Miles experiment in the basement serve to position Milland as a surrogate Peter Cushing, but unlike Baron Frankenstein's obsession with the creation of life, Guy is obsessed only with avoiding death. The honeymoon which Guy and Emily never manage to go on was to have been in Venice, an entire city which has been slowly dying for centuries.

Even the dog dies.

Or, at least, poor old King *appears* to die, before recovering from the lightning strike which seemed to have killed him, only to further deepen Guy's fear of being buried alive.

Death lurks in every corner of the narrative – just as you'd expect from a film called *The Premature Burial* – but even more startlingly it exerts a presence in almost every frame. The production design foregrounds it from the opening shot onwards, tracking across a mist-shrouded, consciously artificial and studio-bound graveyard, flecked with lifeless, twisted stick-trees and framed against a sickly painted night-sky backdrop. It's in the eerily whistled version of 'Molly Malone' which continues to echo hauntingly throughout the film, and in the top-hatted mourning dress of the scene's grave-robbing doctors. Most of all, perhaps, it's in the livid red blood-smears on the bottom of the coffin lid and in the crash zoom onto the frozen, screaming face of the corpse, now revealed to have been buried alive.

It's not only the magnificent first sequence however. As the opening credits roll we cut to the stately progress of a jet-black horse drawing what appears to be a black funeral carriage through the same fog-blanketed landscape, and then move inside to focus on the black, mourning-clad Hazel Court as Milland's fiancée Emily.

There is, as we are soon to discover, no narrative reason why she should first appear in mourning dress when she is simply going to see in person why Guy has broken off their engagement by letter. Corman and designer Daniel Haller have made a production decision based purely on atmospheric, rather than narrative, logic, choosing to use the costume design to keep the idea of death before our eyes at every moment. The only flicker of colour is provided by the striking scarlet feathers in Emily's black bonnet, calculated to create, perhaps consciously, an association with the bright red flare of her lips, and vividly contrasting her black-clad and bustled respectability. Sex and death. Sex and death.

The reds and blacks that continue to dominate the production design once we are inside Guy's mansion have a clear symbolic function, which point towards Corman's use of Hazel Court throughout the film. Her amoral sensuality is the flash of red on the black palette, the flicker of Eros in the face of Thanatos. Emily is Desire in the kingdom of the Dead.

It's an opposition that runs throughout the film, but one that is never embodied more clearly than in the wedding night sequence. Having had a funny turn at the reception, Milland is laid out on the couple's four-poster, black-suited and still as death, while Hazel Court, diaphanous nightgown floating softly around her, leans over her unmoving husband, gently caressing his forehead, his cheek, his chin, and lends a desperate, sensual urgency to the soft, deep, lingering kisses she offers her corpse-like groom.

Hazel Court occupies an exceptional place in the history of the horror film, working for Hammer on *Curse of Frankenstein* and *The Man Who Could Cheat Death,* before crossing the Atlantic and becoming Corman's leading lady of choice, appearing with equal power for the director in *The Premature Burial* and *The Masque of the Red Death,* and even revealing a talent for comedy in *The Raven.* What unites her performances across these disparate films, and what develops increasingly powerfully from one to the next, is a much more full-blooded and potently sensual quality than was often to be found elsewhere in the films of the period.

Female sexuality in films is often synonymous with youth, conveying a rather dubious connotation that sexual desire is the preserve of young girls barely out of high school and that, much past twenty-five, a woman is sexless mother or nothing. What Hazel Court is able to do, much more unusually, is the unabashed sexuality of the grown woman. The contrast between the two ideas is one which is drawn very boldly in *Masque of the Red Death* – embodied in the casting of a wide-eyed and fresh-faced Jane Asher as the young girl Vincent Price lusts after and aims to corrupt, which is perfectly balanced by the maturity of Court's stellar performance as Price's lover.

There is no 'younger woman' in *Premature Burial*, but Court's performance here is, if anything, even more exceptional. Although she is revealed by the end as the film's nominal villain, I can forgive Emily any amount of duplicity and manipulation – Court's performance is such that she holds my complete sympathy throughout the film. I'd far rather side with her rich, earthy sensuality and hedonism than with Milland's dreadful, self-absorbed and selfish fetishisation of death. If I had the misfortune to be married to Guy I'd certainly be plotting his speedy demise too. The waste of Emily's life as he takes his psychotic revenge seems to me a far worse crime than anything she does to him. At least Emily was alive in the first place, which is more than you can say for the death-fixated Milland.

The film's final track across the graveyard, away from the dead bodies of both leading actors until the frame is filled with the words 'Rest in Peace' carved into a weathered stone seems to suggest the meaningless inevitability of death's triumph over us all. Yet it was the sheer, unashamed sexuality of Hazel Court that was to be the film's most lasting impression on me. The red feathers rather than the black dress. The red lips rather than the clammy tomb. In memory, at least, sex triumphs over death.

And, just to say, Court is *spectacularly* sexy in the film. Not just in her first appearance, nor only in the wedding night sequence. There's also a fabulously telling little moment when the servant announces a call from Miles Archer (the doctor to whom she has taken a fancy, despite her marriage to Guy) and Hazel Court looks down thoughtfully, stands, checks her reflection and adjusts her hair before receiving him. The moment speaks volumes about Emily's instinctive worldview that desire is natural and should be embraced, not repressed. There's no guilt or indecision, just a complete, unselfconscious acceptance of her own sexuality.

The moment is echoed even more strongly later, after Guy's apparent death, when she reclines on the bed in front of a bizarrely oblivious Miles, the tight framing emphasising the bareness of her shoulders as though she were naked. But much more than the hint of flesh, it's in her eyes. The knowing, poised and unashamed gaze Hazel Court gives the scene is extraordinarily erotic.

Sometimes there's a tendency to argue that these things are always relative. 'Yes', the idea goes, 'Lana Turner may have smouldered in the context of the 1940s but it's hardly Sharon Stone in *Basic Instinct* is it?' As though the modern attitude to censorship and permissiveness has a monopoly on the genuinely seductive, like each new generation of teenagers demanding the right to believe that they invented sex. Hazel Court in *The Premature Burial* gives the lie to the relativism as far as I'm concerned. The look in her eyes as she lies, bare-shouldered and eager, in front of her prospective new lover is more overt and explicit for me than any number of erotic thrillers filled with fleshy but soulless montages. The scene is sexy by the standards of any day or age because of the knowing desire and sexual confidence Court lends her performance.

It all combines to make Hazel Court's Emily, for me, horror cinema's most perfect femme fatale (I'd spare an honourable mention for Linda Hayden's brilliant performance as Angel Blake in *Blood on Satan's Claw*, but Hayden's youth at the time makes it a very different kind of role) and a performance which was more than enough to make a startling and lasting impression on the adolescent me watching breathlessly from his parent's sofa in the summer of 1977.

Now, flash forward twenty years.

A late 90s January morning, stupidly early, struggling out of sleep under a steely, slate-grey sky. The phone rings, harsh and metallic in the early morning silence. The phone. A sudden, lurching, sick in the stomach moment. We're all afraid of early morning phone calls, aren't we? Afraid that they'll be *that* phone call, the phone call we never even want to think about receiving. And this time, just this once, it is.

My mother's voice, far away on the other end of the line, sounding oddly distant and emptied. 'Michael?' she says. She's hesitant yet urgent at the same time.

'There's something wrong with your dad.'

'What is it? What do you mean?'

'He's in his chair. He was eating his porridge, and then he started shaking. He stopped eating his porridge and he was shaking and then he just slumped and he made this awful noise...Michael? Michael? I think he's dead.'

The porridge is the thing, isn't it? I don't know why, in that context, mum felt it important to specify the particular breakfast involved, but she did. We think about death coming in many forms, sudden or violent, brutal or tragic, dramatic or peaceful, but never quite so banal. We don't picture the Reaper popping round over the Quaker Oats. We tend to leave those sort of details aside.

Shakespeare understood it though, as he did so many other things. For me, the most unbearably moving moment at the end of *King Lear* isn't the hideous juxtaposition of 'the gods defend her' with the immediate entrance of Lear carrying Cordelia's dead body, nor Lear's desperate denial of the undeniable, nor his anguished 'howl, howl, howl, howl.' It is the moment Lear truly accepts the horror of his loss, and the profundity of his tragedy is punctuated by a spot of bother with his collar: '..thou wilt come no more/Never, never, never. – Pray you, undo/This button here..' It's that sudden interjection of the trivial and the mundane which renders everything else so human and so anguished and so desperately, unbearably true.

'Oh God,' I mumble helpfully into the phone, and then 'Oh Christ.' Ha! the God-botherers cry triumphantly – proof that there are no atheists in foxholes! The argument rather neglects the fact, however, that had I been speaking to anyone other than my mum, I would almost certainly have said 'Oh shit... Oh fuck' instead, demonstrating as an alternative hypothesis that there are no constipation sufferers or celibates on that metaphorical front line.

I've always felt Hemingway's phrase about the earth moving during sex to be a bit overblown (oo-er). But this phone call shows me that death can do what sex can't. I have the distinct sense of a shift in the axis of existence at exactly this moment. The ceiling and the sky beyond it seem to move oppressively close while the rest of the world recedes into long shot, and I have a sickly falling sensation that I'm lost, and standing on some kind of conveyor belt carrying me further and further from home and that there's no getting off, not ever.

I hold it together enough to mutter that I'm on my way. 'Please hurry' she says, beginning to cry properly.

Fortunately, at the time I was living only a handful of streets away from my parent's home – a five-minute drive at most – but, unfortunately, I couldn't drive back then, having failed my test at 18, then left home and been without the money or the pressing need to take it again at any point since. At this moment however, the sensation of helplessness and inadequacy is overwhelming.

Not overwhelming enough for me to actually do anything about getting my licence in the immediate aftermath though; that doesn't happen until, almost ten years later, I am faced with a similar sense of my own humiliating uselessness when my wife is allowed home from hospital only on the proviso that someone can drive her back at a moment's notice if need be, and we have to ask her stepmother to come and stay for a few days as designated driver.

I ring a taxi. I speak numbly to my partner of the time. After some centuries the taxi arrives, and we head round more or less in silence. I don't really remember that short journey at all, except for one specific moment, staring bleakly out of the window at the passing privet, and clutching somehow at the presence of a robin in the hedge as a sign that this was all just a terrible mistake. That, as in all those cruel, cruel films, he wasn't really dead at all, and would open his eyes to pass humorous comment on the tears of all those gathered around the body.

We arrive. We go in. I remember nothing of what is said. I'm in the living room, somehow, and there he is. He is sitting in his big brown leather armchair, his head lolling back and his mouth hanging open. His sightless eyes are wide. There's no question of doing anything. He is so completely gone. It doesn't even look like him. This is the dead body of my father. This is how Death looks.

My hand moves to my mouth. I look away because I have to and look back for the same reason. That bloody bowl of porridge is resting on a shelf between the chair and the fireplace.

My feelings come like this. First, there is shock. Not shock in quite the usual sense though. Not shock at the loss and what it means and what life will be like now and how mum will cope, though that's all buried in there somewhere deep down.

No, it's the shock of the visual that dominates the moment. It's the sudden instant of horror that sears itself onto the retina and stays there like the shock reveal in so many, many of these horror films I cradle and clutch to my inadequate heart to try to explain and understand so much that is wonderful and frightening and terrifying in the world around me, and here they are again, these strange old movies, even here, even now, these strange old films I first encountered so long ago with my dad snoring peacefully upstairs.

I react to him now just as if he's Karloff framed in those James Whale trademark three tightening close ups, or Lon Chaney turning to Mary Philbin, finally unmasked in *The Phantom of the Opera,* or the crash–zoomed face of the 'poor wretch' buried alive in the opening sequence of *The Premature Burial.*

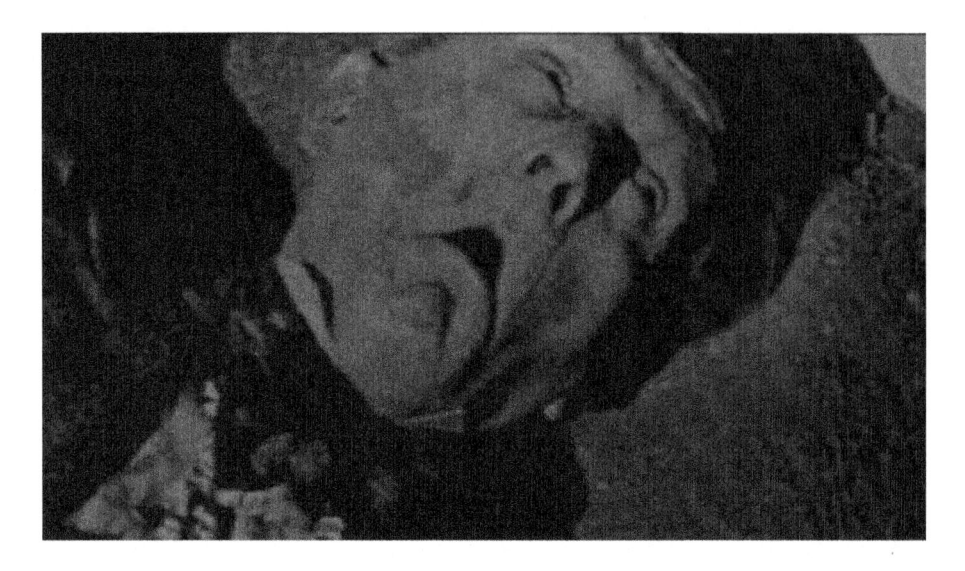

Hard on the heels of the shock is the tiny, shameful, guilty, giggling flicker of relief. 'So close, so close, but it's him not you', whispers that still, small, and utterly self-centred voice from the back of the brain. 'You're still here. You're still breathing and sucking up the present tense. Alive.'

And then, above and beyond it all, the sudden and absolute certainty of conviction that I'm looking at a vision of the future. One day, who knows how far away, this figure in the chair, cold and ugly and lifeless, will be me. I am but my father's son, and to this same favour I must come. In that moment, I become Ray Milland's Guy, absolute in his conviction that his father's terrible fate is now his own. My death ceases to be hypothetical, ceases to be a projection, and is made concrete in those split seconds at ten past seven on January 22$^{nd}$ 1999.

Of course, that revelation has grown less raw and immediate with each passing year, but I carry it with me now, and have done through every second I've lived since that slate-grey January morning.

Finally, shamefully late, it stops being about me, and becomes about mum and dad, and doing what I can to make this one iota less appalling and unbearable. I make a couple of phone calls, to medical people. I'm told I mustn't move him. Something to do with the fact he'd had a hospital appointment recently means there's likely to have to be an autopsy. A doctor will be along soon. I ask, and am given the concession that I can turn the chair around, so that at least my mum doesn't have to be staring at the body for the next hour. I do that, and start phoning people to let them know.

Then I ring work, and, get this, *I set cover lessons for my classes.* It's either a sign of the impossibly high standards expected of the modern era's teaching machine, or of my continuing and debilitating fear of being told off or found out as the unprofessional faker I really am. Either way, it suggests that my head has stopped functioning properly. At the end of the phone call the school secretary tells me how sorry she is and for the first time I feel tears beginning to steal up on me.

A lot of the rest is a blur. A cold, numb, nagging empty. Moments and impressions remain. Mum insisting on starting to clear out his clothes, there and then, that day, and burying her face in a bundle of jumpers that hold his scent. Aunts and sandwiches. A camply oleaginous registrar who seemed to take a bizarre shine to me.

I fell into something of a black pit in the days and weeks and months following dad's death. Nothing remarkable or unusual in that, I know, but no less oppressive for being commonplace. Ordinary, run of the mill actions – going to work, putting the kettle on, climbing the stairs – all seemed to carry with them a backwash of futility and inauthenticity. Life emptied itself of meaning. There was no point in anything.

Of course, in the larger, existential terror of the human condition, this is simply facing up to the inescapable reality of the universe. Our insignificance is a given; of course there is no meaning or purpose to anything we do, and if we fail to accept this then we never really emerge from the nursery. To assume or hope for anything else is simply a failure of courage, or of the imagination: childish and contemptible. Even so, to continue to function we need to be able to tell ourselves that what we are doing is somehow worth doing, and I found it impossible to do so for a time.

I was Ray Milland in *The Premature Burial,* frozen and terrified to the point of paralysis.

Strangely, however, in one of those curious moments of synchronicity which would annoy me intensely if a novelist tried to put them over on me and yet which do actually occur from time to time in life, the days which followed hard upon dad's death contained within them the specific experience I needed to sow the seeds of recovery. Red feathers against a black dress.

The day after the funeral, and now back at work, the office passed me a phone message from an Emma Brown who had rung and left a number asking me to ring back if I could.

This was quite out of the blue. I'd known Emma pretty well a few years earlier, and we had carried on a mildly flirtatious relationship which a combination of my own lack of courage and a range of tricky personal contexts – I was unmarried, but in a long-term relationship at the time, amongst other things – prevented from ever developing into anything else.

Perhaps, in truly clichéd vein, it was this perceived unattainability that had fuelled my longing. At the time I had known her, I had also become fixated with the rich, playfully sexy qualities of David Lynch's *Twin Peaks*, which was casting its lush, mysterious spell over the world back then. Fanboy to the end, Emma became entangled in my head with coffee black as midnight on a moonless night, Angelo Badalamenti's hauntingly sensual soundtrack, and Sherilyn Fenn's hauntingly sensual Audrey Horne.

Since then, however, Emma had moved to Southampton, and worked for a while in a school somewhere in Guildford. During the early part of this time we'd exchanged letters, and met up a couple of times when she visited Norwich, but had inevitably lost touch after a while.

Life moved on, as it should, and while I still spared the occasional wistful daydream for what might have been, I hadn't given any serious thought to Emma for years. There's an Elvis Costello song called *Just About Glad* on his 1994 album *Brutal Youth* which I remember had felt like my last shrug of goodbye to all that.

> *I'm just about glad that I knew you once*
> *And it was more than just a passing acquaintance*
> *I'm just about glad that it was a memory*
> *That doesn't need constant maintenance*
> *There are a few things that I regret*
> *But nothing that I need to forget*
> *For all of the courage that we never had*
> *I'm just about glad.*

This mysterious phone message was the first contact we'd had since the early 90s. When I returned her call we arranged to meet the following lunchtime in a pub at the end of the road – teacher pub lunchtimes seem to have sadly disappeared in today's OFSTED-quaking education system, but those were different times.

My head was full of dad and death and depression, and perhaps surprisingly, I can say truthfully that I'd not really dwelled on the prospect of seeing her again and there wasn't a particularly strong tingle of anticipation as I stepped into the darkened bar.

I saw her immediately, talking to two tall, much older men in suits at the bar, and there was something strikingly erotic about the tableau, something about her absolute power and control of these two figures towering above her, something about the way they leaned into and over her that suggested an almost magnetic allure. Quite unexpectedly, I felt my stomach lurch in that hardly-ever-experienced-as-an-adult first love adolescent way.

A few moments later, and she was sitting opposite me. Her hair was shorter than it used to be, but otherwise she was almost unchanged. The sun was slanting in from the window beside our table, catching the satin blouse she was wearing and making it sheer enough that I found it rather hard to concentrate.

I didn't have much to say, but she filled me in on some of the things that had happened to her since we'd last met. Sitting beside Cecil Parkinson – former Chairman of the Conservative Party and all-round randy old goat – at a young Tory dinner she'd organised and him telling her she was the sexiest girl in the room. Having to leave her last teaching job as a result of the brief affair she'd had with a PE teacher who was married to the Deputy Head – 'The poor man had never had oral sex. I mean it was *cruel*.' And then the laugh, dry and dirty.

And I saw it all clearly, quite suddenly. The socially ambitious tory. The unrepentant hedonist. Both of them aspects of an unquestioningly egocentric view of self and appetite as the only relevant things in the world which should have been deeply unattractive but in fact had me all but trembling like a schoolboy.

And as I looked into that open upturned face, its rounded cheeks, its bold eyes and its delicate, fine-boned nose, it came to me that I was sitting opposite Hazel Court in *The Premature Burial*, and that I was overwhelmed by the kind of yearning that I hadn't really felt for a long, long time; perhaps not since I'd actually *been* a trembling schoolboy.

With something like the force of revelation, this moment of Joycean epiphany revealed to me quite suddenly that not only was this the first time I'd felt alive since my dad's death, it was also the first time I'd felt alive in a lot longer than that.

At the time all this happened I'd been in a stable, ostensibly happy relationship for many years. My partner of the time was thoughtful and clever, our views on life, politics and people were in accord, and we had a long shared history. I admired and respected her and liked her very much. But in that moment, sitting opposite a young woman I wasn't sure I liked at all, but *wanted* with every atom of my being, I realised that 'happy' was not the right word for my life, or for the state of our relationship. We were comfortable. Companionable. Content. Colourless.

The overwhelming guilt I felt as Emma's eyes gazed into mine with the same potency Hazel Court leant Emily's bedroom scene with Miles in *The Premature Burial* was not only about how desperately I wanted to sleep with her, but about my sudden awareness of how pathetically little of myself I was able to offer to my partner, and how much more she – and everyone – deserved.

In other words, we'd both been guilty of *settling*, and it took the death of my dad, with its reminder that life is just the flare of a match in an eternal night, plus the electrical jolt of desire I felt sitting at that unremarkable pub table, to open my eyes to the fact. Sex and Death, Sex and Death. Red feathers and a black dress.

'Comfortable and content', it was instantly clear to me, wasn't giving either of us what we really needed. Schopenhauer and the pessimist school may argue that the human condition is one of inevitable suffering, that to be comfortable and content is to be one man picked out of ten thousand and that happiness can only ever be defined negatively as the absence of pain - but Schopenhauer had never watched Emma Brown turn eating a smoked salmon roll into an act of seductive temptation so erotic that it would have made even Hazel Court blush.

The riot that had quite suddenly erupted in my heart was not only the opposite of the despair and paralysis I'd fallen into while failing to deal with my grief, it was also an absolute prefiguring of the need for change. Were life as straightforward as most stories, I might be able to tell you that Emma and I walked hand in hand into a rosy sunset. But it isn't and we didn't.

I went back to work for the afternoon, and I only ever saw Emma once more, later that night, by which time I was so helplessly drunk I could barely move. The other, slightly less Joycean epiphany I had that day was that it wasn't a good idea to mumble paralytic, incoherent and squirmingly embarrassing confessions of your depth of feeling to the object of your obsession while trying not to dribble on her chest. Then I went home, never saw her again, and spent the next few months attempting, ultimately unsuccessfully, to repress and ignore the lesson I felt I'd learned and to go on with life exactly as it was.

A bit more significantly, however, a year or so later I found myself sitting alone one night outside a café in Venice, drinking red wine at a table on the Piazzetta opposite the Doge's Palace and listening to the house band play a smooth piano, bass and sax instrumental of *La Vie en Rose* punctuated by the relentless tourist buzz and the percussive slapping of water from the Lagoon. Drunk and more than a little maudlin, and contemplating the by now unavoidable breakdown of a fifteen-year relationship that had turned out, for each of us, to be more of an evasion of life than an expression of it, I took a bleary-eyed look around me.

Venice. A fantasy city built on stilts in the water, a Disneyland for grown-ups. A city Emily and Guy never got to for their planned honeymoon, but a city simultaneously sexually extravagant and death-haunted enough for them each to have loved it, encompassing as it does both the Eros of Casanova's exploits and the Thanatos of Thomas Mann's mournful parable. And of course, horror film fans, also *Don't Look*

*Now,* which features both the most powerfully affecting sex scene and the most powerfully affecting death scene the genre has to offer. A city built on the very idea of transience, thrown into existence in defiance of time and tide and possibility.

From where I sat, surrounded by the fantastical folly of the Doge's Palace and the Basilica, the whole absurdly beautiful edifice of St. Mark's Square, and all of it, by infinitesimal but irrevocable degrees, all of it, slowly sinking into the water, I knew that everything was dying. Nothing could last. Nothing was forever. All things must pass. Simultaneously I knew that it didn't matter. What might be gone in a year or a decade, a second or a century, was here *now* and that the experiencing of it, of life and existence, here, now, in this single unique and irreducible instant was all that mattered.

I finished my wine and walked away – but I left the Ray Milland part of me at the table.

Life isn't neat, and the journey wasn't over. No, the long and winding road that stretched all the way back to watching Hazel Court flirt with Guy and Miles in *The Premature Burial* in the second half of a 1977 BBC2 horror double bill and forward to a bottle of wine on the Piazzetta, and back to a leather armchair in a living room with a bowl of porridge on a shelf and forward to a pub table, sunlight, a window, a satin shirt, and a smoked salmon roll, would continue to twist and turn, the consequences of all this playing out even more uncomfortably and painfully over years because of my own lack of courage and indecisiveness.

Even so, it was a road that led me forwards. It meant movement, not paralysis. It was a road that led me to the place where I am today, which, with all the imperfections and frustrations and disappointments that every life contends with, is a life that has room in it for the riot in the heart, for love, for the brevity of human life and the urgency of the present tense.

For that, Emma, Hazel, and dad – amongst others – my thanks.

# DOUBLE BILL SEVEN

## Saturday August 13<sup>th</sup> 1977

THE RAVEN                   23.05 – 00.05

THE BLACK CAT               00.05 – 01.10

# 15. PERFECTION

The Raven            (1935, Universal, Louis Friedlander)
The Black Cat        (1934, Universal, Edgar Ulmer)

*'We understand each other too well. We know too much of life. We shall play a little game, Vitus. A game of death, if you like.'*
**Hjalmar Poelzig (Boris Karloff)**

*'Death is my talisman. The one indestructible force. The one certain thing in an uncertain universe. Death.'*
**Richard Vollin (Bela Lugosi)**

Perfection. It's a slippery and difficult concept, isn't it? Such an elusive, even absurd, idea – something that can never be anything other than an unattainable dream in this too too sullied world of ours. As Woody Allen has it, 'if even one guy is starving somewhere it puts a crimp in my whole evening'. We know it's impossible, we know that life is compromise, is compromised, is compromising. And yet it nags at us. We just can't quite let go of that pale and insubstantial shadow. Perfection. We dream of it, we search vainly for it, all the time knowing that we're tilting at windmills. But at least in our daydreams, and our most secret wishes, we tilt anyway.

Interestingly, it's through the secret alchemy of *combination* that we dream most potently that such elusive, impossible perfection might be found. We dream that it can be found in that one other person. Mr Right, the soulmate, the impossible girl.

In the good old days when compilation tapes were a key component in any self-respecting sensitive young soul's weaponry of mass seduction we all understood the magic of combination so much better. Is it possible to achieve the same effect with iTunes Playlists, do you think? I doubt it. The mechanism's too easy; it doesn't speak of nights spent diligently recording and sequencing to achieve the perfect result, which couldn't then be shuffled into a new state of being with the tap of a finger on a touchscreen. There was nothing random about it, not in the long hours spent agonising over exactly which tracks most perfectly represented your heart's truth, and even less so in the even more difficult task of establishing the perfect running order.

Combination, again, you see. The segue from shoegazing introspection, to upbeat but heartfelt, to wittily ironic, and always taking tone and tempo, lyric, and first and last chords into the reckoning. Every element was crucial. The inexplicably magical combination that would make the tape that little bit more than the sum of its parts, and would allow your scratchy C60 to transcend the temporal and touch the hem of the eternal. The slightest misstep and the compilation tape crashes and burns, its power mysteriously dispelled in an instant of Neil Young slipping awkwardly into Everything But the Girl. It was always impossible of course – the perfect compilation tape has never been made, any more than the perfect life has ever been lived, or any more than anyone ever slept with me because of my impeccable taste in music anyway.

Even so, the double bill of the 13$^{th}$ August that offered the magical *combination* of *The Raven* and *The Black Cat* represents this for me; a shimmering single vision of perfection. A strange kind of Platonic ideal, glimpsed not in shadows on the cave wall, but in black and white flickering ghosts on a little screen in the corner of a small living room in a Norwich suburb.

At the risk of sounding even more like a candidate for Pseuds Corner than I usually do, there is something that approaches the divine for me in watching these two beautiful films *together*, the magic wonder of combination making my experience of this double bill about as close to spiritual experience as I'm willing to admit to.

And so I'd like to talk about these two films together rather than one at a time, because in some strange way that's how I've always thought of them, not as separate entities, despite their entirely unconnected and distinct characters and plots, but somehow mystically conjoined into a single whole, like Fish'n'Chips.

*TheBlackCat'n'TheRaven*.

Perhaps this is even stranger since this double bill represented a departure from BBC2's typical – and wonderfully effective – combination of an old one and a new one. *The Black Cat* and *The Raven* were made only a year or so apart, and although 30s Universals both, neither is typical of the Universal cycle in that there is no supernatural monster (despite Karloff's bizarre appearance in *The Black Cat* and heavy makeup job in *The Raven*). Wonderful horror movies though they are, neither is a Universal Monster movie in the vein of *Dracula, Frankenstein, The Mummy, The Wolf Man* or any of the proliferation of sequels to the great originals.

*The Raven* tells the story of Richard Vollin, a brilliant doctor, with a morbid fixation on the work of Edgar Allan Poe. His surgical genius saves the life of a beautiful young woman, played by Irene Ware, and upon her recovery, she becomes mildly infatuated with Vollin, while he develops a madly intense erotic obsession with her. Her starchily conventional father and fiancé stand in the way of the relationship however, and denied the chance to fulfil his love, a crazed Vollin uses his Poe-inspired torture chamber to wreak revenge on those who thwarted him.

*The Black Cat* centres on the conflict between Vitus Werdegast, a prisoner of war returning to seek revenge, and Hjalmar Poelzig, the

Crowleyish leader of a satanic cult who betrayed him to the enemy and stole his wife and daughter.

There is nothing to connect them really, except for the almost entirely spurious reference to Poe in their titles, a certain shared morbidity, and, crucially, their casting. Both films were designed as vehicles for Universal to pair Karloff with Lugosi, thus enabling lots of promotional ballyhoo along the lines of 'The screen's twin titans of terror – together!', or 'Karloff the uncanny and Bela 'Dracula' Lugosi – twice the chills!' And for once, the ballyhoo was expressing an extraordinary truth. The combination is magical. The films shown together as a double bill combine into something greater than the two component parts, and so too do Boris and Bela themselves.

Both Stan Laurel and Oliver Hardy had perfectly acceptable solo careers in the silent cinema, and when they were pressured into forming a double act, it was Stan alone who took artistic control of their films, while Ollie simply turned up, did the job, and went home. For all that, however, it is the indefinable joy of the two of them together, in combination, which lifts the experience of watching their films beyond the everyday and into a realm very close to perfection. Just as is the case with Morecambe and Wise, the only comedy double act worthy of mentioning in the same paragraph as Stan and Ollie. And just as it is with Boris and Bela, horror cinema's greatest double act. Something inexplicable happens to me when they are joined on screen.

I don't believe in God, but He's there, if He's anywhere, in those moments of ineffable wonder when something adds up to more than the sum of its parts, opens a door, however briefly, on the transcendent, and points us, however uncertainly, towards a world which is better and cleaner and purer than the one we're stuck with most of the time.

Setting aside the chance to see the face of God though (because I'll reluctantly concede that might be just me), what *The Black Cat 'n' The Raven* does undeniably offer is the chance to see the first pairings of the two great horror stars of the golden age, and the only collaborations which were on equal terms at a time when each was at the height of their powers.

There were many later outings for the deadly duo, admittedly. *The Invisible Ray* in 1936 is a terrific film, but it's a Karloff vehicle with Lugosi – very effectively, and sympathetically – heading up the supporting cast. The same was planned for *Son of Frankenstein*, but in the end it's Lugosi's film, with Karloff's Monster playing second fiddle – although, Karloff being Karloff, he plays second fiddle like Stephane Grappelli.

Considerably less distinguished than either is 1940's *Black Friday*, planned as another more or less equal match before being scuppered when Karloff got the collywobbles, rejected the dual role written for him and was given Lugosi's mad scientist part instead, with the relatively unknown Stanley Ridges being drafted in to play the Jekyll and Hyde lead and Lugosi bumped into a meaningless supporting turn.

A much, much better film – and the couple's final pairing – was Val Lewton's 1945 *The Body Snatcher,* directed by Robert Wise. By this time, however, Karloff was unquestionably the star, and Lugosi, on whom age, alcohol, and a temporary separation from his wife Lillian were taking a visible and heavy toll, is given not much more than a cameo – although you wouldn't have known it from the RKO promotional campaign. The front office knew Lugosi could still be a draw, particularly alongside his old rival.

By contrast there is a delightful *fairness* about the two films in this double bill. The gleeful perversity Karloff brings to the characterisation of Hjalmar Poelzig in *The Black Cat* is so brilliant and bizarre that most observers would agree with me that he takes the film on points, although the justified riposte is that the tormented yet heroic role of Werdegast allows Lugosi to show some of the range he was rarely given the chance to display. *The Raven* provides the perfect counterbalance, however, showing a dominant Lugosi at his bravura best, which is perhaps another reason I can only think of the films together. Lugosi's brooding Vollin is a tour de force from the outset, and he barnstorms his way through the increasing hysteria of the later scenes with a maniacal delight that Karloff's more subdued Bateman offsets very effectively.

Even in my own private preferences I find it impossible to separate the two films, despite the critical consensus that *The Black Cat* is vastly superior. I love *The Black Cat* for its wonderfully expressionist set design, effortlessly demonstrating the peculiarly Gothic heart beating beneath its ultra-modernist Bauhaus; I love *The Raven* for its brooding, morbid Romanticism. I love *The Raven* for the intensity and commitment that it lends – through the screenplay and Lugosi's performance – to the portrait of the 'tortured genius'; I love *The Black Cat* for the sly perversity that Ulmer's inspired direction and Karloff's knowing performance sneaks spectacularly past the censors. I love *The Black Cat* for the bleak pessimism of its moral vision, revealing profoundly that both the virtuous Lugosi and the corrupt Karloff are equally trapped and doomed, both, as Poelzig puts it, 'the living dead'; I love *The Raven* for the dualism of its moral structure, as Lugosi's initially sympathetic Vollin slides into damnation and Karloff's truly monstrous Bateman finds redemption at the last. I love them both for their wonderfully atmospheric lighting, literate screenplays and for the uniformly excellent performances.

All wrapped up together, it makes the experience of watching them both – as I always have to – a blissful and a beautiful thing, and for all their darkness and morbidity the films make me profoundly happy.

I'm led to the question of where and when I've been happiest, apart from when watching these two films on the 13th of August 1977. If you ask people that question, more often than not they will tend to tell you a particular period of their lives. 'I was happiest at school,' or 'in my university years,' or 'when I was working at such and such', or 'when me and so and so were together…'

I think they're missing the point. By definition, perfect happiness is a matter of isolated moments, of single instants. It simply cannot be sustained across any length of time, no matter how positive your general circumstances might be. The ordinary and the mundane have to intrude, as certain as breathing. It's not happiness you're talking about – it's contentment maybe, or wellbeing, but that's just not the same thing.

So for me I was happiest one day sitting alone on the upper deck of a bus between the Irish coastal towns of Portrush and Portstewart, a copy of Richard Ellmann's biography of James Joyce in my hands, while the sun danced and sparkled on the waves, and again as the sun danced on the water across the Dorsodouro, it seeming a matter of the most perfect joy that the light should arrange itself just so, and once more that moment in 1996 as Gascgoine flipped that ball up and over Colin Hendrie's head and volleyed a sublime finish in the Wembley sunshine, and again as I bellowed the words 'Now I'm your old man, and you are my missus' from behind my Dylancirca66 Rae-Bans and hit the chords at the end of *Greetings to the New Brunette* on my Burns Steer, bathed in sunlight on my wedding day.

And what is it that these fleeting moments have in common? Freedom. Complete personal determination. A sense that, at that exact moment, my life was fully and entirely my own, owing nothing to anybody. I could step off that Portstewart bus and go – *anywhere*. Nowhere I had to be, nothing I had to do – the choice was my own. The dancing Venetian sunlight carried me momentarily to a place beyond circumstance, beyond mortality, beyond the passage of time. And Paul Gascgoine, just briefly, lifted me outside the cares of the world, outside my job or my not entirely happy relationship of the time, and I stood uplifted in the middle of a screaming pub, drenched in the beer of a hundred similarly and suddenly sky-rocketing pint-clasping hands, and for a few seconds was allowed a glimpse into a better and a truer world. I was, in those moments, my own sovereign self, and life was one limitless opportunity.

But have you spotted the odd one out? A wedding is about any number of things, and mine was an expression of perfect joy, but whatever else it may be, a wedding is not a declaration of freedom or of owing nothing to anybody. Those perfect, absolutely unsullied moments belong to an altogether different phase of life, before every moment, whatever kind of gift it may be, comes bundled up in responsibility and worry and commitment.

There's a moment in Anne Tyler's beautiful bittersweet novel *The Accidental Tourist* which sums it up so much more eloquently than I could ever manage that I'd like to cop out and offer you her words rather than my own. Following the death of his child, the end of his marriage and his own desperate attempt to find safety in emotional isolation, Tyler's hero, Macon Leary, rescues a small boy he has become somehow responsible for from a group of bullies and begins to find himself, almost against his will, reconnecting with life and the world.

> *But when they started walking again, he slipped his hand into Macon's. Those cool little fingers were so distinct, so particular, so full of character. Macon tightened his grip and felt a pleasant kind of sorrow sweeping through him. Oh, his life had regained all its old perils. He was forced to worry once again about nuclear war and the future of the planet. He often had the same guilty, secret thought that had come to him after Ethan was born:* **From this time on I can never be completely happy.**
> *Not that he was before, of course.*

Maybe that, in the end, is why perfect happiness is not what defines our lives. Not because happiness is an ideal we can never reach, but because life – compromised, compromising life – with all its fears and failures and responsibilities, is so much better than perfection. So I'll never be completely happy again? Good. I'll mix my freedom with love and commitment and terror and laundry and washing up, and through that *combination* (as surely as Boris and Bela and *TheBlackCat'n'TheRaven*) I'll get as close to fulfilment as I can ever reach.

Perfection is just a shadow on the wall. I'll take flesh and blood any day. *TheBlackCat'n'TheRaven* has plenty of shadows and walls, and plenty of flesh and blood too.

That'll do for me, in the end.

# DOUBLE BILL EIGHT

## Saturday August 20th 1977

FRANKENSTEIN MEETS THE WOLF MAN  22.00 – 23.15

THE RAVEN                                                    00.05 - 01.30

# 16. IF I EVER FIND PEACE I'LL FIND IT HERE

**Frankenstein Meets the Wolf Man**
**(1942, Universal, Roy William Neill)**

*'He is not insane. He simply wants to die.'*
**Maleva (Marya Ouspenskaya)**

*Frankenstein Meets the Wolf Man.* It sounds like a joke, doesn't it? A comically bad title, designed like a satirical comment on the worst kind of brainless formulaic Hollywood nonsense.

In fact, if you believe screenwriter Curt Siodmak's account, that is indeed exactly how it started out. When producer George Waggner buttonholed him in the studio commissary and asked him for his ideas for a new Universal horror movie, Siodmak indulged his sardonic instincts with a throwaway gag. 'How about Frankenstein Wolfs the Meat-Man... I mean Frankenstein Meets the Wolf Man' he suggested.

Much to Siodmak's surprise, rather than seeing the joke, Waggner signed him up to the project on the spot, thus opening the door to 'Alien vs Predator', 'Jason vs Freddy' and in fact the whole concept of the 'Shared Universe' so important to modern-day Hollywood thinking. Marvel Studios and Warner brothers' DC franchise both owe a lot to Curt Siodmak's sceptical gag.

So too does modern-day Universal, despite currently admitting defeat over their unsuccessful attempt to launch their own shared universe with the false start of the 'not especially good' *Dracula Untold* and the 'even less especially good in fact downright not good at all' Tom Cruise version of *The Mummy*.

Siodmak was always pretty cynical about the quality of his own work, even more so about the horror genre, and most of all about Hollywood in general. He'd have fallen about laughing at the idea of a pretentious idiot like me taking any of it seriously, let alone thinking it worthy of thousands of words of exploration. And even I would have to admit that the problems with *Frankenstein Meets the Wolf Man* extend well beyond the cheesy formula-driven sequelising logic that Siodmak first mocked, then delivered.

*Frankenstein Meets the Wolf Man* is a film *beset* with problems.

Firstly, the title suggests a balance that the film doesn't deliver. By now, having already racked up three sequels to the 1931 original, the Frankenstein Monster was more than a little tired. The Wolf-Man, on the other hand, had only had one previous and very successful outing, so this sequel is pretty much the ongoing story of Lawrence Stewart Talbot, with the Monster forming a much less prominent element in the narrative.

Secondly, the film, like many another mid to lowish budget quickie of the period, makes up some of its running time with an extended 'tra-la-lee fol-de-rol' Tyrolean musical number set during the Festival of the New Wine, no doubt intended to get maximum value out of Universal's brilliant middle-European village set. In the context of a 40s monster movie though, the thigh slapping lederhosen sequence feels distinctly odd.

More significantly, the casting posed a real problem for Universal. Karloff had quit the role of the Monster unequivocally and irrevocably after seeing the formulaic writing on the wall during *Son of Frankenstein*. The present incumbent, having had a go at filling the Master's asphalt-spreader's boots in *Ghost of Frankenstein*, was Lon Chaney Jr. However, Chaney was also, and much more recognisably, Larry Talbot in *The Wolf Man*.

For a time, Universal considered the idea of giving their favoured Chaney both roles, accomplishing this through a mixture of stunt doubles, split screen, and other trick photography. However, a number of practical obstacles, alongside Chaney's reluctance to undergo dual makeup ordeals, led the studio to abandon the idea. Despite his somewhat vainglorious boast about his one stab at Karloff's most famous role – "I can do anything that guy can" – Chaney had not enjoyed the experience of making *Ghost of Frankenstein*, partly because the mutual dislike between him and his co-star Evelyn Ankers had only increased since their pairing on *The Wolf Man*, and partly because he liked makeup chief Jack Pierce even less. He had, in short, hated the part of the Monster only marginally less than he was soon to hate the equally makeup-heavy role of Kharis in Universal's Mummy series.

Besides which, there was never any question of Chaney abandoning his favourite role as Larry Talbot, a part the actor fondly described ever afterwards as 'my baby'. All of which left Universal in need of a new Monster.

Not unnaturally, the studio turned to the only other horror 'name' fit to grace a poster or marquee alongside the likes of Karloff or Chaney. Step forward, Bela Lugosi. Fortuitously, the climax of the previous film in the series had given us the brain of Lugosi's Ygor being transplanted into the Monster's skull, providing the monster for the final sequence of *The Ghost of Frankenstein* with Lugosi's instantly recognisable Ygor voice, as well as a nasty case of blindness. So if the audience now recognised Lugosi's features beneath the makeup, it was, quite reasonably, simply Ygor's expressions showing through.

Lugosi himself was no longer at a place in his career where he could high-handedly turn down the role of the Monster as some accounts suggest he had done more than a decade earlier in the wake of his *Dracula* success. He readily accepted, despite the physical demands of a role that, by now entering his sixties, the actor was not really best placed to fill.

As a result, a number of key shots, even some of the close ups (including the iconic moment when Chaney first discovers the Monster frozen in ice in a subterranean cavern, and some parts of the ultimate battle between the two monsters) quite visibly don't feature Lugosi, but stunt double Gil Perkins instead. Or stunt double Eddie Parker, depending on which account you accept.

Worse still for the finished film, however, Siodmak's script originally picked up directly from the conclusion to *Ghost of Frankenstein*. The Monster in *Frankenstein Meets the Wolf Man* was given lengthy expository dialogue, which during filming Lugosi delivered, presumably in his Ygor voice.

The screenplay also retained the Monster's blindness, again as established at the end of the earlier film. Lugosi developed the arms-outstretched lumbering walk (so beloved of generations of monster-impersonating schoolkids to come) as a highly effective way of suggesting the sightless creature's caution and vulnerability. It also explains the quite brilliant flourish of sly malice Lugosi gives to the close-up of the Monster on the operating table towards the end. Not only has his strength returned, his sight has been restored.

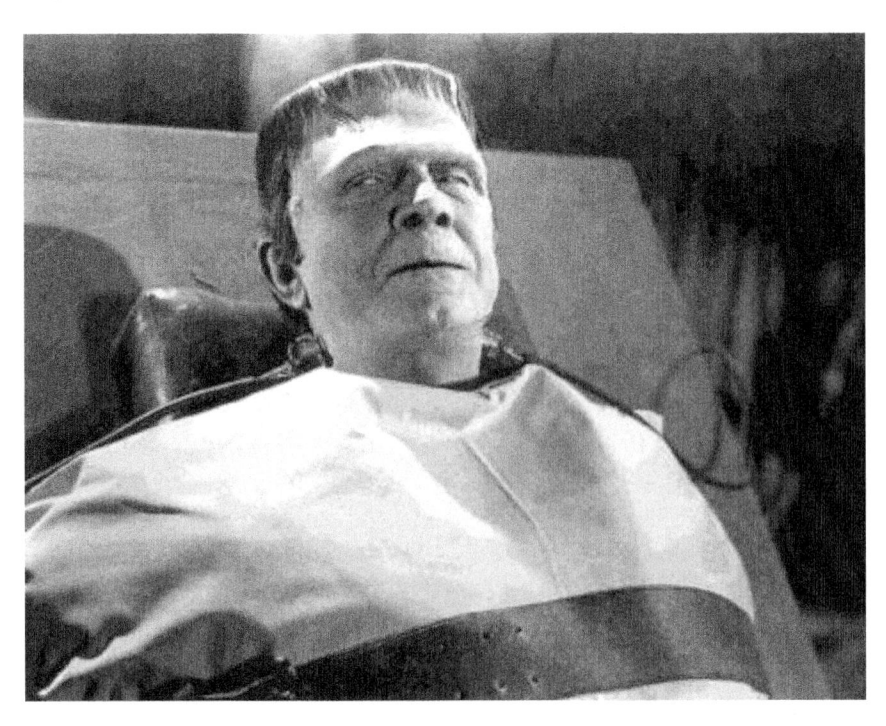

So far so good, and certainly watching *Frankenstein Meets the Wolf-Man* as part of a BBC2 horror double bill season only a couple of Saturdays after seeing *Ghost of Frankenstein,* this twelve-year-old fanboy had no problem retaining the continuity from the earlier film, which made Lugosi's stumbling stiff-armed walk perfectly logical.

However, back in 1942, audiences hadn't necessarily seen the previous film for a couple of years, if at all. Hearing Lugosi's heavily accented voice emerging from the Monster's mouth without the benefit of the narrative build-up that *Ghost of Frankenstein* had given to the same effect in its concluding scene, struck audiences at the test screenings as hysterically funny.

Universal's bosses panicked, and the film's soundtrack was re-edited in post-production, excising all Lugosi's dialogue and thus removing all reference to the Monster's blindness. Consequently, audiences were treated to the Monster lumbering around with his arms extended for no apparent reason, while occasionally and wordlessly opening and closing his mouth like the world's deadliest goldfish. The apparent absurdity is exacerbated by the fact that, while Lugosi adjusted his performance according to the development of the narrative, the stunt doubles simply aped the straight-armed Lugosi stomp even in the fight scenes after the Monster's sight has come back.

As a result of all this, through no fault of his own, Lugosi's performance was rendered bizarre, even risible. He would not appear in another role for Universal until six years later in the last dying gasp of horror's Golden Age, 1948's *Abbott and Costello Meet Frankenstein.* This is perhaps the only example in cinema history of an actor being blacklisted by a studio for having had the audacity to have stuck strictly to the script the studio had given him.

Given the range of problems the finished *Frankenstein Meets the Wolf-Man* is unable to hide, it's extraordinary that I love the film as much as I do. But I do.

The film's director Roy William Neill, best known for his briskly efficient and hugely effective helming of Universal's exquisite Basil Rathbone and Nigel Bruce Sherlock Holmes series, delivers some wonderfully inventive and imaginative visuals.

The opening sequence in the Welsh graveyard where poor Larry Talbot has been laid to rest is as atmospheric a feast for the eyes as anything Universal ever did. The set for the Llanwelly cemetery is magnificently realised, the crooked gravestones offering a suitably morbid punctuation to the sloping landscape, darkened skeletal trees rolling across the foreground as Neill's camera tracks the nervy progress of our two opportunistic graverobbers.

The scene is just as wonderful once the two men break into the Talbot tomb, hoping to liberate Larry's gold valuables from the coffin in which he was interred after being beaten to death by Sir John at the end of *The Wolf Man*. The lighting is moody and powerful, and the sense of encroaching doom as the full moon flits across the sky outside the little window and the wolfbane is lifted away from Talbot's perfectly preserved corpse is genuinely intense. The eventual fate of the first graverobber, caught in the iron grip of the rejuvenated and transforming werewolf and pleading in vain for help as his terrified friend scrabbles his way back out of the tomb creates a real degree of pathos.

Curt Siodmak's cheery cynicism notwithstanding, I also love the film for the exceptional and courageous willingness of the writer to embrace rather than evade the deep pessimism and despair at the heart of the subject matter. Talbot's only goal in searching for Frankenstein's secrets is to discover the means by which he can die; if we're rooting for Chaney – as we certainly are – then what we're rooting for is his successful suicide.

There aren't many mainstream Hollywood genre movies where the narrative drive stems from something so unremittingly bleak; the film's philosophy is essentially Schopenhauer plus yak hair.

In this regard, *Frankenstein Meets the Wolf Man* goes one step further than its near contemporary, Frank Capra's *It's a Wonderful Life*. The joyous sentimentality of the conclusion to Capra's masterpiece tends to lead audiences to forget the tone of disillusion and despair which dominates the middle section of the film. Jimmy Stewart's subjective sense that he has wasted his life may be shown to be objectively false in his triumphant snowy return to Bedford Falls, but that doesn't make it any less real while he experiences it. Chaney's Talbot also despairs, but he has no Clarence to console him, and no Christmas bell to signal an angel getting its wings. Siodmak follows the suicidal logic of his story remorselessly to the end, the film's tragic monsters locked in conflict as the castle collapses around them, but even more than its bitingly effective screenplay it is Chaney's performance which renders the film as powerful as it is at the human level and which, like Stewart's, magnificently exudes essence of Everyman.

Lon Chaney junior is the least loved and the most underrated of the great horror stars. He's very good in *The Wolf Man,* and for my money he's even better here. Given the chance, as he is this time, to hit the tortured soul button from the word go rather than a third of the way through the movie as in the previous film, he makes Talbot's plight touching, human and genuinely affecting. In lesser hands the performance might easily have slipped into bathos but Chaney never puts a hairy paw wrong. His humanity lends a truly tragic element to Talbot, fully engaging our sympathies, and is a tribute to Chaney's considerable skill and charm.

It's not the actor's fault that Universal overused him in the 1940s, or that some of the vehicles he was offered – the couple of Mummy films he did, or the *Inner Sanctum* series for instance – were poor enough that even Lugosi at his most energetic and histrionic would have struggled to lift the limp corpses of their narratives out of the mire.

Admittedly Chaney's take on the Monster in *Ghost of Frankenstein* is oddly flat, but then he had the misfortune to be the first actor faced with the unenviable task of following Karloff's era-defining performance. Hopelessly miscast in *Son of Dracula,* he does his level best to make as decent a fist as he can of it despite the natural disadvantages of his bulky physique and evident all-Americanness.

But it's his performance as poor tormented, doom-laden Larry Talbot on which a defence of Chaney's right to be mentioned in the same breath as Karloff and Lugosi must depend, and although he played the part – with equal conviction and commitment – on five separate occasions for Universal, the definitive version is here, in *Frankenstein Meets the Wolf Man.*

It's not only Chaney though. The rest of the cast is also excellent. There's Marya Ouspenskaya reprising the role of Maleva and Illona Massey replacing Evelyn Ankers as Elsa Frankenstein (much to Chaney's delight no doubt). There's Dennis Hoey, known and loved by generations of Sherlock Holmes fans as the pompous and dunderheaded Inspector Lestrade in the Rathbone/Bruce movies, here effectively playing the same role in all but name. Briefly, and in his last role before a tragically early death, there's Dwight Frye, who had been there at the beginning in both the 1931 classics that had set the whole cycle in motion; a role the bulk of which, sadly, hit the cutting room floor with much the same force as Lugosi's dialogue and later career. And, inevitably, there's Lionel Atwill.

Skilled direction. Atmospheric visuals. A powerful script. A magnificent central performance. An excellent supporting cast. Hopefully this represents more than enough to establish that there are many logical and rational reasons for loving *Frankenstein Meets the Wolf Man.*

However, it wasn't really until I had children that I began to understand that the *il*logical, *ir*rational ones are much more powerful.

I became a parent for the first time more than a decade ago, and am now the proud father of two daughters, one ten and one twelve. Over those years, they have taught me many valuable lessons. In the early days, they taught me that the 'bigger on the inside' dimensional transcendentalism of the TARDIS is more scientifically plausible than it seems, since tiny babies can apparently produce two hundred times their own bodyweight in poo. A related lesson; they taught me that if the price of Protecting the Environment is washing re-usable nappies then the Environment can fuck right off. Global apocalypse is much the lesser of two evils. They taught me that long term sleeplessness is a viable life choice if incapacity, incompetence and incandescent irritability are no obstacles to your day to day existence. In fact, if you want to be a President or a Prime Minister those qualities are positive advantages. More recently, they have taught me that a single episode of certain children's television programmes can last for thirty-seven months. Or seem to at least.

Mostly though, they've taught me what the phrase 'Unconditional Love' actually means.

I'm not at all certain that such a thing actually exists in any other form, or even if it should. However completely and passionately in love with your partner you may be, that love is still subject to the possibility of change. Even if it survives time, and circumstance, then, hypothetically at least, the actions of the other person could alter the nature of your love for them. Your love now may be total, absolute and overwhelming, but there are unspoken conditions attached to it. And so there should be. I love you this much while you don't hurt me, while you don't abuse my trust, while you don't betray me.

That's the proper basis for any adult relationship; we should all have sufficient self-respect to make our love conditional in that way. If we don't, we lay ourselves open to being one of those people who stays in an abusive relationship out of 'love'; neglecting to notice the glaringly obvious truth that if someone hits or humiliates you it tends to suggest they don't even like you very much. Of course, we lucky ones never have to think about the unspoken conditions on which our relationship is based. But that doesn't mean they're not there.

With my children however, those conditions simply don't exist. There is absolutely nothing either of my daughters could do that would alter my love for them by the tiniest fraction of an iota. The love of parent for child is divorced from the conditional, from any semblance of rationality, from the very notion of cause and effect.

You see, in truth – and whisper the secret quietly – neither of my girls is completely without flaw. Of course they are kind and clever and funny and utterly brilliant, but that's not the whole story. One is so shy and withdrawn that she will barely speak outside the house, and inside the house is prone to tantrums of quite indescribably terrifying proportions. The other is pathologically incapable of shutting up for a nanosecond at a time, and yet deeply insecure and craving approval beneath her apparent social confidence. Aware of how completely different they are, at times they can be utterly horrible to one another. Like most of us, they can both be prone to a degree of self-interest and neither is above the occasional self-serving lie. They are not total strangers to materialistic greed.

They have flaws drawn from me. They have flaws drawn from their mother. They have flaws entirely their own. They have flaws stemming from nature and flaws stemming from nurture and flaws stemming from any other bloody place flaws might be lurking. The same is true of me and of the rest of the human race, but the difference with children is in the nakedness of their flaws. They're just not as well-trained in the arts of dissembling as the rest of us.

A year or two ago, in my own hideously ill-advised version of the love trial from *King Lear*, I asked my daughters what they wished for. My eldest, having learned the value and rewards to be gained through offering up the right answers, smiled sweetly and replied "I wish for happiness for my whole lovely family." Her younger sister, marching to the beat of a deeper drum, replied "Cake."

But the point is this. Not one of those flaws undermines the inescapable and undeniable truth that my daughters are the two most wonderful creatures this world has ever been lucky enough to have walk upon it. And more. I don't love my children *despite* their flaws. I love my children *because* of their flaws. I wouldn't wish for an atom of them to be other than it is. And that love never burns more fiercely proud and protective than when those flaws are most evident. When they're making mistakes, when they're failing or falling, when they're upset or isolated or making wrong choices and choosing the wrong road, when they're some way from the top of their game; those are often the moments when I'm most aware of how profoundly and proudly and desperately my heart aches with love for them.

And to those of you wondering what any of this has to do with *Frankenstein Meets the Wolf Man* – my own tangential fault, not yours – my answer is this. Although different in *degree* (even my fanboy heart couldn't *really* love a monster mashup movie from 1942 *quite* as much as I love my kids) it was something of the same *kind* of 'unconditional all flaws happily accepted' love that my twelve-year-old self felt for the film, and that I've found myself eventually working my way back towards.

For many years in between the 1977 season of BBC2 horror double bills and today, whenever I watched or thought of *Frankenstein Meets the Wolf Man* (which was, of course, far more often than any sane man would admit to) I found myself wishing for a different film. I was wishing for a film that retained Lugosi's dialogue, for a film that explained the Monster's blindness and made sense of Lugosi's performance. I was wishing for a film that cast Karloff instead of Lugosi and spared the Hungarian's blushes. I was wishing for a film that gave the monster a fairer deal, or for a film that didn't have *Far-o-la Far-o-li* running infuriatingly around my head for days afterwards. I was wishing for a film that was a bit more tastefully titled, that didn't wear its formulaic intentions quite so obviously on its sleeve.

If the 1977 me could have met and talked with the 2020 version, perhaps sitting amiably around a campfire like Talbot and the thawing Monster, my twelve-year-old self would have laughed at the poor, unfortunate, myopic creature he was to become. "It's *Frankenstein Meets the Wolf Man!*" he would have reminded me. "The Frankenstein Monster meets the Wolf Man in it!! They have a fight!!!! What more do you want?!!!!!"

And the middle-aged father I am now would nod sagely and agree. Why wish for a different film when the one you've got is fantastic? Why bother with might have beens at all? Why waste precious time wishing for things in life to be different at the expense of seeing the brilliant stuff that's right there in front of you?

It's *Frankenstein Meets the Wolf Man*. What's not to love?

# 17. QUOTH THE RAVEN....

**The Raven (1963, AIP, Roger Corman)**

*'Are you some dark-winged messenger from beyond? Answer me, monster, tell me truly! Shall I ever hold again the radiant maiden whom the angels call Lenore?'*
**Dr Erasmus Craven (Vincent Price)**

*'How the hell should I know? What am I, a fortune teller?'*
**Dr Bedloe (Peter Lorre)**

Okay, let's get this straight. As those of you who have been happily guffawing your way through the previous chapters will readily attest, I am a funny guy. A *very* funny guy. In fact – if you'll permit me – I am a fellow of infinite jest, of most excellent fancy. I am wont to set the pub table on a roar at any available opportunity. I am the sultan of the sarcastic retort. The wizard of the witty riposte. The aristocrat of the acerbic aphorism. The duke of the devilish double entendre and the clown prince of punning parody. Oscar Wilde and Woody Allen purloin my polished one-liners. My *mots* could not be more *bon*. My sense of humour, in other words, is finely honed.

Even so, there is a kind of broad, overly assertive comedy which leaves me completely cold. Jim Carrey, for instance, is an actor whose work I can admire very much in more restrained, dramatic vehicles like *The Truman Show* and *Eternal Sunshine of the Spotless Mind*. The moment he begins to try to make me laugh, however, he has something like the effect on me of nails being scraped along a blackboard. It's not just Carrey. There are whole genres of humour that feel to me like being grabbed by the throat, banged over the head, kicked in the nadgers and told to think it's funny. Gurning and screeching comics straining for impact set my comedic teeth on edge.

To offer a double-act example of what I mean, for those of a certain age and nationality: Morecambe and Wise were simply funny, while Cannon and Ball were *being* funny (American readers may need to mentally substitute 'Laurel and Hardy' and 'The Three Stooges' respectively to reach the same conclusion). The *being* shows, and just ends up feeling uncomfortable. It's why I hate pantomimes.

It isn't just professional funny folk. Enforced jollity in its amateur form is equally painful to me. There's a particular breed of joyless personality, who is always somehow nerve-shreddingly in search of 'fun'. People who regard the novelty tie as a perfectly acceptable substitute for a personality. Overly keen Secret Santa organisers. Fiercely devoted fancy dress fans. Anyone who describes themselves as 'wacky'. They tend to find men dressed as women hilariously funny in and of itself and hurl themselves into comedic charity events with an utterly humourless enthusiasm that borders on the maniacal. My usual approach if faced by one – or worse, several – of these irritatingly frolicsome fuckers is to explain through gritted teeth that, as a long term and committed adherent of the Miserabilist faith, my religion demands that I am surrounded at all times by a five-hundred-yard fun-free exclusion zone.

Bringing it closer to this book's home territory, this is the reason I can never really enjoy, for instance, *Abbott and Costello Meet Frankenstein*. Many later critics have been generous to Universal's final monster mash-up, this time played completely for laughs, seeing in it an affectionate farewell to the Golden Age. For me however, good though both Lugosi and Chaney are while reprising their best known roles, the film is an unpleasant watch due to the laboured, grating gag-fest Bud and Lou bring to the material. Having said that, in its defence the film has the comedic elegance of P.G. Wodehouse if measured against the ghastliness of the post-millennial comedy-horror farrago that is the *Scary Movie* series.

Of course I recognise this says more about me than it does about anyone else. Humour is, by definition, subjective. If someone finds something funny, then it *is* funny, whether or not I happen to agree with them. It doesn't make them 'wrong', and me objectively 'right'. Even though I am.

But all of this would seem to make it likely that Roger Corman's 1963 *The Raven* is simply not for me.

Any film that features Jack Nicholson dressed as a pantomime Robin Hood, complete with feathery hat, scores dangerously high on the jollity scale in my book.

You see, by this point Corman had begun to feel almost as trapped and frustrated by the conventions of his Poe cycle as he had previously been by the endless round of low budget black and white AIP quickies which he had created the Poe films in order to escape from.

Desperate to find something new in the formula, Corman remembered the humorous 'Black Cat' segment he had added to his 1962 portmanteau film *Tales of Terror,* as well as the pairing of that segment's stars, the ubiquitous Vincent Price and, for the first time, Peter Lorre. For his adaptation of *The Raven*, Corman had screenwriter Richard Matheson heighten and extend the tongue in cheek tone to feature length. Perhaps he was emboldened in the approach by the fact that, even more than the narratively slight short stories the previous Poe pictures had used as inspiration, Poe's famous poem had almost no narrative at all, so there was no plot to depart *from*.

Of course, the connection to Poe in Corman's tale of battling mediaeval magicians is no more tenuous than that in Universal's 1935 vehicle for Karloff and Lugosi, but the mood of the two films could not be more different. Where Universal had responded to Poe's verse with a dark, morbid take on tormented genius and obsession, Corman's film works as broad, knockabout farce. As such, with my hard earned 'Mr Picky' persona when it comes to comedy, I could be expected to find AIP's *The Raven* a gratingly unpleasant experience.

In fact, I love it. I loved it then, and I love it still.

Here is why.

Back in 1977, viewing it for the first time, Corman's film had more than enough brooding gothic trappings to delight my morbid adolescent heart. Of course even as a twelve-year-old, I could see the tongue in cheek, almost *Scooby Doo* tone of the film, but there were still a series of beautifully realised crypts and coffins and decaying corpses. It still had gothic castles and haunted palaces aplenty. It didn't matter to me that it wasn't played straight; the production design was *absolutely* straight, and the trappings were more than enough for me. In fact, viewed later, and with greater knowledge of the film's production history, *The Raven* has even more of these things than the earlier, more Poe-faced (see what I did there?) movies, since a typically canny and cash-conscious Corman had stumbled on the strategy of re-using sets from the previous Poe pictures alongside a new build for each subsequent production, thus delivering incrementally richer environments with each successive film.

It was more than just the sets though. The film had Price and Lorre and Karloff, a piece of dream casting so good it was repeated, with Basil Rathbone thrown in for good measure, for another AIP knockabout horror comedy, the even more enjoyable Jacques Tourneur directed *Comedy of Terrors*. And the dream casting begins to meld into another reason I continue to love the film, despite its slightly forced and over-eager attempts to amuse: Saturday night nostalgia.

Corman's film, with its big guest stars and its juvenile lead (Nicholson had become a huge celebrity by 1977) all hamming it up in silly costumes, slotted beautifully into the wider landscape of the seventies Saturday night British television on which I grew up. The BBC's iron domination of the Golden Age of Saturday TV was all built around the cult of personality. That was the common factor running through all of the programming now so fondly remembered: big, bold personalities that burst off the screen. From Basil Brush and Tom Baker in the early evening, through Brucie or Larry on *The Generation Game,* to the Two Ronnies, to Gemma Jones's fantastic embodiment of the larger than life Louisa Trotter in *The Duchess of Duke Street,* to Parkinson and his superstar guests. The larger than life quality was even shared by the malevolent and predatory teatime pervert Jimmy Saville as he fixed it for kids each Saturday on his early evening show *Jim'll Fuck It*.

These were actors that seemed almost too big for the small screen, presenters that were bigger than the shows they presented. It wasn't, for instance, anything particularly witty in the scripts or anything exceptionally skilled in the technique of puppeteering that made *The Basil Brush Show* such a fixture of Saturday night children's entertainment, but the manic ebullience of Basil's own misguided conviction in the unrivalled hilarity of his material. 'BOOM BOOM' he cried repeatedly, collapsing sideways in sheer joy at the magnificence of whatever cringeworthy punchline he had just delivered, and a nation felt his joy, and shared it.

Similarly, it was not, in the end, the fantastic, dark, engrossing script work of Terrance Dicks or Robert Holmes that will have hard-edged grown men in their 50s – and I count myself a proud member of their number – grow misty-eyed when recalling how much *Doctor Who* meant to them as children, but the ferociously daring intensity of Tom Baker's goggle-eyed commitment to the role. Or, if you prefer, Jon Pertwee's earlier, effortlessly commanding ability to reassure for England, were reassuring an Olympic Sport.

It was into this context that Corman's *The Raven* dropped as the second feature of a BBC2 horror double bill in the early hours of August the 21st. The heightened, knowingly hammy performances of Price and Lorre and Karloff were far more about personality than about 'acting' – just of a piece, in other words, with the rest of the BBC's Saturday night schedule. No-one could argue that the actors are carefully subsumed and effaced by their characters here; in fact, it's just the opposite. The effect of the whole piece is precisely because it *is* Price, and Lorre, and Karloff, just as though the old ghouls were guesting in a creepy comedy sketch on *Dave Allen at Large* or *The Two Ronnies*. It's possible to watch the entire film as though it were 'a play what Ernie wrote' while mentally picturing Eric Morecambe in Jack Nicholson's role using the props to badly ventriloquise the opinion that the whole thing is 'Ruggish'.

The beautiful dovetailing of the personalities on screen was not entirely reflected off-screen, however, if Corman's recollections of the set are at all accurate. The problems ran a little deeper than Nicholson's understandable dislike of being crapped on by the production's trained raven – although he evidently became a little less fastidious later in his career. He didn't seem to mind being crapped on by the screenwriter of *Man Trouble,* or the director of *Wolf,* for example. It wasn't even the difficulties surrounding the ageing Boris Karloff's increasing physical discomfort and incapacity – by this point the actor could barely walk in real life.

No, the main issue came in the shape of Peter Lorre's free and easy approach to minor matters like the dialogue. Improvising furiously, he irritated the normally affable Karloff by failing to offer up any of the lines which the by-the-book Englishman was waiting for. Karloff, ever the consummate professional and the epitome of the old-school 'trained actor' felt wrong-footed and uncomfortable with never knowing where the next cue was coming from. According to his own account, Vincent Price was forced to act as a kind of emollient in soothing the troubles between his two antagonistic co-stars.

In the end, sadly, the last laugh is on poor Boris, since Lorre ends up comprehensively upstaging everyone and walks away with the film. His Dr Bedloe, by turns pompous, cowardly and wonderfully self-aggrandizing, is a joy to watch, even in the moments when he is physically represented on screen by the raven (when it wasn't busy whitewashing the set), and Lorre's performance is by some distance the most enjoyable and entertaining thing in a massively enjoyable and entertaining film.

Perhaps this might also be the most opportune place to consider Lorre's place in the horror stars' pantheon, since it was his only appearance in this 1977 season of BBC2 horror double bills. For one thing, unlike say Lugosi or Karloff or Chaney or Price or Lee or Cushing, Lorre was never predominantly a horror film actor. Yes, it's true that you could point to non-genre roles for all of the others (even Lugosi had *Ninotchka* opposite Greta Garbo), but I think it's fair to say that these always feel like interesting side-roads or footnotes to what was basically a horror film career.

In Lorre's case, however, his position is probably more indelibly associated with eye-catching supporting roles opposite Bogart in both *Casablanca* and *The Maltese Falcon,* or with the series of subsequent, Bogartless, noirish thrillers he made with his other co-star from those classics, Sydney Greenstreet – wonderful films like *The Mask of Dimitrios* in which Lorre played against type as the film's writer hero.

Starting in Germany with an unforgettable performance as the eponymous child killer in Fritz Lang's *M*, Lorre's screen image is also strongly associated with his wonderful line in psychopathology, with key roles in early Hitchcock pieces like the original *The Man Who Knew Too Much,* or the Hollywood adaptation of *Crime and Punishment* for instance, but these were still clearly not operating within anything that could meaningfully be considered part of the horror genre.

In fact, Lorre's status as a major horror star is based on only a handful of performances, notably as Dr Gogol in Karl Freund's 1935 *Mad Love,* and in Robert Florey's wonderfully atmospheric *The Beast with Five Fingers* in 1946, before parodying this image in horror-comedies like *Tales of Terror, The Raven* and *Comedy of Terrors,* a tendency that began with his magnificent comedic turn as Raymond Massey's cringing co-conspirator in the 1940s screen adaptation of *Arsenic and Old Lace.* Nonetheless, so powerful was the impression Lorre generated in a relatively minor number of excursions into the genre that it seemed natural for RKO to throw him into a largely forgotten 1940 comedy called *You'll Find Out* alongside Karloff and Lugosi as an equal part of the film's 'spooky' element. And Lorre looms large alongside both Chaneys, Karloff, Lugosi and Price, never feeling out of place in their company, in *Heroes of the Horrors,* Calvin Thomas Beck's biographical approach to the genre, a book beloved of all monster kids everywhere.

There's much to enjoy in Corman's *The Raven,* but Lorre is right at the heart of most of it, justifying the director's feeling that the actor had not only all the horror credentials required to sit so beautifully alongside Karloff, Price and Poe, but also the quality of *knowingness* to judge exactly the degree of campery and ham to lend a performance which would most perfectly enhance a hybrid piece like this.

There's one final, more personal reason I love *The Raven* though.

It was the only film over the entire course of five consecutive years of summer seasons of BBC2 horror double bills which my mum enjoyed as much as I did. More often than not, I would be watching at least the second feature alone, but sometimes mum would sit up and watch with me as she did on this occasion, and this was the single time I can remember her expressing a wholeheartedly positive response to the film in question.

In fact, for years afterwards if one of us was talking too much, or expressing an opinion mum didn't much care for, she would press her thumb and first finger together in a passable impression of Vincent Price's final gesture in the film and pronounce – in a rather less passable impression of Price's silky tones – 'Quoth the raven "nevermore."'

Mum wasn't keen on 'dark', or 'troubling' or 'gloomy'. Certainly not 'scary'. She viewed the world with an essential optimism, and didn't like to acknowledge the dark behind the curtain. When it finally came at her, in the shape of the death of my dad, she chose to grow a tumour and die of a broken heart rather than deal with a new and darker world.

*Mum, Dad and an auditionee for the world's sulkiest teenager award.*

Although, as I've mentioned elsewhere, both mum and dad were extraordinarily tolerant of my obsessions, I think there's no doubt that mum in particular would have preferred me to enjoy a somewhat sunnier mental and emotional landscape than I did. Whenever I chose to share whatever dark fixation was preoccupying me at any given moment, she would give an affectionate but slightly baffled shake of the head, and mutter the word 'Morbid' while wistfully imagining a more clean-cut, athletic, square-jawed path through adolescence for me.

So *The Raven,* its light-hearted silliness counterbalancing its tombs and terrors, pleased her, and for once found us on the same page when it came to the pleasures of the monster movie double bill.

Humour suited mum better than horror. When I try to picture her now, peering back through the fog that so cruelly intervenes when we try to hold the face of a dead loved one in our mind's eye, I can only ever see her laughing.

Which, of course, is just what she would have wanted.

# DOUBLE BILL NINE

## Saturday August 27th 1977

HOUSE OF FRANKENSTEIN     22.20 – 23.30

THE REPTILE     00.05 – 01.30

# 18. THE MONSTER MASH

## House of Frankenstein (1944, Universal, Erle C. Kenton)

*'Who are you? Why have you freed me from the ice that imprisoned the beast that lived within me? Why?'*
**Lawrence Talbot (Lon Chaney)**

I make it a fixed rule never to mix friends from different arenas of my life since it will lead inevitably to disaster. Or at least I would make it a fixed rule if my life were interesting enough to have different arenas in it. Or if I had any friends.

After all, it can be a dangerous proposition to assume that indiscriminately combining your favourite things will necessarily produce good results. A nice prawn curry isn't improved by pouring it over New York cheesecake, wonderful though each separate ingredient may be.

It was this sort of flawed thinking that saw the Universal golden age slip away into uninspired monster rallies like *House of Frankenstein,* so initially enjoyable but ultimately unsatisfying. The Chinese Takeaway of the horror film world.

Even so, it's a wonderfully entertaining movie, with an awful lot to enjoy. Karloff is on form in his only post-Monster return to the Frankenstein franchise as mad scientist Dr Niemann, and so is Chaney, always reliably excellent when reprising the Wolf Man. There is an engagingly sepulchral John Carradine taking his first bow as Dracula, a bow very nearly successful enough to allow me not to spend the next few thousand words lamenting the missing Lugosi, plus George Zucco as the unfortunate owner of Lampini's travelling chamber of horrors and Lionel 'the inevitable' Atwill in the supporting cast.

Perhaps best of all, there is also J. Carroll Naish exuding equal parts menace and pathos as the hunchbacked Daniel in the film's most affecting and memorable performance. There is a genuinely moving quality to the yearning and the sense of loss in his eyes as he recognises that Rita, the dancing gypsy girl he is smitten with, could never return his feelings, a quality which only deepens when the pangs of unrequited love begin to meld into a smouldering resentment as he watches her succumbing to the charms of Chaney's Talbot. I'm also especially fond of Naish's slow murderous advances towards camera, fingers menacingly splayed and pointed in order to sportingly announce his strangulatory intent to his prospective victims, mainly because my old school friend Mark Welch used to do a cracking impersonation of Daniel's not entirely inconspicuous approach to murders.

It's also true to say that I'm not unutterably opposed to the idea of the 'shared universe' so currently in vogue. I loved the cheeky panache with which Russell T Davies was willing to hurl Daleks and Cybermen into the same *Doctor Who* story, legitimising the 'eight-year-old in their bedroom with their toys' approach to narrative strategy for ever afterwards, and Joss Whedon among others had a more than creditable stab at uniting the disparate strands of the Marvel movies into something coherent and entertaining in the *Avengers* films.

The problem in *House of Frankenstein,* for me at least, is that the different narrative strands are barely interacting with one another, creating the (possibly accurate) impression that they have been dropped purposelessly into the feature without any conscious consideration of why they might belong together.

First we have a prison break segment which helps establish the characters and goals of Daniel and Niemann, culminating in Daniel killing Zucco's travelling showman, and Karloff stealing his identity. But Niemann then becomes no more than a plot device to wake the skeletal Dracula by removing the stake from his heart and the Carradine Dracula segment which follows is entirely self-contained.

It's actually quite effective on its own terms, with a particularly nice piece of vampiric mesmerism and an unusually fluent man to bat transformation, but nothing Carradine's vampire count does before being speedily reduced back to a pile of bones by the morning sunlight reflects on or affects the later narrative at all. Instead we simply return to Niemann's mission of self-justifying revenge as though nothing had occurred. Then we thaw the Monster and the Wolf Man from the ice, but it is only Talbot's story which occupies us next, including the love triangle which develops between Chaney, Naish and Anne Gwynne's Rita, with the Monster really only entering the action in the final act.

*House of Frankenstein*, in other words, contrives to be a little less than the sum of its parts.

Not that there's anything intrinsically wrong with the portmanteau form. *House of Frankenstein*'s near contemporary, the British anthology film *Dead of Night* contains a couple of striking episodes, and helped form the template on which Amicus, in the '60s and '70s, was to produce a string of massively enjoyable horror films – things like *Dr Terror's House of Horrors*, *From Beyond the Grave* and *Asylum*. These films make a virtue out of their episodic nature, since the quality of the stories within each film could vary wildly and failure to enjoy one particular episode did not necessarily spoil your enjoyment of the whole film.

However, unlike the Amicus films, *House of Frankenstein* makes a pretence of having a single linear plot rather than cheerfully admitting to being a group of unconnected episodes held together only by a sketchy framing narrative, and as such is almost sneakily a portmanteau movie. It's like buying a novel only to discover it's actually a collection of short stories, and the film can feel a faintly disjointed and disappointing experience as a result.

The failings of *House of Frankenstein*, for me, are thrown into sharp relief by a comparison with the contemporaneous work being done by Val Lewton's horror film unit at RKO. Lewton's work at RKO has, deservedly, garnered a great deal of critical praise and attention, and so I suspect his films will already be very familiar to anyone reading this, but since Lewton's body of work, like that of Amicus, did not feature at all in this 1977 season of BBC2 horror double bills, which focuses exclusively on classic horror's 'big three' (Universal, Hammer and the Corman Poe pictures) it might be worth me dwelling on them a little here.

In the wake of the commercial failure of the studio's brief association with Orson 'wunderkind' Welles, and under the auspices of a new studio management whose watchword was 'showmanship in place of genius,' RKO found themselves casting envious glances in the direction of the highly profitable and relatively cheap cycle of B feature horrors Universal was creating in the '40s. Val Lewton, who had worked as Selznick's right hand man on '30s classics like *Gone With the Wind*, was the producer RKO turned to in order to grab a share of Universal's monster profits.

Lewton was to establish a production team (which became an invaluable training ground for major talents like Jacques Tourneur, Robert Wise, Mark Robson and cinematographer Nicholas Musuraca), RKO would provide him with a pre-tested schlocky title like *The Leopard Man* or

*I Walked With a Zombie*, a 75 minute running time, a tiny budget and a tinier shooting schedule, and Lewton would do the rest.

Surprisingly, rather than the kind of drek which Monogram and PRC were churning out in a similarly motivated but even more low-rent attempt to get in on a little of the Universal action, from this inauspicious beginning Lewton's horror unit produced some of the most distinctive and atmospheric films of the era, films which belong every bit as much to the 'genius' school of filmmaking as *Citizen Kane* and *The Magnificent Ambersons* – an irony given RKO's desperation to dissociate themselves from any hint of their recent past with Welles.

Lewton took the attitude that suggestion and suspense would work better than the more conventional, overt monster movies Universal was specialising in. This was partly out of financial necessity, since a $150,000 production budget was never going to run to a convincing Jack Pierce make-up job, but partly also from a personal sensibility that favoured subtlety and restraint.

That Lewton was allowed to continue consistently giving RKO material which was so much better than they had either asked for, wanted, or deserved, is largely down to the fact that the first of these films, 1942's *Cat People,* was a huge commercial success. With a massively profitable and cheaply produced hit under his belt, Lewton was by and large left alone to produce the kind of work he wanted to. Even to the extent that when presented with the title *I Walked With a Zombie* for his second film, Lewton felt sufficiently empowered to deliver RKO an unofficial adaptation of *Jane Eyre*. And it was also *Cat People,* brilliantly directed by Jacques Tourneur, Lewton's first and most crucial collaborator, which established the template which, in varying ways, the succeeding films adopted.

Firstly, the 'monster' – if there even is one – remains shadowy and unseen. Secondly, there is a psychological depth and complexity to the characterisation which is rare for any film of the period. Viewed in a certain light, *Cat People* is not only a film about a woman turning into a black panther (although it *is* undeniably about that, despite the determination of certain critics to pretend they are watching a Bergmanesque psychodrama rather than a supernatural horror movie), but also a deeply acuitive study of sexual dysfunction within an unhappy marriage.

The decision, taken early on by Lewton, not to go for a period adaptation of the Algernon Blackwood story *Ancient Sorceries*, but instead to adopt a determinedly realistic and recognisable contemporary American setting differentiates the film very strongly from Universal's geographically and historically vague middle Europe. The striving for modern-day realism and rounded characterisation aligns the film more closely to the developing noir aesthetic than to the traditional horror film.

The 'horror' elements are restricted to a couple of astonishingly effective set piece moments. In *Cat People* itself the first of these is the scene in which the heroine is followed down a street at night, signalled by a series of shots of feet moving into pools of streetlamp light and then plunging into deeper pools of darkness once more. The sound and the editing build the tension to a crescendo which is broken both visually and aurally by the sudden, shocking interjection into frame of a perfectly innocent bus, accompanied by a hiss of hydraulic brakes, a jump scare technique so familiar now within the horror film that its use has become referred to as a 'Lewton bus.' The second, even more remarkable set piece is the virtuoso handling of light, shadow and sound when our heroine is menaced in a deserted swimming pool at night. Nothing is shown, nothing is made overt, and yet the sense of genuine menace is astonishingly powerful.

Once the formula was established, the Lewton films redeploy such highlights again and again. The night-time journey in *I Walked With a Zombie*, among the most hauntingly beautiful sequences in the whole of 1940s cinema, or the 'girl outside the door' scene in *The Leopard Man*, for instance. In fact, my own favourite of all the Lewton films, the 'sequel in name only' *Curse of the Cat People*, is no kind of horror film at all but an evocation of childhood, with all its terrors, delights and fantasies, every bit as resonant and poetic as Richard Hughes' novel *A High Wind in Jamaica*, Dennis Potter's play *Blue Remembered Hills*, Charles Laughton's film *Night of the Hunter*, Golding's *Lord of the Flies* or Harper Lee's *To Kill a Mockingbird*.

Perhaps the contrast between *House of Frankenstein* and the approach of the Lewton films can be seen most tellingly through the lens of Boris Karloff's acting. As I've already said, I find a lot to enjoy in Karloff's Dr Niemann, and would go so far as to suggest that, even if the portrayal lacks some of the light and shade he brought to classic '30s performances like Ardeth Bay in *The Mummy* or Poelzig in *The Black Cat*, it is Karloff's sustained study of a monomaniacal sociopath that pointed the way to Peter Cushing's later take on the monster-making Baron in Hammer's Frankenstein films a little more directly than had either Colin Clive, Ernest Thesiger, Basil Rathbone or Cedric Hardwicke in the earlier Universal movies.

Still, a number of critics have found Karloff's tongue slipping a little too far into his cheek in *House of Frankenstein*, and have drawn attention to the idea that unlike Lugosi, who brought a furious, sometimes overwrought, sincerity to even the most appalling of scripts, Karloff was a little too willing to distance himself from material he was unimpressed by, either with a too-knowing wink of condescension or a self-conscious and self-parodying hint of ham. While I don't entirely agree, it seems to me undeniable that there's a touch of both in his Dr Niemann.

Now look at the work Karloff did for Lewton. An awkward plagiarism court case surrounding 1943s *The Ghost Ship;* a couple of commercial failures; and a drift away from even the most tangential relationship to the horror genre into period drama with *Mademoiselle Fifi* and juvenile delinquency in *Youth Runs Wild,* both released in 1944, had weakened Lewton's position at RKO and led the studio to revisit its usual policy of non-intervention. They pushed Karloff, coming straight off *House of Frankenstein,* onto an initially horrified Lewton, partly as a punishment and partly in an effort to get him at last to make the kind of straight horror film Karloff was associated with.

Perhaps surprisingly, however, unlike the kind of fractious and openly hostile relationship that occurred between director Michael Reeve and Vincent Price on the set of the 1969 *Witchfinder General* after a very similar piece of studio interference had seen AIP foist their established star on an unwilling Reeve, Karloff and Lewton hit it off from the first, and found a shared sensibility. Lewton came to view Karloff as one of the all-time great character actors, and Karloff, forever grateful for the opportunities at genuine artistic expression which the RKO films afforded him, simply said that Lewton had saved him from the living dead and given him back his soul and self-respect.

Though each one is entirely different, the performances Karloff gives in the three films he made with Lewton all rank as among the very best of his career. The first, and least showy of these, Nikolas Pherides in *Isle of the Dead,* is a model of the steadily accumulating power that comes through depth and, most of all, restraint. His tour de force as the grave-robber Gray in *The Body Snatcher,* probably the most memorable performance of the three, has everything: wit, sly charm, intelligence, malice and a genuine monstrosity, and all in a film which has a decent case to make for being the best horror movie of the 1940s. It may well be the finest acting Karloff ever did; it's certainly his best work since the mid '30s. Their final collaboration, and the last of the Lewton films, was *Bedlam* in 1946, and Karloff's work as the sinister and manipulative asylum director is, once again, exceptional. The common factor across the three performances, so superficially different, is nuance and subtlety; the contrast with the entertaining, but essentially cartoonish Niemann in *House of Frankenstein* could hardly be more evident.

Technically and narratively ambitious, stylishly realised, with a potent understanding of human psychology, acted with precision and power and showing a sophisticated and creative sensibility at work, it is easy to see with hindsight that the Lewton films were cutting edge, *modern* even when set in period, and pointed a fruitful way into the future of film-making, while *House of Frankenstein* shows Universal's Golden Age in its last dying moments.

In essence, Lewton was making films for grown-ups, while *House of Frankenstein*, at its core, is a kids' film.

Certainly when I first encountered the Lewton movies in a block, as the first screened film each week in the last of the original run of BBC2 horror double bills in 1981, this is how they presented themselves to me. In 1977, for *Dracula, Frankenstein – and Friends!* I had actually *been* a kid, and so kids' films like *House of Frankenstein* were entirely to my taste. By the summer horror double bill season of 1981, I was going on seventeen, and although looking back now I can see just how much of a kid I still was, at the time I thought quite the opposite.

The intervening years had given me, through the educative power of television, and in particular the BBC, an understanding and awareness of film history it would be much harder to achieve for a similarly inclined adolescent today. I'd seen plenty of classic noir. I knew Bogart's films particularly well. I'd seen a lot of Hitchcock, and some Welles. I'd encountered screwball comedy, and the women's melodramas of the '40s. I knew westerns and musicals and gangsters and silent comedy and British '60s kitchen sink movies. I didn't have to make an effort, all of that stuff was just *on*.

Additionally, by the early eighties I'd begun to encounter a lot of the key films from New Hollywood, usually in Sunday night BBC2 movie seasons called things like *The Great American Picture Show* which I'd come to value almost as much to my growth and development as the younger me had valued *Doctor Who* and the annual horror double bill – early 70s movies by Altman and Coppola and Scorsese and Bogdanovich and Pakula and Woody Allen. *Real* films, *proper* films, *serio*us films rather than silly little genre pictures as, with a very young man's lack of perspective on the value of the things he once loved, I was beginning to think of them.

Beyond television, I had seen *The Elephant Man* at the cinema, my first encounter with Lynch. And since the opening of Cinema City, the first – and still only – arthouse in my hometown, I'd also begun to discover foreign films. I'd certainly seen some Herzog and Truffaut by 1981, and though the exact chronology is a bit vague in my memory perhaps also a bit of Bergman and Bunuel.

So by the time I saw the Lewton movies in the 1981 season, with their sombre, elegiac, doom-laden and above all adult sensibility, it felt somehow miraculously right to me. A perfect circularity, and a perfect sense of the end of an era. They felt like a jumping off point, bridging the gap for me between the things I used to love and the things I was moving towards. When I became a man, I put away childish things, or something along those lines, and those childish things included Universal and Lugosi and Karloff and Hammer and Cushing and Lee. I was too old for kids' films. Even if the '81 horror double bill season hadn't actually been the last, it probably would have been for me, now that I'd grown up.

Edgy, sophisticated and film-literate, the Lewton films struck me as everything the Universal films no longer were, both in their actual production history – the films of the Universal era tended to get progressively less complex and less sophisticated as they went on – and in terms of what they had once meant to me, but were gradually ceasing to. I saw my dwindling ability to appreciate the monster movie any longer as a symptom of moving, as I was convinced I had, from innocence to experience, from a child's perspective to an adult one.

But here's the twist. Over the years since my 1981 first encounter with Lewton – rich, enigmatic, sophisticated Lewton – I could count the numbers of rewatches I've undertaken on the fingers of one hand. There was a separate season of Lewton films on the BBC in the late '80s, and again in the late '90s I believe, and I would have dipped back into those films on both occasions.

Since the growth of home video though, a certain truth emerges. I never owned any Lewton on VHS tapes – I don't even know if any of his films came out on that format, because I never tried to find out. I had lots of the Universals on tape though, because I bought any I could find almost as soon as I had a VCR. By the mid '90s a number of the Universals were available in a uniform Classic Collection edition – not all in the UK though – but those I owned I played until the tapes were all but unwatchably worn.

I eventually replaced the tapes with the Universal legacy collection on DVD, which I had to import from the US because the versions available in England contained the nailed on '30s classics, but did not include most of the later films. The first time I performed a multi-region hack on a DVD player was not out of a vague desire to be able to see any old American region DVDs, but specifically in order to be able to watch the lesser sequels and mash-ups of the second wave Universal era.

And watch them I did, all of them, many, many times. As I did all over again when I bought collections of the same films on Blu-ray.

I don't know exactly how many times I've seen *House of Frankenstein.* Considerably more times than some of the Universal films I've come to feel I undervalued – like 1932's *The Mummy* for instance – or some that I still just don't like quite as much, like *Werewolf of London* or any of the later Mummy films. A few less times than my real, real favourites, like the Lugosi *Dracula*, the first three Frankenstein films, *The Black Cat, The Raven, The Wolf Man* and *Murders in the Rue Morgue.* Even so, I've probably seen *House of Frankenstein* at least a couple of times a year since the available technology allowed me to make that choice. That means in all probability I've seen the film perhaps 25 times, maybe more. The figure would be about the same for most of the other '40s Universals, and a bit more – perhaps three or four times a year – for the real '30s classics.

When the Lewton films became available as a DVD box set – an accolade I'm not aware of having been bestowed on any other producer, as opposed to director – of course I bought it. Of the five films I already knew best, four – *Cat People, I Walked With a Zombie, Bedlam,* and *The Body Snatcher* – I have watched just a single time since then. My personal favourite, *Curse of the Cat People*, I've watched twice. A couple I knew a little less well, either because I'd missed one or other of the later TV screenings or simply hadn't found them as memorable, like *The Leopard Man, The Seventh Victim* and *Isle of the Dead* I've probably watched twice since too. *The Ghost Ship*, which I'd never seen before it became available on DVD, I've still seen only once.

Which means that, for all I've said about the relative technical, creative and storytelling superiority of the Lewton films, there is something in *House of Frankenstein* that means I want to watch it again and again. There is some property in what is by any objective measure a work of much lesser merit which has enabled me to experience it without boredom, not because I needed to remind myself about the film in order to teach it, or write about it, or any other borderline rational real-world reason like that, but simply because *I wanted to see it again*, something like *twenty times* more often than I could face any of the artistically superior Lewton films.

I think it comes down to this. The Lewton films are just that, beautiful, atmospheric, sophisticated *films*. To want to see a really good film once, twice, maybe even three or four times in a lifetime, as I've watched the Lewton films is, I think, a normal, rational response. To be able to watch a film twenty, thirty, forty times – more, to want or even *need* to do so –suggests that I'm responding to something different. To something more than just a film.

The Universal movies, and in particular the later, and lesser Universal movies, have stopped being just films and have become myths instead, a broader element of our culture. Once Universal began throwing their monsters rather randomly into shared narratives, however flawed their formula-driven sequelising might have been, they created a world in which Dracula and the Monster and the Wolf Man were no longer simply characters within a film, but cultural giants whose presence would not later be out of place on postage stamps and lollies, in fanzines and plastic modelling kits, in advertising and comic books and on T shirts and lunchboxes and collectors cards.

It was in these narratively uninspired later monster mash-ups that they became finally, irrevocably a part of the landscape of all our dreams and imaginings, that they truly began to live and breathe beyond the confines of the screen and inhabit a world of their own. *House of Frankenstein* liberates the monsters from the source material, frees them from the context of the specific film or story in which they are appearing and sets them off about their business of becoming truly immortal. The undying monsters indeed.

*House of Frankenstein* is when the monsters stop belonging to Universal and start belonging to all of us, like all of the great storytelling myths which underpinned earlier cultures. Just as no ancient Greek ever moaned 'Not Zeus *again*…' when the bard began to intone, and no self-respecting young Viking ever declared 'I'm fed up with Thor and Loki…can't you tell us a *real* story, for grown-ups?', so I can quite happily press 'Play' time after time after time and wallow joyfully once more in the cosily familiar, hyperreal world of Professor Lampini's immortal chamber of horrors.

Maybe next time I'll accompany it with a nice plate of curried prawn cheesecake after all.

# 19.  A LOATHSOME THING

## The Reptile (1966, Hammer, John Gilling)

*'A hideous parody of herself ... A loathsome thing using her body ... My daughter, my lovely Anna ... My only happiness ... My dearest possession.'*
**Dr Franklyn (Noel Willman)**

Most fans of classic horror will already know the specific production context of Hammer's 1966 quartet of films, but just in case anyone has accidentally stumbled their way here while trying to find the best terrarium in which to house their pet gecko, I'd better begin by explaining that *The Reptile* emerged out of a new experiment in cost-cutting at Bray studios. It was shot back to back with *Plague of the Zombies*, re-using the same sets, locations, crew and some of the same cast members – notably Jacqueline Pearce and, inevitably, Michael Ripper. Meanwhile *Dracula, Prince of Darkness*, featuring Christopher Lee's first return to the role of the vampire count, was shot alongside *Rasputin the Mad Monk* (both starring Lee opposite Barbara Shelley) on the same model.

The idea was that by pairing productions like this it was possible to create substantial economies through re-use and recycling – making Hammer an inadvertently eco-friendly production company – while avoiding the likelihood of the film-going public noticing the unnatural resemblance between the films by releasing them separated by a couple of months on a double bill with one of the other pair. Thus *Plague of the Zombies* was released as part of a double bill with the long-awaited Dracula sequel, while *The Reptile* went out alongside the rather less enticing Russian melodrama.

As a result, fewer people saw *The Reptile* at the time of its initial release than its demon twin, and it has remained in many fans' minds a kind of poor relation to *Plague of the Zombies.* This inability to view the film on its own terms as a self-contained, and actually rather wonderful piece of work has only been heightened by the enormous changes in technology and viewing habits the passing years have brought. My *Reptile* Blu-ray, for instance, sits right beside my *Plague* one, with about the same degree of separation in terms of shelf space as there was in terms of production schedules back in 1966. Proud fanboy that I am, I'll quite happily admit that I'm not above watching the films in a similarly back to back fashion as they were shot; an approach to viewing which was quite impossible to foresee in 1966 and one which renders the cost-cutting plan quite glaringly obvious.

Back in 1977, for the eager twelve-year-old watching a summer season of BBC2 horror double bills, the gap between screenings was only a couple of weeks, and although I was unaware of the specific production background and the full extent of the similarities, I was certainly conscious of a shared DNA between the two films. As part of the *Dracula, Frankenstein – and Friends!* season, I didn't really have a preference however. If *Plague* had a beheading, and a grisly dream sequence, and zombies, well, *The Reptile* had maybe a bit more atmosphere, and with its gleefully close-upped black crusty bite marks and foaming mouths, was even more satisfyingly gruesome.

So I adored both films equally, and perhaps it was easier to do so since, in memory at least, the broadcast image back then tended towards the murky and suggestive, slightly disguising the fact that the make-up job in *The Reptile* was a bit more obviously artificial and therefore a bit less impressive than the zombie faces in *Plague*. Today's shiny flat-screen Hi-Def world is not so forgiving. In more ways than one, as I'm reminded every time I glance into my shiny flat screen Hi-Def mirror. Fortunately, however, the same ageing process which has superglued some fat old bloke's face over my true boyish good looks has made my eyes strictly Lo-Def, which kindly conceals at least some of the damage.

I still adore both films today, and if pushed I might even express a hairsbreadth preference for the less lauded *Reptile*. There's a subtlety and complexity at work in the ways the themes are approached which rewards repeated viewings and perhaps offers even more to the mature viewer than to the excited adolescent who didn't notice much beyond John Laurie's wonderfully eye-rolling Mad Peter and his foaming-lipped close up demise.

Firstly, to acknowledge the great big snake in the room, like *Plague of the Zombies*, *The Reptile* indulges in an unhealthy dose of the borderline racist 'fear of the foreign' trope which had underscored much of the late Victorian gothic literary revival upon which Hammer drew so heavily for inspiration, tapping at the same time into a whole new set of British 1960s post-Imperial anxieties. Pulling all the strings on behalf of an obscure Indian snake cult, the most overtly sinister character in the film, The Malay – denied even the individual dignity of a name – may seem on the surface to be no more than a straightforwardly racist stereotype playing into all those clichés about the mysterious, unknowable and exotic East.

However, if you accept that with its woman to snake transformation the film's most specific (though unacknowledged) source is Bram Stoker's final, and very odd, novel *The Lair of the White Worm*, the much greater subtlety at work in John Gilling's film becomes immediately apparent. The fear of the foreign, implicit in Stoker's earlier *Dracula* with its atavistic East European invader (a quality it shares with a number of invasion metaphor fin-de-siècle novels, including some by writers such as Conan Doyle and H.G. Wells who, like Stoker, would have regarded themselves as relatively liberal, humane and progressive) has become, in Stoker's final novel, an outright racism which is almost laughably overt to a twenty first century reader. Stoker's portrayal of the African servant Oolanga is so filled with unrecognised bile and bigotry that it becomes self-parodying, an unfortunate stain, even for the time, on what is otherwise a surprisingly gripping if sometimes bizarrely surreal novel.

In contrast, *The Reptile* can at least in part be seen as a sly critique of the arrogant assumption of cultural superiority which underlies all colonialism. The film makes very clear in its expository dialogue that the Malay, and the India he represents, are in fact responding to an initial aggression against "the primitive religions of the East" on the part of Noel Willman's Dr Franklyn. Seeing himself unproblematically as the representative of 'civilisation', Franklyn has made a series of colonial excursions into territory which he has no right to interfere with in order to stamp out beliefs which do not accord with his own. It is just as possible for an audience's sympathies to lie with the calmly powerful superiority of the Malay's retaliation against Western imperialism as it is to see Franklyn as the entirely innocent victim of the evil alien; a point given an added emphasis by the decision to cast an actor of the appropriate ethnicity, Marne Maitland, rather than adopting the more common practice of the time to have prominent roles of this sort played by white actors blacked up.

The emphasis is further strengthened by the way the film raises, and neither confirms nor denies, the possibility that the central character of Franklyn's daughter Anna, with her penchant for saris and sitars, and her conspicuously absent mother, is herself mixed race.

However, it's not only in its treatment of race and colonialism that *The Reptile* repays close attention. If, as I've reflected earlier, *Plague of the Zombies* offers quite an acute examination of class anxieties, *The Reptile* is, perhaps even more interestingly, a film that explores the issue of gender.

For one thing, most obviously but also most unusually, we have a female monster. A single, central monster that is, not the kind of decorative female vampires, subservient to a dominant male big bad, that we tend to see in the Dracula films. Hammer experimented with a not entirely dissimilar premise in what, for me, is a fascinating but flawed misfire, 1964's *The Gorgon*. Despite that film's re-uniting of the original Hammer dream team of Lee, Cushing and director Terence Fisher (for the very last time as it turned out), it rather loses itself in an unresolved uncertainty as to whether it wants to play out as traditional Hammer horror film or as a more restrained fantasy of doomed romance and ends up falling uncomfortably between the two.

*The Reptile* is an altogether more assured, fully-realised attempt at the reversal of the traditional gender roles. Interestingly, *The Reptile's* director, John Gilling, had written the script for the earlier film, and had reportedly been annoyed that the directorial duties had been offered to Fisher rather than to him. Perhaps Gilling saw *The Reptile* as a chance to show what he might have made out of his earlier screenplay.

It's been suggested, and rightly I think, that *The Reptile*, like the Tourneur/Lewton film *Cat People* before it, is in fact just a werewolf movie in disguise. A sympathetic central character periodically and reluctantly transforming into a predatory animal – for Simone Simon's Irena or Jacqueline Pearce's Anna, read Larry Talbot. The premise is essentially the same.

However, this in itself raises the question why not just make a female werewolf movie? Why panthers and snakes instead? While possibly the best known example of the werewolf in literature is female, in Clemence Housman's cod-mediaeval *The Werewolf*, the werewolf movie gives us very few such examples.

There's an interesting parallel with the development of the mummy film, where again the literary original, Bram Stoker's *The Jewel of Seven Stars*, features a female mummy, although you wouldn't know it from the succession of Karloffs, Chaneys, Tom Tylers and Chris Lees that stomp their way through the sub-genre. In fact, it wasn't until Hammer staged a direct adaptation of *Jewel* in the 1972 *Blood From the Mummy's Tomb* that the female mummy finally emerged from the sarcophagus, and even then I think it's fair to say that Hammer's interest by that stage in the company's history lay more in the prurient possibilities arising from the casting of the statuesque Valerie Leon than in any attempt to challenge the culturally dominant gender stereotypes. Imhotep never looked that good in a sheer nightdress.

It seems as though, in the minds of filmmakers and of audiences, certain types of monster, and entire species of the animal kingdom (or queendom) are specifically gendered. Wolves are male monsters, cats and snakes female. I remember Basil Rathbone's Sherlock Holmes – it may have been in *Woman in Green* or perhaps in *Sherlock Holmes and the Spider Woman*, itself a significant title in the current context, being able to deduce that his suspect must be a woman (probably Gale Sondergaard) because, he murmured thoughtfully, 'the murder had a *feline, rather than a canine* quality.' I'm not sure even the Great Detective himself would be able to satisfactorily define the difference, but the meaningless distinction passes unchallenged and unexamined in the dialogue because of the accurate assumption that we all, at some level, know what he means.

Lon Chaney could not have become a panther, any more than Simone Simon could have become a wolf – although some irritatingly pernickety smart-alec will certainly want to quibble by pointing to the 1946 film *She-Wolf of London* and to the fact that our ever more fluid post-millennial sense of gender has begun to allow for interesting exceptions to the rule like the strikingly original and extremely effective 2000 Canadian horror film *Ginger Snaps* or the TV series *Bitten*. Even so, I think the essential point still stands.

Anthropomorphists all, we perceive a sinuous and sensuous quality to cats which we assume to be essentially female, while the overt bare-toothed aggression of the wolf is essentially male. And the snake women of *Lair of the White Worm* and *The Reptile* (and to go a bit more highbrow, of Coleridge's *Christabel* and Keats' *Lamia*) lies undeniably on the former side of that equation, with an interesting touch of the phallic to further muddy the waters.

It's an association that runs back at least to the dubious implications of the myth of Eve and the serpent, the Fall stemming from both an external male tempter and from a woman's apparently greater susceptibility to temptation. The snake is both out there in the Garden and within Eve, both male and female. Certainly, as someone who has always felt that, like Prometheus before her, Eve did the right thing in defying the gods and chomping down on that juicy apple, thereby bequeathing us knowledge rather than ignorance and freedom rather than subservience, I find Jacqueline Pearce's snaky turn as Anna Franklyn to be the most engaging and empathetic element of the film.

I think the film's exploration of gender runs at an even deeper level than simply offering us a female monster with some heavy symbolism attached, however. It is the relationship between Franklyn and Anna that is the heart of the film, and it is a complex and troubling one.

Initially we are introduced to an icily patrician Noel Willman as Franklyn who seems determined to assert an unsettling, stern and domineering control over his recalcitrant daughter Anna. Willman's performance is consistently excellent – the actor had demonstrated a similarly cold and sinister quality in Hammer's earlier *Kiss of the Vampire*. The disturbing quality of Willman's otherwise conventionally Victorian patriarchal authority becomes clear when we meet the 'rebellious' daughter herself.

Anna is in fact beautiful, soft-spoken, mild, gentle and kind – almost the only member of the little community to offer any sort of warmth or welcome to Harry and Valerie Spalding, the young couple (played by Ray Barrett and Jennifer Daniel, who had also played a pivotal role in *Kiss of the Vampire* alongside Willman) who have inherited a cottage after the mysterious death of Spalding's elder brother. She is also apparently devoted to her domineering father; clearly mortified by the sinister impression he has previously made on Jennifer Daniel's Valerie, she insists plaintively that 'he's a very *good* man' and when he arrives at the Spalding's cottage to sternly order her home she is as meek and submissive as any patriarch could wish, barely able to make eye contact while pleading that her father might allow the couple to dine with them that evening. When the Spaldings finally arrive at the Franklyn house, Anna remains upstairs while they eat with her father, Franklyn explaining casually that 'she is being punished', and is only allowed to join them after dinner when Franklyn consents.

The overtly stated narrative reveals that Franklyn's apparently brutal parenting regime in fact comes from concern and love. Knowing of her snaky transformations only too well, and tormented by the secret they are harbouring, he is merely trying to protect the daughter he loves – as well as her potential victims. The preferred reading, in other words, is that Franklyn becomes a warmer, more human and more sympathetic figure as the film goes on. Sub-textually, however, the symbolism and the visuals, in two scenes in particular, suggest something much darker and more disturbing at work, and for me at least I find Willmann's character increasingly sinister rather than increasingly sympathetic.

The first comes in the scene immediately after the dinner, when Anna is finally released from her punishment and runs girlishly and delightedly downstairs. Despite the fact that she is clearly a grown woman, there is something extraordinarily child-like about Pearce's performance here, which offers a subtle hint at a peculiarly twisted quality to the relationship her father has created with her. This strangely child-like quality returns, bizarrely but affectingly, at the film's climax, in which the fully reptile Anna plaintively intones 'Cold..I'm cold'. The sub-text becomes quite overt, however, in the moments that immediately follow her belated arrival at the dinner party.

Franklyn invites Anna to entertain their guests with a performance on the sitar. She quickly shows herself to be a virtuoso, in the days just before George Harrison and Ravi Shankar rendered the instrument familiar rather than outlandish to the Western audience. Her skill, along with the striking sari she is wearing, positions Anna as a direct, exotic contrast to Daniels' conventionally English Valerie, who has earlier pointedly observed that she has 'never eaten curry.'

The performance begins calmly enough, but as the speed and intensity of Anna's playing increases, Gilling's skilled point counter point cutting economically establishes a strikingly eroticised power struggle unfolding between father and daughter. Their eyes lock as Anna plays, and while Willmann's expressions shift from a smugly complacent dominance, underlined by his self-satisfied puffs at a phallically inclined cigar (this time it actually *is*, Sigmund!) to an almost hypnotic enchantment to horrified outrage, Pearce lends each successive close up an increasing degree of confidence, defiance and seductiveness, until Franklyn's turmoil explodes into impotent rage and violence as he smashes the sitar on the fireplace.

One can read the scene as working at the level of post-imperial critique. Cutaway shots are used to connect Anna's increasing power to the influence of the onlooking Malay, accompanied by some eerie non-diegetic Indian music underscoring the diegetic sitar, utilising the signifiers of the colonised culture in defiance of the colonial power represented by Franklin, until the scene explodes into reactionary and violent but ineffective repression.

More powerfully and more troublingly however, I think it's impossible not to register the sexual tension which is the heart of the scene's powerful and disturbing tone. The intensity of their mutual gaze, Franklyn's increasing loss of control cut against the increasingly knowing and overtly sexual quality Pearce injects into her eyes, all speak to a relationship that exists beyond the bounds of parent and child. Whether or not an actually incestuous relationship is being implied, there seems little room for doubt that Franklyn's rage reflects at the very least the frustration he feels over his own illicit desire for his daughter, or quite possibly the self-disgust turned outward of an actual abuser. In this sense, it is certainly Franklyn, rather than his 'half-woman half-snake' daughter who is the film's monster.

The dark sub-text becomes, if anything, even more disturbing in the later scene in which Franklyn enters his daughter's bedroom and approaches her bed only to find that she has shed her skin, which, rather bizarrely, retains the shape and form of her body inside her nightdress. Appalled, Franklyn proceeds to beat and flail at the outline of his daughter's body with his walking stick, the ugly symbolism of which hardly needs deeper examination.

Anna's sole point of human contact and sympathy in the midst of all this lies in the tentative friendship she seeks with the only other female character in the film, Jennifer Daniel's Valerie Spalding. Jacqueline Pearce, a gifted actress who was terrific in her brief appearance in *Plague of the Zombies* and is even better here, lends an exceptional pathos to these moments, giving Anna a haunted, tragic quality which the practical, conventional Valerie instinctively recognises and responds to without really understanding. The lost, mysterious quality Valerie senses in Anna draws her sympathy, but also underlines the ultimately unbridgeable gulf between them.

The contrast in their characters is a trope which echoes through the long and controversial history of the horror film's relationship with women. It seems to me that there are essentially two types of female star in the classic horror film. One is characterised by a specific, constructed kind of 'innocence'. Although there is a sliding scale from 'helpless' at one end to 'plucky and resourceful' at the other, with *The Reptile's* Valerie Spalding embodying the latter end of the spectrum, all bustling, practical common sense, calmly clearing up after the break-in at the cottage and capably cutting the reptile's poison from her husband's neck after he has been bitten, the type is ultimately defined by being positioned in the narrative as bait, as victim, as beauty to the beast.

Fay Wray first and best embodied this form of scream queen in an extraordinary run of films in just a couple of years in the early thirties – *Dr X*, *The Most Dangerous Game*, *Mystery of the Wax Museum*, *The Vampire Bat* and, of course, *King Kong*. A skilled, convincing actress, and strikingly beautiful without seeming to convey an aura of constructed 'glamour', Wray's girl next door persona, alongside her talent, rooted the most unbelievable of situations in sincerity and reality.

I remember vividly the effect a couple of stills from the end of *Wax Museum* had on me as a twelve or thirteen-year-old – Lionel Atwill leering over a supine Fay Wray, wrapped in a sheet, her wrists strapped to a table and her naked shoulders exposed. Those were more innocent times. Or times requiring greater exercise of the imagination, at any rate.

Fay Wray's mantle was passed to Evelyn Ankers, who fulfilled essentially the same role for 1940s audiences in films like *The Wolf Man*, *Ghost of Frankenstein*, *Son of Dracula*, and *Captive Wild Woman*.

In her seminal critical work *Men, Women and Chainsaws*, the theorist Carol Clover brilliantly dissects the slasher movie and posits the figure of 'the final girl' who invites audience identification, and is best exemplified by Jamie Lee Curtis in *Halloween*. I'd argue that the final girl has her origins in Wray and Ankers and the other scream goddesses of the '30s and '40s, but in a less than progressive twist the prerequisite of survival for the horror heroine by the '80s was a kind of androgynous, asexual quality that differentiated her from the pot-smoking promiscuous slasher fodder around her. It's possible to see a different, and I think a healthier, concept of 'innocent' 40 years before; sexlessness was not a quality required of Fay or Evelyn to justify their survival.

The second female trope might be defined as the 'exotic'. Usually, though not always, dark-haired and 'foreign' in appearance; usually, though not always, sexually seductive, combining that siren quality with a sense of mystery, of the enigmatic; and usually, but not always, posing some kind of direct or indirect threat to the forces of 'normality' within the narrative, the trope can be seen as a variant, or perhaps even a precursor to the femme fatale of post-war noir.

Many of the characteristics of the exotic female are shared in the horror film with the figure of the monster – and in some instances the role is combined. Think of Gloria Holden as Marya Zaleska in *Dracula's Daughter*, Simone Simon in *Cat People*, Barbara Steele in almost anything or for me most powerfully of all, Jacqueline Pearce in *The Reptile*.

At other times, the exotic woman is not herself the monster, but in some kind of thrall to a dominant, and monstrous male figure – again, in her less scaly moments, Pearce embodies this in *The Reptile*.

It is a typical narrative device to use the 'exotic female' trope in conjunction with and in contrast to the 'innocent female' trope – Simone

Simon against Jane Randolph in *Cat People*, Gloria Holden against Marguerite Churchill in *Dracula's Daughter*.

Perhaps most interestingly of all, picking up on a single throwaway line from Stoker's novel, in which Dracula's soon-to-be first victim Lucy expresses the shocking wish to be married to more than one of her suitors, much to the consternation of the rather more primly middle class Mina, some responses to *Dracula* – the Coppola movie for instance – have positioned an exotic, sexualised Lucy in contrast to staid Mina in exactly this way. Without insisting on such an initial reading, what seems to me undeniably true is that Dracula's influence on Victorian womanhood is precisely to transform them from the construction 'innocent' into the construction 'exotic.'

At times the exotic character is sympathetic, at others sinister, and frequently a combination of the two, but in whatever context the defining characteristic is a carefully constructed sense of otherness. In her highly influential essay 'Visual Pleasure and The Narrative Cinema' film theorist Laura Mulvey propounded the idea of the 'male gaze' – the theory suggests that in conventional narrative cinema the camera, and therefore the viewer, is specifically gendered. Thus the male gaze. Films are a place where men do things and women are looked at.

Within the horror film, this intrinsic sense of the exotic woman as *other*, as an enigmatic, unknowable mystery, drawing the audience to investigate, is the clearest exemplification of Mulvey's point one could ever wish for. Anna Franklyn is a mystery for us to look at from the outside, to be entranced and intrigued by, but not to identify with.

I like to think of myself as a fairly thoroughly reconstructed male. I'm not consciously sexist in either thought or action and I at least try to be aware of the sexism in the world around me, and to challenge it where I can. Perhaps just as importantly, I don't expect a medal or anyone's gratitude for what doesn't amount to more than saying I try to be a decent human being rather than a knob. Feminism is just another word for fairness, and I find it baffling that many apparently intelligent people I know, of whatever gender, seem to regard the term as a dirty word. I am the father of daughters, and spend a fair bit of my time trying to explain to my eldest that it's fine that she's much more interested in football and superheroes and fighting aliens than she is in pretty shoes and princesses, and decrying an advertising industry that seems to need to market even something so beautifully innocent of gender as Lego into pre-defined pink or blue boy or girl packages. After all, I matured during the right-on culture of the 1980s when it was almost impossible to get an erection without worrying that you were oppressing somebody.

And so of course it's sexist nonsense to posit women as dark, mysterious, and 'other'; a stereotype just as demeaning as 'the mysterious

Orient' or 'darkest Africa' in the kind of white colonial discourse with which it shares a more than borderline racism, given the tendency of casting directors to assign the role to actresses whose look is redolent of a typical WASP's idea of 'foreign' – dark-haired, dark-eyed, dusky maidens.

Women can only be seen as 'mysterious' because, as I myself am in the process of demonstrating here, men *just never shut the fuck up about themselves*, whereas women, even when they have been granted the luxury of speaking, have also had to contend with the simple fact that no-one was listening to them. That's why they're so sodding mysterious. Of course, of course, it's pernicious, sexist nonsense. And yet, and yet…

And yet, for all that, something in that imagery, something in that exotic 'other' calls to something deep within me. It echoes powerfully through the work of my favourite filmmaker, David Lynch, for instance. And if you had asked me to name my favourite actress back in the 1970s or early eighties I would have replied without a moment's hesitation "Caroline Munro," an actress whose extraordinary beauty might have been specifically drawn up by a committee of perverts to fulfil their design requirements for the exotic woman.

Never quite a household name, she was nonetheless one of the most recognisable stars of the time, having first come to prominence as the face, and body, of Lambs Navy Rum, adorning billboards across the country for a decade in carefully constructed 007 style exotic poses in exotic locations. Spotted on one of these by Hammer's chief executive, James Carreras, she was placed under contract and appeared in eye-catching roles for the company in *Dracula AD 1972* and the criminally underrated *Captain Kronos Vampire Hunter,* confirming her iconic status in the genre with brief, but crucial appearances as Vincent Price's dead wife in the two *Dr Phibes* films, and going on to leading roles in more family friendly fantasy films like *At the Earth's Core* and Ray Harryhausen's *The Golden Voyage of Sinbad,* before finally confirming her obvious status as Bond-girl-in-waiting in *The Spy Who Loved Me.*

Although a capable actress, and actually an extremely good one at times – her all-too-brief performance is the one moment of real sincerity and conviction in the otherwise ill-judged *Dracula AD 1972,* and when given a little more to do she's terrific in the unappreciated *Kronos* – even her greatest admirers would admit she was never likely to trouble the Academy. My adolescent fan-worship was to do with her look, rather than her acting abilities, and it was crucially centred around a specific publicity shot from her Hammer days. It's a full body shot, in costume (and it's quite a costume) from the Dracula film – but it wasn't just the black bikini or even the thigh length PVC boots which fascinated me. It was her eyes. She was gazing into the camera, and there was something in her eyes which was at once defiant and seductive, overt and yet self-contained,

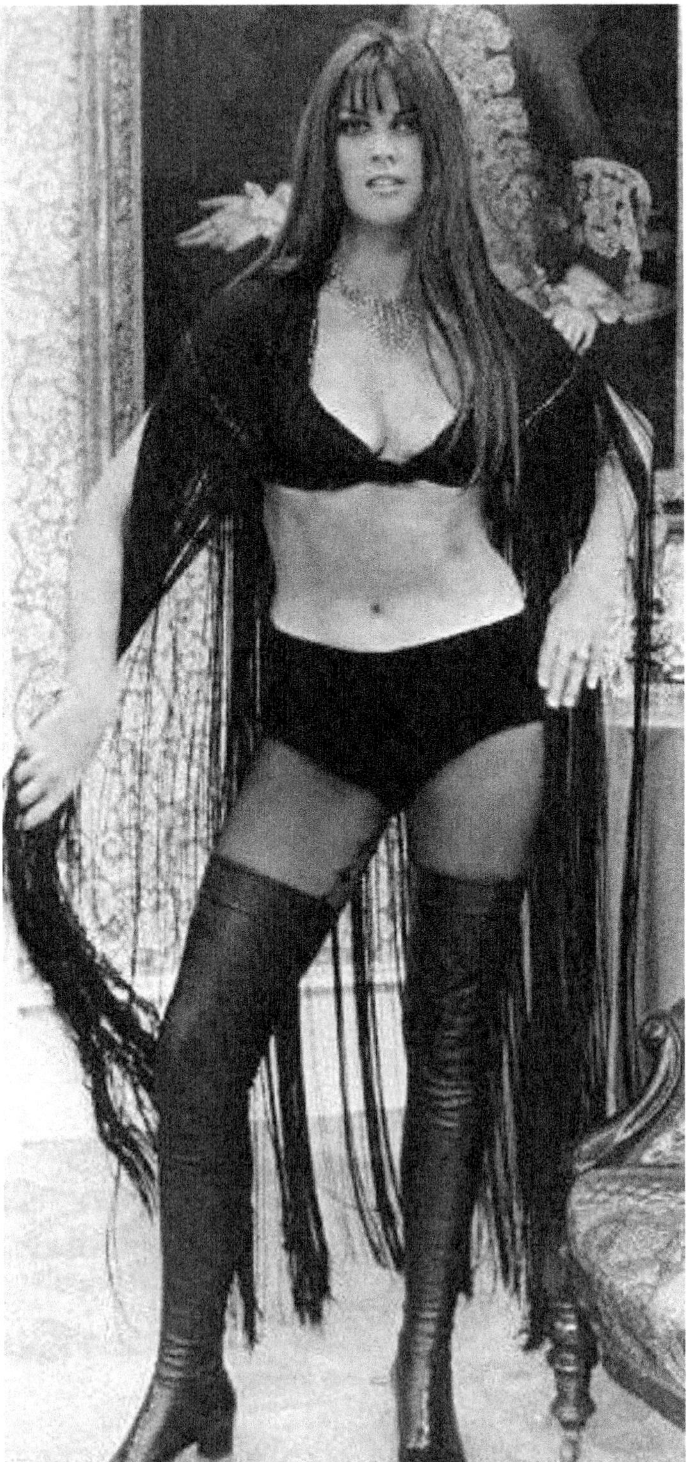

empowered and enigmatic, knowingly sexual and yet distant and faraway. They were *dreaming* eyes, and they seemed to suggest to my hormone engulfed teenage self something of the whole yearning, exotic, unknowable mystery of it all.

Easily dismissed, of course, as the immature daydreaming of a naïve adolescent who never spoke to actual female people. Except that a year or two back, as a man in his early fifties, I ordered a DVD from Caroline Munro's own website. When it came, rather than being just an anonymous online order, it was accompanied by a personally written card, which used my name and was signed with love from Caroline Munro.

I almost fainted.

The impact she had on me as that naïve adolescent runs somewhere deep down inside me, even now. The love of 'the exotic', however much the critical and analytical and grown up part of my head knows it to be an illusion, and perhaps a pernicious one, still speaks to me, even today.

To illustrate my point, I'd like to conduct a little thought experiment around the casting of Jodie Whitaker as the new Doctor Who. I wonder what it says about me that I would not have had even a nanosecond's difficulty in accepting a black Doctor, but I know, buried deep deep down in that tiny part of my psyche which lies beyond received opinion and is just pure, uncensored me, feeling what I *actually* feel rather than what I know I *ought* to feel, my first reaction to the revelation that a female Doctor had been cast was the briefest of flickers of disappointment. And just to be clear, this is not to say that my rational self could or would object, and in conversation I immediately and sincerely advocated the idea as not just perfectly acceptable but as a positive and exciting move. I quickly talked myself into seeing what a good and interesting idea it was – but the point is that I'd had, however briefly, to actually do that talking to myself first.

It had been in the air for so long that I'd mentally rehearsed my reaction for some time. In those first moments when I imagined Zoe Ball announcing in a charmingly shambolic live show that 'the next Doctor is … Olivia Colman…' (oddly it was always Olivia Colman I pictured, meaning I was precognitively tuned in to the wrong star of *Broadchurch)* my first reaction, a couple of split-seconds before reminding myself what an exceptionally gifted actor and all-round wonderful human being she was and what a perfect ambassador for this silly old show I love so much she would be – just before all that, I'm ashamed to admit, I knew I'd feel that momentary sense of loss and disappointment, and in fact when the equally brilliant and equally talented Jodie pulled back that black hood in a brief promo at the end of the Wimbledon final it was exactly as I'd imagined. On the other hand, my only and immediate reaction as Zoe paused dramatically before shouting 'the next Doctor is…Idris Elba…or Shaun Parkes..or Adrian Lester…or Chiwetel Ejifor..' would have been a whoop of unalloyed delight.

What does this suggest to me? Using myself as a test case, the idea that, exposed to the infallible Occam's razor that is *Doctor Who,* the sense of racial difference as somehow 'other' does not exist. In other words, it's entirely a cultural construct, socially created. No-one is born racist, as the cliché goes, they're made that way. On the other hand, it seems the idea of women as intrinsically 'other' seems still to lurk somewhere down deep in my DNA, stubbornly refusing to be eradicated by education or conviction. I would genuinely love this not to be true, but it is. And if it's true of me, I have to suspect it's true of other men too. Perhaps it's a biological imperative, though that sounds like a bit of a cop-out and an abdication of responsibility to me.

I'd hasten to add that this is not in itself a problem. It's perfectly possible to ignore that reptilian voice from the back of your head, and to view and treat people kindly and with a bit of respect no matter what gender they, or you, are. To say there's a sense of difference between genders that I can't quite eradicate doesn't mean I therefore have to act like a dickhead in the real world, and it doesn't excuse anybody else who does.

But what I think it does do, somehow, is to account for the response I can't help but feel to Caroline Munro in *Kronos,* or Jacqueline Pierce in *The Reptile,* or Simone Simon in *Cat People,* or Laura 'filled with secrets' Palmer or Audrey 'cherry stalk' Horne, rather than 'girl next door' Donna, in *Twin Peaks.* Or perhaps most potently of all, since the film itself is a conscious exploration and expose of exactly this form of male desire, my response to the dream-like, mysterious – and entirely illusory – Madeline, rather than the clever, common-sense, and knowable Midge in Hitchcock's *Vertigo.* Woman as exotic, mysterious, *other,* speaks directly to that tiny little unreconstructed part of myself that refuses to quite go away.

Given all that, perhaps the trope of the exotic woman will be around for a while to come, and maybe it doesn't matter much after all, so long as we're also developing and creating better alternatives. We just need more female heroes. As one shining example, I've already referenced my love of Buffy many times. As another, if you consider Jonathan Demme's *Silence of the Lambs* a horror film – and if you do then it's by far the best horror film of the last thirty years – then what makes it special for me is not Anthony Hopkins' headline-grabbing performance as Lecter, but the fact that at its heart, and still all too unusually, it is a *female* epic narrative. Brilliantly played by Jodie Foster, the film is Clarice Starling's quest to rescue the princess and destroy the ogre. Starling is the perfect modern hero, knocking David Manners into a cocked hat (though that's damning with faint praise) and more than fit to stand shoulder to shoulder with Cushing's Van Helsing. Perhaps we just need more Jodies being Clarice or the Doctor to prove that heroism is not a gender specific concept.

I would have concluded there, but for the news that the incomparably talented Jacqueline Pearce, star of *Plague of the Zombies, The Reptile* and *Blake's Seven,* died at the age of 74 during the time I was writing this. She was able to offer her roles for Hammer a rare degree of nuance and subtlety – not qualities one automatically associates with Hammer horror – and I'd argue she was among the most talented actors ever to grace the genre. Thanks to the immortality celluloid confers, I can joyfully continue to use the present tense when I say she is the true beating heart of both *Plague of the Zombies* and *The Reptile*, and she is the reason the latter film offers a real, raw, wounded humanity below the surface of its silly little monster movie trappings.

But my final tribute is to point out that like many of my generation, I will often find my mind wandering in an idle moment - a moment at the edge of sleep, a daydream or an aimless drift in a chain of thought - and quite unexpectedly but not infrequently, an unbidden and utterly indelible recollection of a strikingly beautiful woman in white with an ice cold heart, a ruthless smile and a knowing glint in her eyes will return to me and the sudden unsought recollection of Jacqueline Pearce as Supreme Commander Servalan brings a nostalgic, and more than a little naughty, gleam into my own eye. Thank you Jacqueline. God speed.

# DOUBLE BILL TEN

## Saturday September 3rd 1977

SON OF DRACULA            21.55 – 23.10

THE EVIL OF FRANKENSTEIN     23.45 – 01.10

---

### 9.55 Dracula, Frankenstein and Friends!

A season of *Midnight Movie* double bills of fantasy and horror.

**Son of Dracula**
starring **Lon Chaney**
with **Robert Paige**
**Louise Allbritton, Evelyn Ankers**
Temporarily forsaking Transylvania, a mysterious and sinister Count arrives in America (with luggage labelled ALUCARD). Lon Chaney, taking time off from playing the Wolf Man is soon causing consternation in the New World by turning into a bat at night, and disappearing by day . . .

Count Dracula............LON CHANEY
Frank Stanley..........ROBERT PAIGE
Katherine Caldwell
               LOUISE ALLBRITTON
Claire Caldwell......EVELYN ANKERS
Doctor Brewster......FRANK CRAVEN
Prof Lazlo.......J. EDWARD BROMBERG
Judge Simmons....SAMUEL S. HINDS
Madame Zimba
         ADELINE DE WALT REYNOLDS
Sheriff Dawes....PATRICK MORIARTY
Sarah......................ETTA McDANIEL

Director ROBERT SIODMAK
(Black and white). Films: page 21

### 11.10 News on 2
Weather

### 11.15 Cricket
*The Gillette Cup Final* from Lord's
PETER WEST introduces highlights of cricket's 'Cup Final'.
Commentators RICHIE BENAUD
JIM LAKER, GEOFFREY BOYCOTT
Producer DAVID KENNING

### 11.45-1.10 am Evil of Frankenstein
starring
**Peter Cushing**
In Hammer's excursion into the Frankenstein legend, the Baron discovers his monster of many years ago perfectly preserved in ice – and enlists the help of hypnotist 'The Great Zoltan' to restore the creature's brain to activity.

Baron Frankenstein.PETER CUSHING
Zoltan...............PETER WOODTHORPE
Hans.....................SANDOR ELES
The Creature.........KIWI KINGSTON
Chief of Police......DUNCAN LAMONT
Beggar girl................KATY WILD
Burgomaster.......DAVID HUTCHESON
Burgomaster's wife.CARON GARDNER
Body-snatcher............TONY ARPINO
Hypnotised man..TIMOTHY BATESON

Director FREDDIE FRANCIS. Films: page 21

# 20. PUT IT OUT! PUT IT OUT I TELL 'YA!

## Son of Dracula (1943, Universal, Robert Siodmak)

*'I like old houses, and I like your countryside and the swampland. My land is dry and desolate. The soil is red with the blood of a hundred races. There is no life left there. Here you have a young and vital race.'*
**Count Dracula (Lon Chaney)**

I've never been quite sure whether I think *Son of Dracula* is a very good film disguised as a bad one, or the other way around. It's certainly a rather curious mixture of the two.

There are elements of the film which rank as some of the very best things Universal accomplished in any of their 1940s monster movies. The decision to transplant Dracula to the American Deep South is inspired, decades before Anne Rice's Lestat or Charlaine Harris's Sookie Stackhouse demonstrated the Southern Gothic possibilities inherent in just such a scenario.

Director Robert Siodmak, brother of writer Curt, utilises the setting brilliantly, unleashing some superbly atmospheric lighting and demonstrating many of the expressionistic touches which were shortly to make him among the finest of all exponents of film noir. The night time run through the Everglades undertaken by Frank Stanley, the film's broken hero, is every bit as evocative as the similar and much better known scenes in the Val Lewton movies at RKO, or Dana Andrews' midnight run through the woods in Jacques Tourneur's best post-Lewton film *Night of the Demon*.

It's not only the film's use of setting which distinguishes it however. By embracing rather than glossing over the darkness at the heart of the sub-text, Curt Siodmak's original story once again finds something powerful and novel within the mythology with which he is working, just as he had earlier in the 'suicide as narrative drive' motif of *Frankenstein Meets the Wolf Man*.

In this instance Louise Allbritton's Katherine Caldwell, all too morbidly aware of the fleeting transience of human life, consciously embraces and seeks out immortality as one of the undead, and it is her desire which powers the narrative engine of the film.

Eric Taylor's script (sibling rivalry seems to have resulted in director Robert bringing in a different writer to polish his brother's story) offers the central female character a range of complex and quite sympathetic motives. In this regard, *Son of Dracula* belies its apparent status as a thoughtless potboiler sequel. It is actually a rather sombre, pessimistic, emotionally mature work, and the bleak philosophy at the film's heart contributes at least as much as the moody visual style to the argument that it can be seen more as an early example of film noir than as a 40s monster movie. In its grown-up tone, *Son of Dracula* feels closer to the output of Lewton's unit at RKO than to much of the horror product coming out of Universal at the time.

Also weighing in heavily on the plus side of the scale are some of the best special photographic effects achieved in any of the Universal horror films, supervised by John P Fulton who had made such an eye-catching job of *The Invisible Man* and *Bride of Frankenstein* in the 30s and who would go on to do some exceptional work with Hitchcock, notably on *Vertigo*. For me the sequence in which Dracula's coffin rises to the surface of the swamp from the murky depths below, billowing otherworldly mist which coalesces into the imposing figure of the Count himself, who then silently rides the coffin to the bank like an eerie gondolier, is perhaps the best visual introduction of Dracula in all of cinema.

Or rather it would be, if it were actually our introduction to the character. But it isn't, because, in an example of the occasionally poor judgement which flaws much of the film, Dracula has already been introduced to the audience through the rather less visually stylish device of knocking on a door and giving a grumpy look to the servant who answers it. This symptomatic mishandling of the vampire Count himself is the film's central failing.

There's a more than a little cringe-inducing lack of trust in the audience – not once but twice characters are shown laboriously spelling out Dracula's feeble reversed anagrammatic alias 'Count Alucard', when truth be told even the more intellectually challenged members of the audience for a film called *Son of Dracula* would probably have been able to crack this most abstruse of cryptograms without the need to borrow the Enigma machine for too long. Though in fairness 'Alucard' is all but impenetrable compared to 'Dr A. Kula' (geddit?), as the character was called in the script for Universal's unmade project *Wolf Man vs Dracula*.

A similarly odd quality marks the film's approach to the character's chronology. We're clearly told that the vampire's reign of terror was previously brought to an end in the nineteenth century, thus erasing the timeline of Lugosi's *Dracula* and its sequel, *Dracula's Daughter*, both of which had a carefully established contemporary 1930s setting, and instead restoring continuity with Stoker's original novel which, even more bizarrely, one of the characters is shown reading in an effort to gather further clues about how to combat the Transylvanian bloodsucker.

More damaging than these minor irritants however, is the decision to make Dracula's role in the narrative essentially that of a film noir patsy, not really much more than a gullible dupe in the machinations of Louise Allbritton's femme fatale to grab a slice of vampiric immortality for herself and her fiancé, Frank Stanley. Dracula here is pretty much Walter Neff in a cloak.

And, to cap it all, there's Chaney.

It's been persuasively argued that Chaney's Dracula represents a kind of missing link between the bizarre, ethereally unsettling and alien qualities of Lugosi and the entirely corporeal, physical ferocity of Christopher Lee.

Lee's Dracula is an imposing presence, but he's essentially human, rather than supernatural, existing in a solid, flesh and blood world, and he's frightening largely because of the fairly clear sense of physical threat he embodies. Dracula, in the hands of Lee, scriptwriter Jimmy Sangster and director Terence Fisher, is scary mainly because he could beat you up.

It was a deliberate strategy by Hammer to humanise and de-mythologise the vampire – Lee's first introduction in the brilliant 1958 film is almost a mission statement – the dark silhouette at the top of the stairs, accompanied by James Bernard's famous three-note fanfare (composed to echo the syllables in the name – DRA-CU-LA) seems to suggest a stereotypical excess which is immediately defused by Lee's brisk, earthly and unremarkable walk down the stairs, and the crisp unaccented normality of his urbane dialogue.

Later we're told vampires can't become bats or wolves, Van Helsing describing the belief, with just a hint of academic disdain, as 'a common fallacy'. Hammer's whole agenda was to humanise the myth, to strip away some of the more overtly ethereal, supernatural trappings, almost in effect (so profound was the actor's impact in the role} to *deLugosi* Dracula.

All this is undeniably powerful, giving the fantastical elements of the story a grounding in the solid and the concrete. It's a very effective strategy, and one which has met with considerable critical approval ever since David Pirie's landmark study *A Heritage of Horror*. Pirie and the others who followed him pointed to the heightened, outlandish grotesquerie of the Lugosi version as a terrible flaw, effectively removing the threat of the vampire Count due to the fact he would be incapable of walking down the street without drawing sniggering attention to himself, and citing this as the source of their preference for the much more convincing threat of Lee and Hammer.

For me though, the power of Lugosi lies precisely in his remote, inhuman *otherness*. Even on a contemporary street, surrounded by cars, Lugosi is a creature from another plane. It's the frisson of the ghostly – the sense that the veil has been briefly lifted and we are led to shudder at the complexity, the strangeness, the fearful mystery at the heart of it all. The essential weirdness of existence is momentarily revealed. Lugosi's Dracula peers through the screen at us from another dimension. There's an almost Lovecraftian quality to the performance, an awe born of a sense of profound strangeness.

Lee's Dracula is intimidating, Lugosi's is truly uncanny, and Chaney in *Son of Dracula* straddles the mid-point between the extremes. In this specific regard I'd want to associate him with Francis Lederer's less well-known performance in the interesting but largely forgotten and almost entirely Hammer-overshadowed 1958 film *The Return of Dracula*.

None of which alters the fundamental fact that Chaney is horribly, hideously miscast. Both physiologically and vocally he is just about the worst equipped actor ever to broach the role of the vampire count. I've seen Chaney's Dracula, complete with dapper little pencil moustache, described unkindly (but accurately enough to make me laugh out loud) as Ronald Colman's fat brother. His bulky frame, jowly features and good ole boy demeanour make him about as far removed as it is possible to imagine an actor being from anyone's conception of the King of the Undead.

This doesn't make Chaney a terrible actor as one or two very unfair online reviews describe him. I've spoken elsewhere of how much I admire Chaney's performance as Lawrence Talbot. It's hardly the actor's fault that Universal felt it more important to have their biggest horror star complete their full roster of monsters – having already ticked off the Frankenstein monster, the Mummy and the Wolf Man – than to get the actor best suited to the role of Dracula. Ironically, if any further proof of who that actor was were needed (it wasn't), Lugosi spent some of the same year providing it at Columbia playing the lead in a Dracula sequel in all but name called *Return of the Vampire*. In almost every individual aspect, *Son of Dracula* is the more impressive. Script, direction, cinematography, atmosphere; in fact, the sole aspect of *Return of the Vampire* which is superior to *Son of Dracula* is having Lugosi rather than Chaney at its centre. But it's enough. So important is the power and charisma of the lead actor that *Return of the Vampire* is much the more rewarding and enjoyable watch, which, for all the official Universal version's strengths, makes it the better film.

None of that can really be placed at Chaney's door. He didn't cast himself, after all, and he makes the best fist he can of it, offering a bit of physical presence and the occasional steely glare, alongside a greater degree of formality than usually to be found in his otherwise all-American vocal range, but even so the performance is more than a little uncomfortable to watch.

It reminds me of nothing more than a teenager up for a job interview in a suit he's borrowed from his dad. However hard he tries, it just doesn't fit. Which is of course a more than a little ironic metaphor, given that had Chaney's famous father not succumbed to throat cancer in 1930 he, rather than Lugosi, would almost certainly have been Universal's first choice to have played Dracula in Tod Browning's original 1931 film. Viewed in this light, watching Creighton Tull Chaney (as he was christened, only reluctantly agreeing to become Lon Jr. at the studio's insistence, with even the Junior being dropped after *Ghost of Frankenstein*, again at the studio's behest, to simply rechristen him with his father's name) attempting to directly fill the shoes of the father with whom he shared an awkward, distant relationship and whose shadow he spent much of his life trying to escape from, only to fail more completely than he did in any other film in which he appeared, becomes oddly affecting.

All this generates a strong sense of fellow feeling in me. After all, don't most of us labour for much of the time with a sense of having been somehow miscast in our own lives?

Oh, not today's brand of sickeningly smug strivers and achievers of course, no, not them. Given half a chance – and my advice is never give them that half-chance; if they look like speaking, punch them hard in the face and run away – these goal-oriented, solution-focused, outside-the-box blue-sky-thinkers and self-proclaimed succeeders tend to trot out a clichéd mantra along the lines of 'I don't do regrets. I look forwards, not backwards. Failure's not in my vocabulary. I'm a dickhead' (no, sorry, that last bit is subtext, isn't it?).

Whenever I hear that kind of nonsense I always find myself looking at the speaker slightly aghast, feeling a bit like the last survivor in *Invasion of the Body Snatchers,* because if there's one thing in this life of which I'm certain it's that anyone who 'doesn't do regrets' is no member of the human race. They're monsters, with their bright and shiny plastic faces and their cold dead eyes, polluting our spirits and our souls, spreading the last and nastiest con of them all – that success is compulsory, that failure is not an option, and that we're now all supposed to feel guilty about feeling guilty, to be ashamed of our own sense of shame. Their bright shining lie must be fought, I tell you.

No, it's the rest of us I'm thinking of – people who come from a little place I like to call the planet Earth. United in crapness, we, the inadequate masses who struggle to live up to any of the roles our apparently randomly cast lives throw at us. In our jobs, in our relationships, in our families – don't we spend most of our time struggling with that inner voice whispering reminders of our own fundamental 'not up to the taskness?'

As a spotty adolescent happily losing myself in BBC2 horror double bills my idealised dream self may have been Lugosi's Dracula, but my actual self was a lot closer to Chaney's poorly cast attempt at a role that was just a bit beyond him.

There's some old photographs and even some grainy super 8 footage of me at about 15 or 16 as an usher at my sister's wedding, my specially bought old-man style three piece suit hanging uncomfortably off my hunched shoulders and my awkwardness and insecurity almost painfully evident. I look weighed down, somehow almost folded in on myself. Chaney copes much better than me with the burden of his role, but there's something more than a little hangdog about his performance which suggests he'd rather be doing just about anything than this. It's a quality that allows me to feel a real sense of kinship beneath the ill-fitting waistcoat.

I've been a – by most standards – reasonably successful high school teacher for something like thirty years. I'm not sure there's been a single working day in all that time that's gone by without me feeling somehow misplaced, or as though there's been some kind of wrong turn somewhere and an actor better suited to the part than me should have been cast instead. I've never quite been able to shake off the sense that someday I'm finally going to be found out, that someone will eventually recognise me for the talentless faker I truly am.

And it's not only at work. *'Someone's willing to sleep with me??!'* murmurs my inner self incredulously, or later *'You mean I'm still married??! She hasn't realised who I am and filed for divorce yet? How the bloody hell am I getting away with that?'* And then, a couple of years later still, *'I'm someone's Dad???!!! You cannot be serious. Surely I'm meant to be playing the part of the kid, aren't I?'*

Jung writes about what he calls individuation, the process by which we gradually integrate the different and contrary elements of our psyche to attain a kind of unity and psychic wholeness – the goal being to achieve a fully developed and complete *Self*. Looking back on the boy I once was, I think I could make a fairly convincing argument that in Jungian terms my identification with Lugosi's powerful, charismatic and irredeemable Dracula was the beginnings of an effort to reconcile myself with the shadow archetype, the dark self that stands in contrast to the conscious personality.

But Chaney's less impressive attempt at the role stands as a reminder of just how far from a sense of completeness, or wholeness, I still am. Once upon a time, the twelve-year-old me lapping up *Dracula Frankenstein – and Friends!* thought it was so simple. I was anxious and inadequate because I was a kid, and when I grew up I wouldn't be anymore. I'd be confident and complete instead.

It turns out, however, I'm still too Jung at heart (see what I did there?). In fact, age doesn't help much at all. Despite the grey hairs and the middle-age spread, and despite the fact that I can fake a bit of self-confidence a little more effectively than I could as the adolescent who first saw *Son of Dracula* in 1977, in my heart of hearts I still feel like a small boy in a grownups world most of the time. Like Lon Chaney in a Dracula cape.

The only reassuring thing is I've come to suspect that so does everyone else.

# 21. THEY ALWAYS DESTROY EVERYTHING

## The Evil of Frankenstein (1964, Hammer, Freddie Francis)

*'Why can't they leave me alone? Why can't they ever leave me alone? ... Anything they don't understand, anything that doesn't conform to their stupid little pattern, they destroy. They have to destroy it.'*
**Baron Frankenstein (Peter Cushing)**

At the risk of beginning to sound like the horror film fan equivalent of the cornily religiose song *Deck of Cards*, when I look at *The Evil of Frankenstein* I'm reminded of how important it is to trust your own voice. Important, but not always easy.

Personally, I've never much enjoyed stepping boldly into the spotlight and singing my own song. I'm far more comfortable in the shadowy background, second extra from the left, lip synching to an uninspired cover version of a standard. In every setting, personal, social or professional, I avoid taking the lead whenever I can. A good supporting role is where I'm happiest, something that allows me to stay pretty much unnoticed and unremarkable. I'm the quiet if occasionally funny one at the pub table. My job title at work is *Second* in English, allowing me to hide pretty effectively behind my Head of Department most of the time. Even if he is shorter than me. I'm Spock, not Kirk. Actually, I'm more like one of those entirely anonymous red-shirted bits of Klingon-fodder.

There's a terrific Woody Allen mockumentary from the 1980s called *Zelig*. The title character of the film is a man so desperate to conform that, like a human chameleon, he begins to take on the physical characteristics of whoever he happens to be with. A lot of the time it feels like watching an actual biopic. Of me. It's an unpretentiously prescient little film that cuts profoundly to the heart of a lot of the issues surrounding modern living.

It's one of our greatest dilemmas – we're so determined to fit in, so fearful of giving offence, so keen ourselves to take offence then pour online opprobrium on the offender, so terrified that we'll be just one unacceptable piece of terminology behind the times, so concerned that we'll express an opinion to someone who disagrees with it, so worried about saying the wrong thing, that we stop saying anything at all. And if we stop saying anything then sooner or later we stop *having* anything to say, because we've stopped thinking or believing anything in the first place. And, most dangerously of all, as Zelig's incorporation into Nazi Germany suggests, along with that lack of our own values and our own beliefs goes a willingness to surrender our sense of self to any populist demagogue that seems to have the answer we're so evidently lacking, to anyone who relieves us of the awful necessity of thinking for ourselves. And easy answers grow ever more popular. Let's Leave. Let's build a wall. Let's kill the Jews. Or the Muslims. Or the Christians. As Yeats had it, the best lack all conviction while the worst are full of passionate intensity.

It's not only in our politics. It's there just as clearly at a personal level. Many of the worst mistakes I've made in life have been as the result of listening too credently to well-meant advice. As a green young teacher trembling my way into my first September in my first classroom and scared stiff of the teenage riot I imagined my every lesson becoming, I made the mistake of listening to the cynical old hands in the staff room muttering "Don't smile until Christmas," the idea being that you present an initial impression of stony-faced, iron-fisted discipline which you can then afford to relax a little as the year goes on.

What I discovered of course is that while that approach may work perfectly well for someone else, someone who was able to carry it off with conviction, if, like me, you were only too aware that you were faking it then pretty quickly so were your classes. The kids I taught way back then were the ones who ended up smiling before Christmas. And not in a good way. Eventually I realised that I had to find my own way of doing things, to find what I could be comfortable doing, to find my own voice rather than offering an unconvincing ventriloquizing of someone else's.

Which is where *The Evil of Frankenstein* comes in.

Because, on the face of things, it's an odd choice for this season of double bills with quality and importance the watchwords for selection. *The Evil of Frankenstein* doesn't have much in the way of either. Easily the weakest entry in the season, it's no-one's favourite Frankenstein film, and no-one's favourite Hammer movie. I didn't particularly like the film as a twelve-year-old watching it for the first time in 1977, and to be honest I still don't, although I can see more of value in it now than I could then.

It's not by any means a terrible film; it's just an oddly difficult film to enjoy. The problem is not a technical one. Few would argue against the proposition that Freddie Francis was the finest cinematographer Britain has ever produced, and as a director he brings a characteristic visual flair to all his horror film work, whether with Hammer, Amicus, Tigon or Tyburn, which is fully in evidence in *The Evil of Frankenstein*. The film, and in particular the laboratory scenes, with their striking lighting and their sickly blue-green hues, are a sumptuous visual delight.

Neither is the acting an issue. Cushing is predictably wonderful, and there is some able support from Sandor Eles as Frankenstein's assistant Hans, Katy Wild as the deaf mute beggar girl, and especially Peter Woodthorpe as the deeply unpleasant hypnotist Zoltan.

But there's something uncomfortable about the film, a fundamental insincerity or lack of conviction that runs deeper than Freddie Francis's well-known later avowal that he rather disliked the genre and regretted that horror films were the only opportunities he was ever offered as a director.

Although it comes relatively early – 1964 – it's the odd one out in Hammer's Frankenstein franchise in a number of ways. First and most obviously, it's the only one not to be directed by the ubiquitous Terence Fisher, widely seen as Hammer's true auteur. Or rather it's the only one if you're willing to draw a discreet veil over 1970's *The Horror of Frankenstein,* one of gifted screenwriter Jimmy Sangster's ghastly but thankfully rare forays into directing, and agree to never speak of it again. Which is something I strongly recommend you do, since *The Horror of Frankenstein* is a film so bad it makes you consider removing your own eyeballs and dropping them into a handy surgical jar for having had the temerity to have remained open for the length of its running time. Secondly, the continuity which Jimmy Sangster's brilliant screenplay had rigidly adhered to in the step from *The Curse of Frankenstein* in 1957 to *The Revenge of Frankenstein* in 1958, is thrown aside by Tony Hinds' script for *The Evil of Frankenstein* (credited under his usual pen name of James Elder) making this film effectively an early example of that ugly modern phenomena, the re-boot.

Third, although Peter Cushing remains, as usual, impeccably the best thing in the film, he appears to be playing a different part. The Baron is no longer the cold, manipulative and amoral figure from previous – and subsequent – outings, but a misunderstood and maligned outsider, more sinned against than sinning.

I don't know if I'm alone in this, but I found the Star Wars prequel *Rogue One* nearly unwatchable, almost entirely as a result of how unpleasant and offensive I found the experience of watching the CGI Cushing – but there's just a little hint of an echo of it in seeing him so completely redefine his Baron Frankenstein in *The Evil of Frankenstein.* Such a ferocious intensity did he give to the role in the earlier films, that watching the same actor playing the same part (and playing it very well) but apparently playing an entirely different man, is not a million light years away from seeing, in 2017 in a galaxy far far away, an actor two decades after his own death apparently reprising a role he originally played in 1977.

So what accounts for the film being imbued with this slightly awkward, uncertain feeling? Unusually, there's a simple, one-word answer. Universal.

The early Hammer films – and the most successful of their later ones – derive some of their startling power and originality by consciously defining themselves *against* the Universal films of the Golden Age, and in so doing achieving a unique, idiosyncratic style of their own. It's a consciously developed contrast which is clear and obvious to any kind of audience, but perhaps most strongly evident to a 12-year-old watching them for the first time in the Summer of 1977 in a Saturday night double bill season which typically offered first a Universal and then a Hammer in carefully chosen pairings at a time when the Hammer films were still recent enough to be seen as modern. At its best, the studio truly found a voice entirely its own by not being Universal.

Lee's Dracula is powerful in part because of how unlike Lugosi he is. He's in colour, not black and white. He has a British accent, not a Hungarian one. His movements are crisp and athletic, rather than stylised and heightened. He's physically, rather than cerebrally, commanding. Bernard Robinson's Castle Dracula works brilliantly by not being an echo of Lugosi's crumbling Gothic ruin – with not a cobweb nor an armadillo in sight.

The Frankenstein films, even more so, are defined by this difference, not least because Hammer were originally working under the very real threat of a Universal lawsuit. Any detail drawn from the Karloff films which was not taken directly from Mary Shelley's novel – most notably of course the iconic Jack Pierce makeup design – and Universal's lawyers would have been all over the British upstarts like the fungal growth over Richard Wordsworth's arm in *The Quatermass Xperiment*. The originality and distinctiveness of *The Curse of Frankenstein* was born out of legal necessity as well as artistic inclination.

*The Evil of Frankenstein,* however, comes with the official Universal seal of approval. Hammer's success was always dependent on securing distribution deals and production money from the States. At the same time, a Universal which no longer had any direct interest in making gothic horror looked enviously at the box office success of the early Hammer films and entered into a deal with the British company, investing in a modest production budget and securing distribution rights in return. As a result, Universal opened its back catalogue to its new partners, and faced with this sudden freedom Hammer made the mistake of, in effect, making a 1940s Universal monster movie rather than a 1960s Hammer Horror film.

It's all there. Rather slow carriage ride across mittelEurope towards Castle Frankenstein as in *Frankenstein Meets the Wolf Man* and *House of Frankenstein*? Check, but although it occupies much less screen time, Cushing's coach ride *feels* slower because of its contrast to Hammer's usual sense of narrative pace and urgency – the studio's 1958 *Dracula* drops Harker's coach ride completely for instance. Jack Pierce's square head monster makeup design? Check, though the limited budget and schedule means it's a crude take on the original, lacking almost all Pierce's painstaking subtlety. Buzzes and flashes from a Kenneth Strickfaden early 30s style electrical laboratory as in *Frankenstein* and *Bride of Frankenstein*? Check, and to be fair it works very well, although I for one miss James Whale's accompanying distorted and expressionistic camera angles. Monster frozen in ice below the castle as in *Frankenstein Meets the Wolf Man*? Check, though despite wrestler Kiwi Kingston's physical bulk his monster is a much less interesting take on the role than Lugosi's or Chaney's, never mind Karloff's. Female lead a mistreated gypsy girl who strikes up a touching relationship with a monster as in *House of Frankenstein*? Check, though Ilonka's devotion to Lon Chaney's Wolf Man feels more clearly motivated than Katy Wild's mute empathy for the Monster as a fellow outsider. The problem of the monster's damaged brain driving the narrative as in *Ghost of Frankenstein*? Check, though without the manic energy of the earlier film's brain swaps. Cunning and amoral sidekick exerting psychological control over the monster to further their own vengeful and selfish agenda as in *Son of Frankenstein*? Check, though good as Woodthorpe is as Zoltan he's no match for Lugosi's charismatic Ygor. Baron Frankenstein in a swashbuckling aerial swing across the laboratory, also as in *Son of Frankenstein*? Check, though lack of studio floor space makes Cushing's Douglas Fairbanks impression a bit less dramatic than Basil Rathbone's.

The end result is simply disappointing. It turns out, unsurprisingly, that while Hammer were very good at making Hammer films, they weren't as good as Universal had been at making Universal films.

The hybrid quality of *The Evil of Frankenstein* renders it a film without real heart, a strange mutant bearing the face of Hammer – colour, Cushing, a bit of blood – but haunted by the spirit of much better films from an altogether different time and context. Hammer were defined in the early days of their success by their chutzpah, by an upstart cheek, a cocksure self-confidence which had little respect for reputation or authority. Something of the same quality permeates the best of their later films – the mid period highlights like *The Reptile, Plague of the Zombies, The Devil Rides Out, Quatermass and the Pit* and also the less highly regarded but equally original and distinctive later efforts like *Dr Jekyll and Sister Hyde* or *Captain Kronos Vampire Hunter*, films which have their own distinct tone and blaze their own trail.

From the 50s to the 70s, the finest Hammer films could only be Hammer films. Where they falter is when that self-confidence fails them, as in the early 60s attempts at a bit more costume drama respectability in films like *The Two Faces of Dr Jekyll* or *The Gorgon*; the awkward, rather naff attempts to bring in the kind of contemporary settings used so well by Amicus or the *Count Yorga* movies in an effort at 'relevance' in *Dracula AD 1972* and *The Satanic Rites of Dracula;* or, saddest of all, their desperate and all but bankrupt attempt to follow the blockbusting trend of *The Omen* and *The Exorcist* with *To the Devil a Daughter* in 1976. Or in *The Evil of Frankenstein*, when the chance to play in the toybox of the Universal Golden Age led them to lose the strong sense of identity that defined so much of their best output, and with it all conviction.

Identity – a strong sense of self – was at the core of Hammer's success, as I think it is at the core of much that defines a successful life. It doesn't come easy, at least not in its authentic form, and it takes time. People assume Hammer was an overnight success, bursting suddenly onto the horror scene with *The Curse of Frankenstein* in 1956. In fact, the company had existed in different forms long before, even importing Bela Lugosi to work on *The Mystery of the Marie Celeste* in the 1930s, and spent the early part of the 50s just about getting by with a series of low budget black and white film adaptations of successful radio and early TV shows, often using a somewhat washed up Hollywood name to have a chance at some American appeal.

This was the model that led them to stumble almost accidentally onto their first horror hit, *The Quatermass Xperiment*, starring Brian Donleavy. Hammer were amongst the first to realise that for a new teenage generation thrilled by the hip swivelling antics of Elvis and the rather tamer lip twitching of Cliff Richard, the X certificate with its promise of hitherto forbidden fruit could actually be part of a successful marketing strategy rather than the box office poison much of the conventional wisdom had assumed it to be. They ramped up the horrific elements of Nigel Kneale's smash hit sci-fi BBC TV series accordingly.

The success of the strategy led them to consider full blown Gothic horror, resulting in *Curse of Frankenstein* which begins to bring together a number of the most important elements of the formula – Lee, Cushing, Fisher, colour, gore. Even so, the Hammer identity still isn't fully formed. The sex isn't really there yet, despite the presence of Hazel Court, and neither is the pace. Those don't arrive until their second go, in *Dracula,* and a remarkable string of wonderful films followed in its twenty-year wake.

But even then, Hammer weren't always reliably able to maintain that strength of conviction in the face of a variety of external pressures, from suddenly tightened and more restrictive censorship codes in the early 60s, to changing social conventions and relaxing censorship codes in the late 60s, or even to the undue influence of an earlier horror brand's definition of what a Frankenstein film was all about.

In the same way we can stumble towards a sense of self as individuals, trying on and discarding personas like dodgy fashion choices we now only cringe at in old photographs. There's a well-known phrase of Shaw's which says that life is not about finding yourself, it's about creating yourself, a phrase you often see recently on 'inspirational' posters and power points. There's a lot of truth to it, in that it rightly asks us to see identity as a hard-earned process rather than a simple given, but it also seems to me to suggest we have a lot more conscious control over the process than most of us are able to exert in reality. Certainly not me, anyway.

From a gawky and utterly insecure adolescent in the 1970s, a bullied outsider at school with no real sense of who I actually was, finding a bit of that answer in my love of Doctor Who and horror double bills, to punk rock, and having a try at sneery cynical angry young man, into which eventually left wing politics began to bleed stridently as the 70s became the 1980s. Then there was Morrisey, a flower waving messiah for so many of us back then who were wrestling with the big philosophical questions like why didn't nice girls (or boys) like us, and witty miserabilism began to define me instead or as well. There was the academic, and then in the 90s the boozy bloke and the resurgent football fan, and then domesticity.

None of those versions of me were phony, not quite, but none of those people were ever *really* me either. Not truthfully. Not authentically. They were all small parts of me which I mistook for a while for a self. It took me years of false starts and blind alleys and missteps and stumblings before I began to be able to draw the shards of all of them together into someone who could be a little more comfortable in his own skin, and even then other people – most of all my wife, and then my children – played a bigger and more wonderful part in that process than anything I was able to do for myself.

Because identity is complex. We are large. We contain multitudes. Which is where many of the deep-rooted problems with today's very specific brand of identity politics come in. Because in truth none of us are 'black'. None of us are 'white'. None of us are 'men' or 'women'. None of us are 'gay' or 'straight' or 'trans'. None of us are 'Leavers' or 'Remainers'. At some level we're all one or other of those things, of course. But we're all also so much more than that. Unique, sovereign and irreducible, each and every one of us.

It goes without saying that this ideological position I hold is a luxury which I have in part by virtue of the fluke of being born into the social group that has more power than any of the others. There's no urgent need to build or work through a sense of White Straight Male identity because the whole world does that for me by giving me the privileges associated with those labels. That's a luxury which other groups don't enjoy, and so of course the assertion of alternative and diverse cultural identities is an important and unavoidable stage on the march towards redressing thousands of years-worth of hierarchy and patriarchy. But it's just that. A stage on the way towards equality, rather than a truth in itself.

Those labels of race, or nationality, or gender or sexuality are just tiny parts of each of us. They're not the true basis for political agreement or the creation of specific 'communities.'

The idea that possession of a penis makes me part of a community makes no sense at all, any more than the idea that the lack of one makes anyone else a member (see what I did there?) of another one. And if I make possession of a penis the central element of my sense of self, and the basis of my values, the way I see the world and the way I think, that makes me automatically, and for once quite literally, a knobhead. It can't be other than sexist. Just as surely as if I take 'whiteness' to be a key component of my identity, that makes me a racist. Which is why I can assert with rigidly dialectical logic that the world is full of racist knobheads. Some of them may even grow up to be Presidents or Prime Ministers.

But the contrary, and apparently 'progressive' application of identity politics, however necessary a stage it may be, contains something of the same fundamental ideological fallacy. Whether I see myself as straight or gay or trans or bi or gender neutral, that's fine. No-one needs anyone else's permission for that. But if I begin to base a politics or an ideological position on that one small – and frankly fairly insignificant – aspect of my identity, then it can quickly descend into the lunacies of cancel culture and to something as dark and intolerant as forces I'd see myself as unutterably opposed to. History offers us plenty of examples of identity politics. Aryan identity for one. Apartheid for another.

Because let's make no bones about it. There is a totalitarian subtext of exclusion to the world-view and the discourse of any politics based solely on a single aspect of an individual identity. It's a very long way from the Nuremberg rallies to the Orange marches and even further from there to a Pride parade, but there's simply no way of constructing a sense of group identity based around an issue of individual identity, whether it's race or gender or religion or sexuality, which doesn't involve an element of exclusion. It can't be other than We or Not We.

As Orwell spent much of his later life trying to point out, it is possible to see the corruption of thought in the corruption of language, and both stem from any ideology that defines itself largely in terms of membership of some kind of exclusive group. To take just one ugly example, think about, for instance, the current vogue for the phrase 'Cis Woman.'

Everyone has the inalienable right to live as they choose, to see themselves however they want to see themselves and to ask others to do the same, to dress and be addressed however they wish, to choose whatever pronouns they are most comfortable with and to sleep with whoever they want however they want so long as the other person (or persons – whatever floats your boat) wants the same thing. Most of all everyone has the right to do any and all of those things without receiving or even having to be aware of the kind of disapproval or abuse which is still sadly all too common, and to do all of those things while being treated with a bit of kindness and respect. But to make language choices over someone else's identity because it somehow clashes with yours is neither kind nor respectful. It's fascistic.

I live in Norwich, and as a high school teacher I spend quite a lot of my working day in the company of provincial boys who, all too acutely aware that being a lower middle class white boy from Norfolk is marginally less cool than being a black kid from the inner city, make it a matter of honour to speak and act as though they were grime artists from Brixton. In effect, they're self-identifying as black. And of course, there's nothing wrong with that. It's certainly not as weird as self-identifying as a dead Hungarian actor named Bela, as I've done for half my life.

But if those same boys start demanding that to prevent outraging their hard-earned sense of self someone who actually *is* a black kid from Brixton no longer has the right to be referred to as 'black' based purely on the biology of their skin pigmentation or their quantity of melanin and offer a term like 'pig-black' or 'mel-black' instead, that would be extraordinarily insulting. Just as is the term 'Cis Woman' because it strips identity from another group rather than asserting it for your own. That's the problem with group identity. If we're not very careful, it corrupts our language, our thought processes, and our own basic kindness towards one another. And the duckspeak chorus of abuse directed recently at J.K. Rowling for having had the temerity to suggest that the word 'women' might still be preferable to the absurd use of 'people who menstruate' makes me just as angry as hearing the language of prejudice and bigotry and schoolyard thuggery still being directed against trans people.

In the end we all have to walk the road for ourselves. We are complex, layered, multi-faceted individuals, not easy labels. The road can be hard and winding, but somewhere down it if we're very lucky and the wind is at our backs, we may find at least a provisional sense of ourselves which enables us to follow our own hearts and our own convictions rather than allowing them to be defined for us by all those outside voices vying to own the inside of our heads.

And if we can all get there, if we can find the strength that comes from knowing a bit better who we really are, then we stand a better chance of finding the strength to make a kinder, stronger world; a world that is respectful of differences but aware of the much greater common ground that unites us; a world in which we could all be a bit nicer to one another, and a world in which *The Evil of Frankenstein* would have been a better film.

# 22. 1977 – ANNUS HORRORBILIS

One of my earliest memories is crystal clear and extraordinarily vivid. It is July 1969. I am four years old. I am just on the cusp of dawning self-awareness, the kind of moment so beautifully caught by Dickens in the first paragraphs of *Great Expectations:* the very beginning of memory and of identity. I am in the back garden of our house – a standard 1930s semi distinguished only by its unfeasibly long back garden. A hundred yards of lawn and hedge and borders and, most improbably of all for plebs such as we, beyond the lawn a small orchard, thrillingly and terrifyingly filled with dark shadows and mysteries and overhanging branches. There are plum trees which yield the sweetest plums ever grown, and there are tingling recollections of potatoes cooked in the garden bonfire on Guy Fawkes Night.

This one particular night stands apart from the general, disconnected jumble of random moments, clear and sharp and specific. There are men on the moon.

Like the rest of the world, I have watched the scratchy black and white footage with my family, and despite my tender age the awe-inspiring significance of what is happening is not lost on me. There are men on the moon. Here, now, as I stand in the garden, there are men on the moon. My feet, in their little side-buckled sandals as I look down, are standing here on this earth. Up there, as it hangs full and round in the sky, men's feet are standing on the surface of the moon. I feel almost breathless with the wonder of it as I stand in the soft light of that full moon, big and pale in the nightblue sky.

It may not, strictly, be my earliest memory. There are jumbled moments. Opening a wooden toy chest. A rubber monster in a shop. Mum singing. But it is certainly the earliest memory that is not simply an isolated moment, but rather has some coherent meaning or connection, some understanding. It is the first moment in my life which can really be seen as the beginning of a narrative. Over the years I've spoken to more than one person of about my age who shares it. Not that they all happened to be standing in my back garden at the time, because that would just be weird, but the essence of that memory of awe and wonder beneath a beautiful clear full moon in 1969 seems to be widely shared. Billy Bragg even wrote about it in one of my favourite songs, *The Space Race is Over:*

> *And I watched the Eagle landing*
> *On a night when the moon was full*
> *And as it tugged at the tide*
> *I knew that deep inside*
> *I too could feel its pull.*

But here's the thing. Years and years later, still fascinated by this most extraordinary of all human ventures, in one sense so utterly vainglorious but in another, truer sense a visionary triumph of spirit and ambition, I pick up and read a wonderful book by Andrew Smith called *Moondust,* in which he explores the effect of the experience on the twelve men in human history to have looked at the Earth from the surface of another world, and sets out to interview the nine who, at the time, were still alive.

I am so impressed by it that when the author's book tour comes to Norwich I get tickets and go to see him speak, which he does, fascinatingly and entertainingly. But in the course of the evening he mentions this shared memory, and how often people have felt compelled to share it with him, and then points out that this moment, so visually strong, so indelibly a part of me, never happened.

Because, he says, *there was no night during the moon landing when the moon was full.*

Unlike many of today's vox-popping, you tube reviewing generation, I see no reason to doubt the better informed opinion of a genuine expert. He is right, and my memory is wrong. A false memory, made out of a conflation of vague impressions and later moments, of films and photographs and imagination, and perhaps most of all a sense of poetic truth. The moon should have been full, even though it wasn't.

I've *created* that memory over time, rather than experiencing it in that moment. It has no basis in fact. Yet even now, knowing that, the memory remains in my mind, clear and hard and sparkling and concrete and true as diamond.

So I suppose my memories of the Saturday nights in the summer of 1977 which made up the *Dracula, Frankenstein – and Friends!* season are, in all probability, every bit as flawed, unreliable and quite possibly fictional as my memory of that full moon just eight years before. But still, I have a potent sense of how those Saturday nights were, and how they felt, which goes something like this.

The long summer evening light is just beginning to fade into night. It's Saturday night. After spending the evening with us, my Auntie Cath has just got a taxi back to her flat in 'The Annexe', which is a section of the nurse's accommodation at the Norfolk and Norwich hospital, where she is home warden. My dad, tall, slow moving and gentle-faced, has finished recording the day's mundanities in his Letts half-page-to-a-day diary and, always early to bed, is on his way upstairs. And mum, her warm brown eyes dancing with their usual life and humour, is settled in an armchair with a late night cup of tea and a cigarette.

A twelve-year-old boy, myself, is watching telly. He's watched a run of great shows from early evening until now, filling in the gaps by idly adding a few more red felt tip bloodstains to the two-page spread of a fangs out vampire king in the middle of an old copy of his *Dracula Lives!* comic and flicking through his treasured copy of Dennis Gifford's *A Pictorial History of Horror Movies*. There's been *Tom and Jerry*, or maybe *Basil Brush* just after *Grandstand* (which itself has featured enthralling coverage of Wimbledon and the Ashes), immediately followed by a brilliant dark and scary new episode of *Doctor Who*, with the screen lit up by the manic energy and charisma of Tom Baker's Doctor. Then he's chortled through some family's disastrous efforts at using a potter's wheel or dancing the tango, or perhaps both at once, on *The Generation Game* and enjoyed a bit of early evening character drama with *The Duchess of Duke Street* or fallen about at *The Two Ronnies*. Now it's just a bit before 10, so I don't know. It's *Starsky and Hutch* maybe? And the prospect of an old time Hollywood star appearing on *Parkinson* shortly, all of them enhanced by the ever-present sense that the best was saved for last. Two fantastic horror films, never seen before, are on the way.

    It had been jacket potatoes – butter and cheese, a slice of ham – for tea, but now the aroma of 9 o clock cheese and onion pasties is hanging heavy in the air. Just before that, there'd been a game of cards (rummy for matchsticks), or maybe *Yahtzee*, accompanied by my dad's comically exasperated moaning about everyone else's unnatural luck, and also by an LP's dreamy $33^{1/3}$ circling (not many to choose from at this point – I owned 'Out of the Blue' by ELO and a Bay City Rollers album which I'd had the decency to grow ashamed of by now), with the gentle and wittily nostalgic harmonising of Manhattan Transfer's *Pastiche* serving as the grown ups' preferred accompaniment for Saturday Night Games, the music crooning softly through the mustard coloured mesh of the built in speakers at either end of the enormous dark wood radiogram which runs along most of the length of one wall in the living room.

    The window on the opposite wall reveals the shadows slowly gathering in the enormous garden, filled with mystery and anticipation, that same garden in which I didn't actually look up at a full moon seven years earlier, and yes, overly convenient though it might now seem I swear it's true, bats are wheeling and darting overhead through the encroaching dark.

    More than forty years later, I can still feel the warmth and comfort of those nights lodged cosily inside me.

    But of course, it wasn't actually like that, not at all, not any more than the full moon ever gazed down on an awe struck boy when the Eagle landed.

    There's no way an evening of cards, Yahtzee and Manhattan Transfer could happen simultaneously with an evening of avid family telly watching, not in those days before entertainment became so individual, with an endless choice of devices, platforms and channels in every room. No, it had to be a straight choice between the one TV or the one radiogram in the living room. And anyway, a series of *Doctor Who* was a winter thing, all dark skies and frosty breath, while the horror double bills only ran for a few weeks of Summer, so my two favourite things couldn't have shared evenings as I remember them doing.

Sure enough, when I break my own previously stated intention of not checking or researching facts at all since it's the memory rather than the actuality that concerns me, the memory cracks and splinters. It's easy for me to check, even though I try not to, as I have a little archive of Radio Times editions from the summer of 1977 carefully stored in my sheddy mancave at the bottom of the garden, but if you happen to be a more normal human being than me you can try the same research through the BBCs own Genome site, an unassuming little time machine which allows you to trawl their listings from 1923 to 2009.

The screenings of *Dracula* and *Frankenstein* which kicked off the *Dracula, Frankenstein – and Friends!* season were not the culmination of an evening of nailed on classics from the Golden Age of British Saturday night TV as I remember them being. No *Doctor Who*, but instead *Saturday Night at the Movies,* which was a weekly screening of a never especially distinguished 1950s film, on this particular Saturday a long forgotten cattlemen drama called *The Burning Hills* starring Tab Hunter and Natalie Wood.

Later, no Brucie, no Ronnies, but instead an outside broadcast from the BBC Big Top in Lowestoft of the terminally naff variety show *Seaside Special* with this one featuring Les Dawson, Dana and Bernie Clifton. The following week's edition had Cilla, Vince Hill and Frank Carson. Later headliners across that Summer included massive A listers such as Peters and Lee, Showaddywaddy, the Nolan Sisters and Stu Francis. Val Doonican pops up too. And each week featured a song and dance routine from New Edition, a ghastly spandex atrocity which made you long for the interpretive taste and subtlety of *Top of the Pops'* ardently literal dance troupes Pans People or Legs & co.

Later still there was no Parkinson, and neither Starsky nor Hutch, but instead an episode of *Cannon*, William Conrad starring in the none-too-gripping casefiles of roly-poly American PI Frank Cannon.

So I guess it must have been Yahtzee and rummy and Manhattan Transfer that night, and all across the Summer, since the schedule doesn't vary much through that golden July and August of 1977.

Interestingly though, I can tell you exactly when I must have put down the Yahtzee dice shaker. At 9.50 on Saturday 2nd July 1977, the date that *Dracula, Frankenstein – and Friends!* began on BBC2, BBC1 was showing the fourth of an eight-part series called *Supernatural,* which featured a range of very effective and enjoyable horror themed stories, with the framing device being that each story came from a candidate seeking entrance to the Club of the Damned. I remember the series well, particularly its very gothic, very 1970s opening titles, and I've caught up with it since on a splendid BFI DVD release, but I had no recollection that it coincided with the '77 horror double bills. This particular episode, *Mr Nightingale* starring Jeremy Brett, finished at 10.40, leaving a mere twenty-five minutes to wait for the screening of Lugosi's *Dracula* on the other channel at five past eleven. I wonder now how much of the extraordinary impact the film had on me at the time was as a result of an earlier entree which had stoked (or Stoker-ed, geddit?) my horror appetite but not yet slaked the red thirst.

It's enough to remind me just how wonderfully horror-drenched the 1970s were in Britain – the decade sits in British culture as an equivalent to the 50s for American monster kids raised on *Shock Theatre* and *Famous Monsters of Filmland*. There were the fan mags (*Monster Mag* and *The House of Hammer*) and comics – *Dracula Lives* came as early as Marvel's third British title, following hot on the heels of *Mighty World of Marvel* and *Spider Man Comics Weekly*. There were the Christmastime M.R. James ghost story adaptations, and as many folk horror kids TV classics as you could shake an elder branch at. Things like *Sky, The Owl Service* and *Children of the Stones*. For some of my generation, a crucial couple of years older than me, there was the ITV regional *Appointment with Fear* screening of classic horror movies, a Friday night slot which, for many, holds a similar place in their hearts as the slightly later BBC2 horror double bills do for me. There were the brilliant stillstastic books by Alan Frank and Denis Gifford. And of course there were the ubiquitous Aurora kits, still using the original early 60s moulds but revitalised for the new generation by the inclusion of optional Glow in the Dark sections.

And in many ways, the year 1977 stands as the high water mark of the British horror boom, at least in terms of broadcast television, as a willingness to allow horror programming to occupy a prominent place in the all-important Saturday night schedules for *both* existing BBC channels would indicate.

And it wasn't just *Supernatural* and *Dracula, Frankenstein – and Friends!* 1977 was also the year in which the BBC transmitted my all-time favourite screen version of Dracula. And astonishingly, I don't mean Tod Browning's cinematic landmark with Lugosi.

*Count Dracula* (subtitled *A Gothic Romance*), a BBC adaptation scripted with an unusual degree of respect for the original novel by Gerald Savory and featuring Louis Jourdan in the title role was broadcast as a single piece in December of '77, before being re-edited into three parts and twice repeated in 1979. Though rendered a little quaint for modern audiences by the then standard video/film hybrid production standards and by the addition of some glam rock era Top of the Pops video effects, the inspired use of many of the novel's actual locations in Whitby and the magnificent performances throughout are more than enough to compensate. Jourdan is a quietly powerful and very effective Dracula, both Susan Penhaligon and Judi Bowker are superb as Lucy and Mina respectively, while Frank Finlay's Van Helsing and Jack Shepherd's extraordinary Renfield are even more impressive.

For me there's a pretty unanswerable argument that it never got much better than 1977 if you were a British horror fan, but in fact in some ways I'd also argue that the year of *Dracula Frankenstein – and Friends!* marked a changing of the cultural guard much broader than was visible at the time to a twelve-year-old horror fan.

Because that Christmas night of 1977 – the same Christmas that saw the broadcast of *Count Dracula* – also represents a kind of high watermark in the history of what used to be called light entertainment. That was the night that *The Morecambe and Wise Show* drew an audience of perhaps as many as 28 million viewers – coming as it did as the jewel in the crown of a BBC lineup that also included Bruce Forsyth's *Generation Game* and a Mike Yarwood Christmas special which some estimates – figures weren't quite as precise back then – suggest was watched by even more people than Morecambe and Wise. The bits that everyone remembers are the sketch with Eric and little Ern in top hat and tails descending a Hollywood style staircase in the company of *The Good Life*'s Penelope Keith only to find the stairs don't reach the ground, and a musical sequence in which a number of the most recognisable faces on BBC at the time do a version of *There is Nothing Like a Dame* while some highly skilled editing creates the illusion they are also undertaking a madcap gymnastic dance routine. That night Eric and Ernie, their writer Eddie Braben, and the BBC itself, solidifying the idea of a common culture and truly fulfilling the remit of Public Service Broadcasting, delivered to more than half the population the Christmas gift of shared and simultaneous laughter, all of us believing in and loving the same things at exactly the same time. It was the apotheosis of British popular culture.

An apotheosis but also an ending.

Heeding the call of Independent Television's filthy lucre, Morecambe and Wise abandoned the BBC and its dream of community and Public Service, and decamped instead to the materially richer but culturally poorer world of Private Enterprise. After that special Christmas of 1977, which with a touching sense of melancholy had ended with a scene of Eric and Ernie moving out of their now empty flat, they never made another show for the BBC and their work was never either as good, nor as central to the culture again. Bruce Forsyth made the same journey the same year with an equal lack of success.

And in that move from Public Service to Private Enterprise, played out on the small screen by the nation's favourite comedians, I think it's possible to detect the whole decisive shift in the culture that we were edging uncertainly towards at the end of the 70s, the consequences of which we're still suffering today.

Coming off the back of the Winter of Discontent, 1979 saw an election victory for the radical monetarism of Margaret Thatcher, and a few short years later Eric and Ernie were wheeled out among the Conservative-backing celebrities – a roster of shame including the likes of Steve 'Interesting' Davis, Ted '3-2-1' Rogers and Jim 'Racist' Davidson, all underscored by Kenny Everett's infamous "Let's Bomb Russia" diatribe – at the Tory party conference which saw a post-Falklands Margaret Thatcher at her most triumphalist, just prior to destroying Michael Foot's Labour party in the next election to be returned for a second term with the vastly increased majority that enabled her to set the ugly and divisive tone of British politics for the next half century.

One Nation Conservatism, not in its fundamentals so very far removed from a reformist, Welfare State consensus on the centre left, surrendered to the Thatcherite bottom line and as Billy Bragg put it (when not summing up the end of the space race) 'the Great and the Good gave way to the Greedy and the Mean'. And the whole dream of Public Service, of a common culture in which we could all believe in and love the same things at the same time, as we did on that magical Christmas night in 1977, came crashing down into a world in which there was "no such thing as society."

Technology, as well as policy, cemented the drift. Broadcasting fragmented, and so did audiences. Alternatives begin to arrive. New channels and de-regulation. Satellite and cable. Plug in technology for games like Pong paved the way for the ZX and Commodore, and eventually a PC in every home, then an Xbox or a PlayStation and by incremental steps we found ourselves in a place where families may physically be in the same house at the same time, but in fact each individual member is living in the individual world of their own tablet or smartphone.

It's a long way from twenty-eight million people all guffawing at the same time at Eric and Ernie helping Penelope Keith clamber off an unfinished staircase. And that ghost or glimmer of a common culture hovering somewhere beyond our divided and bleeding country … perhaps it was always an empty dream, but it was one that seemed genuinely close and possible in 1977, even alongside the educational division, the industrial unrest and the racial tension. It's further away than ever here in 2020, as we all yell 'Leave' or 'Remain' at a TV no-one's really watching any more.

In other news, 1977 was the punk year, its short-lived incendiary excitement initially masking but ultimately revealing the truth hindsight would show – that this was to be the last time anything genuinely new or innovative could be found in the classic foursquare 'white blokes with guitars' model of rock music. Not to say there hasn't been a wealth of great rock music since then – there has – nor that there haven't been isolated innovators and mavericks finding their own path – there have. But in terms of a consistent movement, punk was the last time. However good and idiosyncratic The Smiths, or The Stone Roses, or any other later band you care to mention were, they were essentially operating within the previously established confines of the genre.

And, in a coincidence so preposterous you'll probably suspect me of making it up, Christmas Day 1977 was not only the date of the last BBC *Morecambe and Wise Show*, it was also the date on which the Sex Pistols played their last ever UK gig.

And much as the Old Skool Punk in me hates to admit it, there was something in Punk's snarling Year Zero aesthetics which echoed the iconoclastic Year Zero mentality with which Thatcherite dogma was so shortly to tear down the old consensus forever. Johnny Rotten may have wanted to destroy the passer-by; so too, for a diametrically opposed set of ideological reasons, did Maggie.

Old horror fan that I unrepentantly am, it reminds me a little of what the critic Siegfried Kracauer argues in his classic study of 1920s German cinema *From Caligari to Hitler*. For Kracauer, 20s expressionist masterpieces like *The Cabinet of Dr Caligari* and *Nosferatu* – while themselves diametrically opposed to a Nazi aesthetic which loathed the 'decadence' of the avant garde – somehow prefigure or precognitively anticipate, and even help to *create* a climate which ultimately gives rise to the Nazi atrocities of the 30s.

Despite the taunts we 'right on' students regularly and thoughtlessly parroted to one another throughout the 1980s Thatcher was no Nazi – she had her own brand of bile, viciousness and malice, but it cheapens and demeans the experiences of those who suffered and died under the Nazi regime to allow our language to conflate the two as I'm now ashamed to admit I frequently did back then. But there is a parallel in the way in which an artistic movement like expressionist cinema or punk rock paradoxically predicted and prepared the ground for a dangerous and destructive political movement with which it was locked in mutual loathing.

So there, perhaps rather depressingly, you have it. 1977 was the last year in which something resembling the dream of a common culture truly existed, and politically and culturally it's been all downhill since then. Essentially it turns out I'm a grumpy old bloke in the corner spouting about how much better it was in the old days.

Oh My God. I am the dream demographic for Brexit and Trump.

And in any case, as the false memory with which I began this chapter suggests, even my recollection of 1977 is probably untrue. Perhaps there never was a unifying sense of being part of a society, perhaps there never was a common culture to be dragged down and destroyed in the first place, just as surely as the BBC2 horror double bills never coincided with the classic Saturday night TV schedule I only seem to remember.

A sadder and a wiser man, I return my old 1977 copies of Radio Times to their protective folder, wondering if anything can ever be as I'd like it to be again, or if it ever was how I thought it was. For old time's sake, I glance at the last issue I have, the one that covers the final double bill – *House of Dracula* and *The Fall of the House of Usher* – rather than the first one.

And startlingly, thrillingly, there it is.

Saturday the 10th of September, 1977. 6.15, *Dr Who* starring Tom Baker in *Horror of Fang Rock,* a four-part story by the wonderful and only recently departed Terrance Dicks, the single individual to whom I owe the greatest debt of gratitude for the pleasure I've taken in a lifetime's reading and writing. Rest in Peace Terrance. Thank you. And, by the way, this is not just any old *Doctor Who,* but a bona fide nailed-on classic. It's the first story in a new series, but actually in tone and mood it's more like the last story of a previous era – the last of the great scary Gothics which had marked the style of the now departed script editor Robert Holmes and producer Phillip Hinchcliffe. The new producer, Graham Williams, was under instruction from his bosses to make the show more Mary Whitehouse friendly, and attempted to replace the dark, gothic tone with a greater emphasis on comedy, achieving only what at best might be described as variable results. In fact, in his BFI guide to the series no less a critic than Kim Newman, a man with a taste for dark and scary even more highly developed than my own, suggests *Horror of Fang Rock* represents the last entry in the Golden Age.

Immediately after this at 6.40, a New Series of *Bruce Forsyth and the Generation Game,* one of those light entertainment classics that defined the television of the age, itself immediately followed by a new episode of *The Duchess of Duke Street,* a wonderfully enjoyable period drama in which star Gemma Jones – a consistently excellent actress across the past forty years of television drama – lights up the screen with an energy no less spectacular than Tom Baker's colossal fourth Doctor from an hour before.

After that it's a near miss – *The Two Ronnies* aren't on, that slot being filled by the less impressive *Dick Emery Show.* A similar genre and demographic, but with just a little less quality, taste and variety in the writing and performances. Next up though, at five past nine, Frank Cannon has waddled off screen leaving room for both *Starsky and Hutch* to take centre stage.

Once the Red Torino with its iconic white stripe has roared through those convenient back alley cardboard boxes for the last time, there's a change of channel (standing up, walking across the room and pressing a button on the telly itself in those days before remote controls) ready for *Dracula, Frankenstein – and Friends!* starting on BBC2 at five past ten, which means missing whoever was on *Parkinson* on BBC1 at five past eleven (no video recorders or On Demand in those days either).

So it really happened. Both the Manhattan Transfer Yahtzee-playing version of a horror double bill Saturday night in 1977 and the square-eyed TV gobbling version genuinely happened. Memory may be unreliable and distorted, but it's not actually false.

Which means, I like to think, that I'm also not inventing the idea that Morecambe and Wise could, briefly and blissfully, unite the nation, a fact that suggests that, however remote and faraway the possibility, this wounded, fractured country could somehow, someway, be united again. The pains of the present need not be permanent. The odds may be against us, but it's not impossible and it's not inevitable.

Nostalgia is not a true escape from present day despair – in fact it only increases it. But an understanding of the past – of what was better and what was worse, of what is lost and what is gained in living every day – an ability, like Scrooge, to live in the past, the present and the future all at once, seems like our best chance to me.

And there are worse places to start than 1977. Bring me Sunshine.

# DOUBLE BILL ELEVEN

## Saturday September 10<sup>th</sup> 1977

HOUSE OF DRACULA                          22.05 – 23.15

THE FALL OF THE HOUSE OF USHER    23.20 – 00.35

---

**10.5**
**Dracula, Frankenstein – and Friends!**

The season of *Midnight Movie* double bills of fantasy and horror comes to an end with two classic spine-chillers.

**House of Dracula**
starring
Lon Chaney, John Carradine
Dr Edelman is engaged on research to discover a culture to correct human deformities. To seek his aid come two new patients, a certain Count Dracula and one Laurence Talbot, the notorious wolf man.

Laurence Talbot.........LON CHANEY
Dracula................JOHN CARRADINE
Miliza..............MARTHA O'DRISCOLL
Holtz....................LIONEL ATWILL
Nina......................JANE ADAMS
Edelman............ONSLOW STEVENS
Monster.............GLENN STRANGE
Steinmuhl..........SKELTON KNAGGS
Brahms..........JOSEPH E. BERNARD
Villager.............DICK DICKINSON

Director ERLE C. KENTON
*Black and white, Films: page 19*
The Fall of the House of Usher is at 11.20

**11.15 News on 2**
Weather

**11.20-12.35 am**
**The Fall of the House of Usher**
starring Vincent Price
with Mark Damon, Myrna Fahey
Madeline, the last female representative of the House of Usher, a family cursed for generations by a hereditary madness, is about to marry the unsuspecting Philip Winthrop, when her brother decides that the tainted family blood must be destroyed for ever.

Roderick Usher.......VINCENT PRICE
Philip Winthrop........MARK DAMON
Madeline Usher.......MYRNA FAHEY
Bristol................HARRY ELLERBE

Based on *The Fall of the House of Usher* by EDGAR ALLAN POE
Director ROGER CORMAN. Films: page 19

# 23. IS THERE NO END TO YOUR HORRORS?

House of Dracula                      (1945, Universal, Erle C. Kenton)
The Fall of the House of Usher     (1960, AIP, Roger Corman)

*'Is there no end to your horrors?'*
**Philip Winthrop (Mark Damon)**

*'No. None whatever.'*
**Roderick Usher (Vincent Price)**

Since this is the final chapter and since it is to be a chapter about the last horror double bill of the *Dracula Frankenstein – and Friends!* season of 1977, it's only fitting to acknowledge that I have a problem with endings. I know nobody likes goodbyes or last times, but I hate them with an intensity quite unknown to the average Joe. I don't feel the need to apologise for this – I've never been too sure about the average Joe anyway. Who is he? What's so average about him? Is he happy about it? Does he constantly wear a beatific 'averager than thou' smile on his unremarkable face?

    To give one small example of how neurotic I can become in the face of last times, I have a compulsive habit just before checking out of any hotel room. I have to sit in every chair in the room – the wooden one beside the writing table, the one without arms by the window, that little chair tucked in the corner. I have to sit in them all because I find myself acutely aware that I'm unlikely to be in this room ever again and if I don't sit on those chairs now I'LL NEVER HAVE THE CHANCE AGAIN, and the prospect fills me with a deep existential dread.

    I don't find myself reduced to tears often, but every reminder that a stage of life is over, is coming to a natural end – or worse, an unnatural one – will have me misty eyed and sniffling before you can say tissue. Every developmental stage my daughters go through as I watch them growing up is a gnawing reminder to me of the passage of time, and all of it's sickening crimes, as Morrisey puts it in *Rubber Ring*. She'll never be five again. She doesn't want that teddy bear anymore. She's more interested in streaming a new Dua Lipa than that toy car that turns into a dustcart she wanted so desperately what seems like only about five minutes ago. Where does it all go? Why can't we hold onto anything, ever? Why must there always be so many endings, so many last times?

    Because, of course, that's what we're talking about here. That's what unites the two films in the final double bill of the season and that's why I've chosen to talk about them together, rather than one at a time – just as I did previously for the Karloff/Lugosi pairing of *The Black*

*Cat* and *The Raven*. Because they are united in my mind, not simply by both having the word 'House' in the title, but by the sense of an ending.

I am irrationally fond of *House of Dracula*. I really shouldn't be. By any objective measure, it doesn't have a huge amount to recommend it. It's not the first of the monster rallies that characterise the Universal cycle in its death throes – that was *Frankenstein Meets the Wolf Man*. It's not even the second – that was *House of Frankenstein,* with which it shares a fairly strong sense of the bottoms of barrels being furiously scraped. As a result, I think it's probably true to say that *House of Dracula* is a little less well-known or well thought of than its immediate predecessor, because it's merely following, rather than creating, a formula established in the earlier film; an 'everything but the kitchen sink' formula that was more than a little uninspired in the first place.

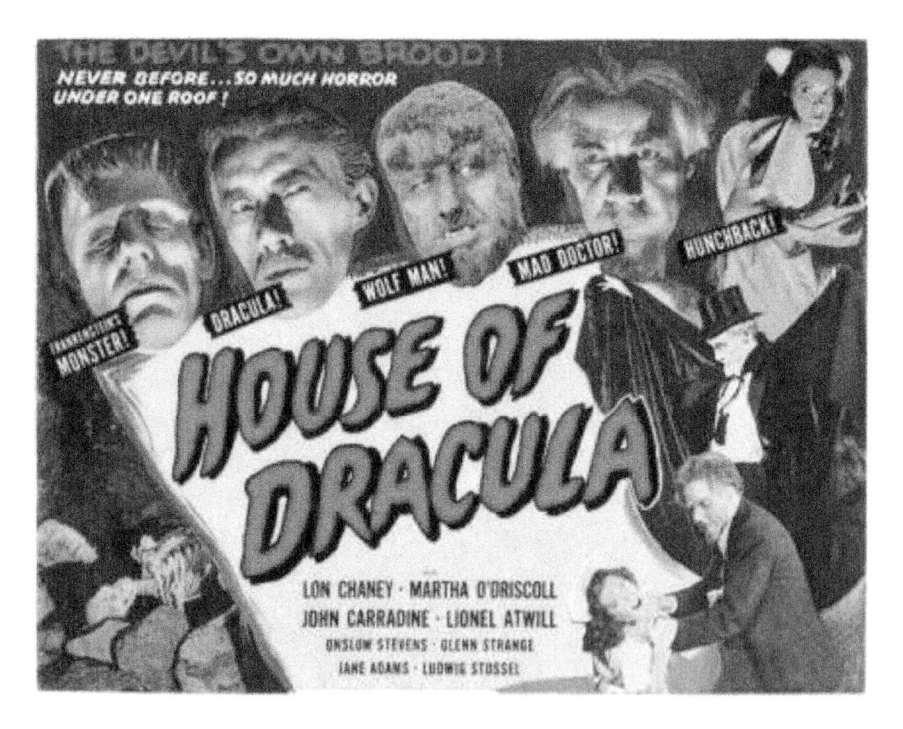

What it does have, however, is John Carradine very effectively reprising his Southern Gentleman version of Dracula, thinly disguised at first here as 'Baron Latos' which is at least a step up from 'Count Alucard' or 'Dr A. Kula' as vampire aliases go. Initially he seems to be seeking a cure for the 'curse' of vampirism in an interesting twist that echoes Marya Zaleska from the 1935 *Dracula's Daughter,* although it takes even less screen time for Carradine to revert to true bloodsucking form. And although *House of Dracula* shares *House of Frankenstein*'s tendency to treat its monsters episodically rather than allowing for much meaningful interaction between them, at least in this instance the vampire Count is permitted to have an impact on the subsequent plot before being – once again – the first of the monsters to be offed.

That impact is to be directly responsible for the Jekyll and Hyde narrative which dominates the film. Onslow Stevens gives an impressive performance as the kind-hearted Dr Edelmann, genuinely attempting to help an apparently sincere Dracula find a cure for Un-Death, offering sympathetic treatment to poor tormented Larry Talbot, and displaying a touching concern for his hunchbacked assistant Nina, played by Jane Adams. Edelmann's kindly altruism is effectively counterbalanced by the emergence of a malevolent dark side, prompted by Dracula's deliberate infection of the doctor with his own vampiric blood. This dark side asserts itself in the film's one genuinely unsettling moment as Edelmann sadistically taunts then gleefully throttles his increasingly terrified coach driver, and subsequently in his brutal murder of the unfortunate Nina and his final reel revival of Glenn Strange's Frankenstein Monster, who this time has even less to do before being engulfed in the by now standard fire which forms the film's climax.

Chaney, back once more in his favourite role, is reliably excellent as the tragic Talbot and this time, fittingly for the film that marks the end of the cycle, he's granted a moment of redemption. It would take a harder heart than mine not to be touched as he gazes untransformed at the full moon and registers that Edelmann has, finally, found him the cure he's been seeking for so long (at least until he's inexplicably back in the yak hair in time to meet Abbot and Costello a couple of years later).

Overall, the disparate parts of what remains, like *House of Frankenstein*, essentially a portmanteau movie in disguise sit together a little more effectively for me than they do in the previous film (although of course Karloff is an obvious miss this time around).

But none of that really accounts for why I love the film. Even at my most winningly eloquent (and as those of you who have made it this far will testify, winning eloquence is practically my middle name) I'd have trouble convincingly defending *House of Dracula* from the charge of being a last desperate attempt to wring the final drop of blood out of an exhausted franchise.

No, it's not the intrinsic quality of the film which leads me to value it so highly, even though it has more intrinsic quality than it's sometimes given credit for. It's precisely the fact that it *is* the last tired gasp of the Universal era which makes the film so special to me.

It's like watching an old dog being taken out in the sun for one last ecstatic roll in the grass before the vet's needle finally releases him from life's burdens.

You see, when you fall in love with something like the Universal films, something *old* rather than something contemporary, a part of the experience lies precisely in the knowledge that the thing you love, the thing you're discovering, is already over. The end is there in the beginning. Nostalgia becomes an intrinsic part of your response, even as you're experiencing things for the first time.

Even back in 1977, watching the slow Saturday night unfolding of *Dracula, Frankenstein – and Friends!* one of the key differences between the Universal movie which typically opened the double bill and the Hammer or AIP film which ended it was the knowledge that most of the cast and crew of the earlier film were long dead. Lugosi was gone, Karloff was gone, Chaney was gone. You were watching, near enough literally, the flickering ghosts of old glories. Whereas in the summer of 77, Cushing, Price and Lee were all very much alive and active, and Hammer was, officially at least, still a functioning production company that might yet continue their gothic horror sagas.

But the Universal cycle was gone, and it wasn't ever coming back. The poetic distance between the once upon a time black and white of the first film and the here and now colour of the second only highlighted the distinction.

So given that the sense of an inevitable ending runs through the Universal movies, even if you're watching them for the first time like the wide-eyed child I was more than forty years ago, there's a certain bittersweet pleasure in reaching the actual, inevitable end. Which, it turns out, is *House of Dracula*.

Oh, I know 1948's *Abbot and Costello Meet Frankenstein* has its apologists and adherents, and it has Chaney's Wolf Man, and Glenn Strange's Monster, and even, for one time and one time only on screen, the return of Lugosi's Dracula, all acquitting themselves with admirable dignity, but it's not truly the last of the Universal horror films. Tonally and narratively, it's a different thing serving a different purpose for a different audience. Whether you like the film or whether you don't – I happen not to, killjoy that I am – despite undeniably sharing a degree of DNA with the studio's classic horror movies I don't think you can really argue that a movie designed as a vehicle for Bud and Lou is a part of that cycle, any more than John Thaw and Dennis Waterman turning up as a pair of tough cops in a comedy sketch with Eric and Ernie makes *The Morecambe and Wise Show* an episode of *The Sweeney*.

Which brings us back to *House of Dracula*. Although the film is obviously a pale shadow of the real classics of the Universal era, it holds a special place in my heart because the monster mash up formula allows for a final fond farewell to each of the three greatest monsters of the Golden Age, and only the most churlish of viewers could fail to enjoy one last hurrah for the old ghouls or deny them the extended curtain call that their past glories so richly deserved.

In total contrast, Roger Corman's wonderful *The Fall of the House of Usher* was the first, rather than the last, of Corman's AIP Poe cycle, but its sickly sense of loss and corruption, its thematic fixation with the idea of death, and decay, and letting go, make it the perfect film to have closed the 1977 double bill season. It's a film *about* endings – about the stagnant waters closing over your head to leave barely a ripple behind. *Usher* is an especial favourite accordingly, its scheduling as the last film of the season (and how could it have belonged anywhere else?) confirming the place of the 'Poe Pictures'[3] alongside Universal and Hammer in the unholy trinity of classic horror.

Although the first of the series, *Usher* was the third Corman film to have been shown in this season. Even so, it was the one which really began to reveal the territory to me. A few weeks earlier *The Premature Burial* had been a revelation, but of course the casting of Ray Milland rather than Vincent Price in the lead made it an anomalous, though fantastic, example of the sub-genre. A couple of weeks later *The Raven* had Price, but it also had an atypical comedic tone. So it was *The Fall of the House of Usher* that finally began to confirm the conventions for me; this

---

[3] The term was coined by Stephen King in his book *On Writing*.

was where I began to catch the style and to form some understanding of what the Poe Pictures actually were.

No more than 'some' understanding though, because although my twelve-year-old self felt the full force of their emotional impact, there was always something shifting and elusive about these Corman masterpieces, with their dream sequences, their occasionally psychedelic visuals, their Freudian subtexts and their uniquely *off*, rather queasy tone. At twelve I felt the power, but I was only partly aware of what I was responding to. In some ways that remains true for me today.

One thing I was responding to that was in no doubt at all, however, was the towering presence of Vincent Price. He is exceptional as Roderick Usher, dominating the screen with a performance which is at once massively heightened and theatrical, and yet utterly convincing. There isn't a false or dishonest note throughout. It's a *fearless* performance which eschews all the play-it-safe dishonesties of understatement, and in its bravura intensity achieves an absolute sincerity. Price, like Lugosi before him, opens himself willingly to the misguided accusation of wild overacting and in doing so demonstrates his absolute conviction in the material.

This is why neither actor has a single moment on screen which is dull or insincere (however weak some of the scripts they were given the task of lifting) and why I'll take the daring, charisma and commitment of 'hams' like Price or Lugosi over anything that more critically lauded but less truthful actors have to offer.

And given really good material to work with, as he is in the Poe Pictures by a director as inventive as Corman and a writer as gifted as Richard Matheson (whose adaptations capture the tormented melancholy of Poe's work perfectly without ever being enslaved by the specific details of the source material), Price is unbeatable.

Walking that tightrope between the necessary and appropriate intensity on the one hand and scenery chewing bathos on the other was a trick Price pulled off again and again throughout the rest of the Poe cycle, and in fact throughout his career. Even so, Price's heightened style makes him vulnerable to misunderstanding and a certain kind of sniggering critical disapproval, most notably in the shape of Michael Reeves, the 'boy genius' director of *Witchfinder General*. Reeves was miffed that AIP rejected Donald Pleasence, his own choice for the role of Matthew Hopkins, in favour of their bankable star, an actor he thought capable of little more than camp tongue in cheek smirking, and he made Price's time on set unbearable as a result. Despite that, Price remains by a distance the most watchable thing in Reeves' cynical and overrated film, and the later *Theatre of Blood* is an especial pleasure for the metatextual chance it gives Price's fallen Shakespearean actor Edward Lionheart to revenge himself on the critics who sneered at him as a barnstorming ham.

It's not just the power of Price's performances that makes the Poe films so special to me though. Corman's work – in brilliant collaboration with his cinematographer Floyd Crosby and production designer Daniel Haller – is a masterclass in making vivid, unsettling, lavish imagined worlds on budgets even more penny-pinching than Hammer's. Crucial to the impact is Corman's decision to duplicate Poe's uncertain, disturbing landscape of the mind by avoiding location shooting altogether and opting instead for a powerfully realised, deliberately artificial, subjective reality created entirely in the studio. It was an inspired approach taken from the outset for *The Fall of the House of Usher* (with the sole exception of Corman's opportunistic use of a recent Californian forest fire for Winthrop's initial journey through a dessicated landscape to the House itself) and pretty rigidly adhered to until the later films *The Masque of the Red Death* and *The Tomb of Ligeia* shifted production to England.

As a result, the films carry an eerie psychological depth which, combined with Corman's love of a dream sequence, makes them feel more profoundly unsettling than either the Universal or the Hammer films which make up the rest of the season. Like Poe's stories, these are films which embody distorted perspectives and deep levels of mental disturbance.

And, perhaps most of all, they are films about death.

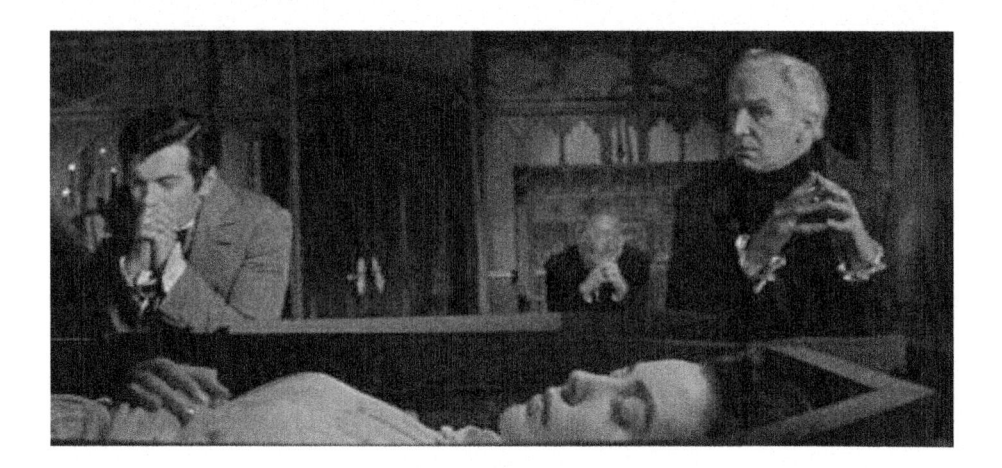

This seems a strange moment to be revisiting them in many ways. I'm writing this final section from the heart of the coronavirus lockdown of 2020 – a surreal and deeply troubled moment of history almost worthy of Poe. The whole world seems to have been brought abruptly face to face with the prospect of mortality, and then given months with little to do other than think about it.

Oddly, for someone whose greatest pleasures include these morbid, death-fixated films, one of the conclusions I've reached is that death holds no grand existential terror for me, as it does for the protagonists of the Poe pictures. I'm fairly convinced there is no life hereafter, and while illness, pain and suffering would be fairly low on my list of welcome guests (though still above Jacob Rees-Mogg), I see no reason to fear the prospect of the world continuing to turn without me. I've yet to meet anyone gripped with nihilistic despair over the fact that 13 billion years passed *before* they arrived at the party, so why worry about the years of oblivion after they leave it? No, it's not death in itself; rather it's the faintly surprising realisation that, when all is said and done, this world suits me very well indeed. It's the small – and not so small – pleasures of life that I find occupying my thoughts in these strangest of strange days.

Death is frightening because I won't be able to get a decent cup of coffee when I'm dead. Death is sad because it means not laughing with my children anymore. Death is terrible because I won't be able to see my wife's face again; because one day I will look into her eyes for the last time. In other words, death is sad because, even with all the obvious caveats and provisos, life is good and worth living. As Marvell says to his coy mistress, the grave's a fine and private place, but none I think do there embrace. The loss of this world is what troubles me, rather than the terrors of the yawning grave.

It's a reminder of the sense of loss and finality that settled over me all those years ago, as the House of Usher sank slowly into a creepily artificial, almost cartoon-like landscape, and I read, and instantly memorised, the film's closing caption superimposed over the final image – 'And the deep and dank tarn closed silently over the fragments of the House of Usher.' It's actually a slight misquote, quietly dropping Poe's use of an alliterative 'sullenly' alongside the 'silently', but, perhaps subconsciously compensating for the omission, my twelve-year-old self provided all the sullenness Poe could have required. The sense of an absolute, irrevocable ending could hardly have been more complete.

This series of films, which over the course of a few short weeks had come to dominate my life and thinking – and as the hundred thousand or so words I've written here might suggest, still do – was suddenly, agonisingly gone. The Summer Holiday was done, the miseries of school had returned and *Dracula, Frankenstein – and Friends!* was over. Nothing had ever felt quite like it. I hadn't really encountered death at that point. My grandparents had died, but I barely knew or remembered any of them. I hadn't even lost a pet.

So I don't think I'm overstating the sense of devastation I felt when I say that this was my first glimpse of a real sense of loss. The French have it wrong when they say that every orgasm is 'le petit mort'. It's not each time you come that's the little death; it's the end of the greatest horror double bill season in history. The end of a series of *Doctor Who* was agony, but there was always the reassuring knowledge that there would be a new one in a few months. When *The Fall of the House of Usher* reached its final fade, however, there was no such reassurance.

And though as it turned out the Horror Double Bills would return, a fixture of the BBC2 summer schedule through the rest of the 70s and into the early 80s, it was never to be, or to feel, quite the same again.

There were, of course, lots of wonderful films for me to encounter, both in and out of the horror double bill seasons, many of which I love every bit as much as the films I first saw across the Summer of 1977. Over the next few years I would thrill to films like *House of Wax, Phantom of the Rue Morgue, The Man with X Ray Eyes, The Devil Rides Out, Quatermass and the Pit, White Zombie, Night of the Demon, Cat People, Theatre of Blood* and *Captain Kronos*.

But I experienced those films more like isolated gems, standing alone. The sense of magnificent perfection I had across the Summer of 77, of film after film after film all occupying an equal and equally intense part of my heart and my head – after the tarn closed over the House of Usher in the early hours of September the 11th I was never to feel that sensation again.

The following season for instance, in the Summer of 1978, opened with Bela Lugosi in the 1932 *Murders in the Rue Morgue* – it's a wonderful, expressionist masterpiece, a criminally underrated and overlooked film from the very early Universal era which thrilled me beyond measure – paired with a minor Hammer classic, *The Man Who Could Cheat Death* with Anton Diffring and Hazel Court. Both films are fabulous, as are most of the films shown in the season – this time given the umbrella title of *Monster Double Bill*. But alongside some nailed on classics, there was a distinctly second division feel to a couple of the older selections, and the season also included Romero's *The Crazies,* which I actively hated, only gradually coming to adore it many years later, and ended with *Superbeast* which I also hated, without in this case ever feeling the need to revise my opinion.

The 1979 *Masters of Terror* season did pretty well by Hammer, but most of the older films felt a bit more like filler than in previous years, while the 1980 season was a mixed bag of a handful of great movies and a handful of fairly forgettable dross. In 1981, the Val Lewton films made for a great opening film each week, but the quality of the later film paired with them was, to put it charitably, variable. So although I adored all of the horror double bill seasons, and found at least a few all-time favourite desert island films in each of them, alongside my love came the chilly fanboy refrain that nothing was ever quite as good as it used to be.

And the Summer of 1977 season became a kind of yardstick, an impossible measure against which all but a few isolated experiences were to come up short. It's the condition and the curse of nostalgia that fangs ain't what they used to be. And they're not. That, I suppose, is why we live in a world of remakes and reboots, a world of new Star Treks and new Star Wars and new Who and film franchises based on the comic books we read when we were kids (Make Mine Marvel); a world in which we're all trying and never quite managing to recapture the things we loved when we were young.

And of course we can't. Of course we can't call back the past, and all the things we've lost, no matter how much we might yearn to at times.

Time passes. It's the fundamental fact of the human condition. We live in a temporal world. Temporarily. The past has gone.

Except in the ways in which it lodges within us.

So here I am, reliving and re-imagining how it felt to be watching this special season of horror double bills so long ago, because, as the closing credits of so many Universal movies almost put it, a good past is worth repeating. I've seen these films many times down the years – I hope I'll see them many more. In different ways I still love each and every one of them.

In some cases, my relationship with the film has deepened and shifted as life has interwoven with the film itself to expand and alter its original power – experience lends a texture innocence can never feel. In others, it's precisely the reverse, and my relationship with the film is all about the fact that, try as I might, I can never again connect with it in quite the open, absolute and innocent way I did on those long gone and long ago warm Summer nights in 1977.

But I'll catch glimpses of it – fleeting half moments when that tingling twelve-year-old excitement flickers into life as a full moon glows behind dark scudding clouds or a bat flutters and flits almost too quick to see against a humid night-blue late Summer sky. Moments where I'm neither entirely in the here and now nor entirely in the past – but a strange monster movie hybrid of the two, my middle aged self and the small boy inside me existing in the same body, the same space and time.

Moments where Dracula, Frankenstein and all my other old friends are always waiting for me, there among the crooked headstones of a shadowy graveyard or at the head of the staircase of a crumbling castle, the full moon flitting behind its broken battlements; Boris and Bela and Lon and Vincent and Peter, all of them waiting, with cloaks and electrodes and bloodied surgical gloves and asphalt spreaders boots and yak hair forever at the ready.

That's why I don't like endings. Because I choose not to believe in them.

That's all folks.

## THE END

The End
It's a Universal Picture

A
HAMMER FILM
PRODUCTION
PRODUCED AT BRAY STUDIOS, ENGLAND

# ACKNOWLEDGEMENTS

First, I'd like to thank the people whose work on the horror film has helped shape my love of the genre – most notably Dennis Gifford, Alan Frank, Carlos Clarens, William Everson, Calvin Beck, Peter Haining, Gregory Mank, Denis Meikle, Kim Newman, Jonathan Rigby, Marcus Hearn, Wayne Kinsey, Bruce Hallenbeck, Gary D Rhodes, David Skal and Mark Gatiss.

Second, the people who made the films – too many to list of course – and, equally importantly, the people who broadcast them. The BBC is an organization under constant attack from venal, mean-spirited and ugly vested interests, but without it I simply would not be the person I am. It is one of our most precious institutions which we should defend at all costs. So that it can start screening horror film seasons again.

I'd also like to thank Deborah, my sister, and William, her husband, who read the manuscript at an early stage and offered some very helpful suggestions and advice. For the same reason, my thanks go to my friend Mark Champion.

Most of all, thanks to my wife, Zoë, and my daughters, Alice and Martha, for making everything worthwhile. All my love always.

And mum and dad, for letting me stay up late forty years ago.

Printed in Great Britain
by Amazon